D1327298

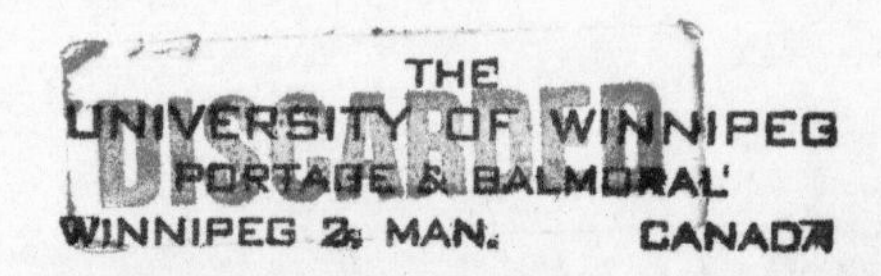
THE
UNIVERSITY OF WINNIPEG
PORTAGE & BALMORAL
WINNIPEG 2, MAN. CANADA

The Newfoundland Journal of Aaron Thomas

The Newfoundland Journal of Aaron Thomas

Able Seaman in H.M.S. Boston

A journal written during a voyage from England to Newfoundland and from Newfoundland to England in the years 1794 and 1795, addressed to a friend.

Edited by Jean M. Murray

Longmans Canada Limited

Longmans Canada Limited
55 Barber Greene Road
Don Mills, Ontario

Printed in Great Britain
by Ebenezer Baylis and Son Ltd
The Trinity Press, Worcester and London

Contents

Illustrations

The last three illustrations are from Aaron Thomas's original watercolours in the Journal. The watercolour by Aaron Thomas which is reproduced on the jacket of this book is of Portugal Cove

Introduction

In the year 1762 three seemingly unrelated events took place. Aaron Thomas was baptized in the parish church of the little Herefordshire village of Wigmore. H.M.S. *Boston,* a 5th Rate 32-gun frigate was fitted at Deptford on the Thames. St John's in Newfoundland was captured by the French and was retaken by the English. Thirty-two years later Aaron Thomas, now an able seaman on the *Boston,* wrote in his journal: "During the night all hands were employ'd in warping the Ship through the Narrows, and on Saturday, 24th May the Boston was safe moored in the Harbour of St John's."

The diary had been begun in March 1794 when the *Boston* was at Spithead with orders to convoy the trade to Newfoundland. The author had just been transferred from the pay lists of the *Suffolk* 74 to the much smaller *Boston,* which was under the command of Captain James Nicholl Morris (see p. xviii). There is no indication in the muster roll of either ship that Aaron Thomas was anything more than an able seaman, but he wrote of his cabin and of frequent shore expeditions to buy supplies. There is internal evidence that he may have been the captain's steward or purser's assistant (see pp. 14, 16, 36, 48). The diary gives a rare account of life on a ship of the Royal Navy in 1794.

The convoy, which consisted of seventy-five ships, was forced to take refuge in the roads of the Scilly Islands for nearly three weeks before the winds were fair. England was at war with France but the long Atlantic crossing was not interrupted by the French fleet, although two vessels were lost in stormy weather. One month later the chief part of another convoy, in the charge of the frigate *Castor,* was captured by the French, but ten vessels of the Newfoundland trade were retaken by the British as they were being escorted to a French port.

The diary, which is addressed to an ex-shipmate of the author, gives an amusing account of the small incidents which occurred on the ship as a result of the rough weather. Through it all the reader is also aware of the hardship and privation which must have been the lot of the two hundred and twenty men who made up the complement of H.M.S. *Boston.* Aaron Thomas recounted day to day events with verve and vividness. "I have related passages and circumstances as they have arose," he wrote to his friend, "at all of which times I have had you in mind. Do you know that as I am writing these sheets I fancy I am telling a Tale? I seting on one side of the table, and you on the other; but what is my mortification on raising my head that I do not behold you. To my observations I get no remark of yours. Alas! on more mature consideration I know that you are some thousands of miles asunder. But still my hope doth not fail me but what your eyes will, at some time or other, be laid on this paper."

There is no way of knowing if his friend ever did read the diary. Since 1882 it has been in the possession of my family in Newfoundland. Originally it was picked up by a Newfoundlander at a second-hand bookstall in Manchester or thereabouts. After passing through the hands of several other Newfoundlanders it was bought by my grandfather, the late James Murray, for four pounds in Newfoundland currency. Its history I have got from an article in the *Centenary Magazine*, a Newfoundland publication which he edited in the latter years of the last century. In this magazine he published two extracts from Aaron Thomas's journal. After his death the book was carefully preserved by my grandmother, who gave it to my father in 1922. To him I am indebted for allowing me to share it with others. The late Judge Prowse included two extracts from it in his *History of Newfoundland*, published in 1895. No other part has appeared in print.

The pages, which measure approximately six and a half by eight inches, are bound in solid brown leather. The volume contains 693 pages in addition to introductory remarks and a full index. There is also a list of the illustrations, a number of which are still in the book. Some have been removed and two were never completed. The whole of the manuscript is written in clear bold handwriting on good paper. The illustrations are in watercolour. It is difficult to know if the sheets were bound after the voyage or if it was written directly in the present volume. Certainly the preface was added after the whole was completed. The outside bears the title "Memoirs of Newfoundland" but on the inside cover (which is quoted on p. 1) the writer called it a history of Newfoundland.

The naval ships of the eighteenth century were manned by all qualities of men. Some had been *forced* from their homes by impressment, others entered to avoid imprisonment for debt and some just wanted to see the world. They sailed in what we would regard as small ships, living at close quarters in conditions which were hard. The food was bad and the pay low. Discipline was harsh. Much of the happiness of the ship depended on the officers. A just and kindly captain had the respect of his men but a bad captain could make the lives of the men intolerable. Such conditions led to the naval mutinies of this period and later. Most of the sailors were sturdy, honest and loyal and only asked for what was their due, as many officers realized. The spartan conditions produced a breed of men who realized that low spirits must be avoided at all costs. Aaron Thomas seems to have realized this when he wrote: "No person who has not been in a Ship can credit the various reports which are flying about every day, or rather every hour. These are termed Galley Packets. A stranger to a Ship wonders what subjects can arise for conversation, but persons who are acquainted with the Royal Exchange or Coffee Houses of capital resort well know the method of starting a topick for the company discanting on. Thus, in a Ship, some transaction is every half hour arising for comment. The Foremast man ingratiates himself with the Wardroom Boys; every word he hears the Officer speak is brought out and immediately told at the Breechen of every Gun in the Waiste, to this is added a thousand falsitys. Everyone who relates the story adds something. If a Servant says that the Chaplain and the Purser today broke a Wine Glass at Dinner at Hob Nob the story goes that the Purser cut the slit in his Tongue with a piece of Flint Glass which the Chaplain put in his Rice Puding. . . . I myself have put some drollery in motion to create a little mirth amongst the men and enliven their spirits. I have always found that it lost nothing in the travelling. . . . So these kind of Tales are told in the Galley (which is like a Barber's Shop or Pott House in London). Here the heat is as great as Wood and Coals can produce, the men around like so many Satellites move off with what fresh News they can catch, and disperse it over the Ship with as much expedition as the Secretary of State transmits good News to the Gazette Office."

Between the end of May and the end of November the *Boston* spent considerable time in St John's Harbour, patrolled the Grand Banks, visited St Pierre, which had recently been taken from the French, and called at such settlements as Ferryland, Aquaforte and Placentia. At each place Aaron Thomas had time ashore and he regaled his friend with descriptions of the places he visited and the people he met. In doing so he revealed his very dry sense of humour, many kindly qualities, and acute powers of observation. What he saw and experienced he described minutely and accurately. It must be borne in mind that as he never actually spent a winter in Newfoundland some of what he tells is hearsay. Despite this he tells much of life in Newfoundland in 1794. The tales of his adventures on shore will ring true to those who know the country. Only someone who has walked through Newfoundland woods on a mild day in May or June could give such vivid descriptions of crossing bog and river bed. A glorious August day spent exploring the coast in a small boat still holds the magic which Aaron Thomas found. His remarks about the lack of a spring of the English kind, and the changeable weather are true.

The return of the convoy at the end of the fishing season was delayed by the murder of Lieutenant Lawry, who had gone ashore with a press gang at St John's. The last of the diary is given over to a description of the time spent in Cadiz and Lisbon. Between Lisbon and Spithead the convoy of twenty-three sail of merchantmen had very bad weather and were scattered, but they seem to have avoided the French Fleet which was then at sea.

The history of the *Boston* together with her specifications is to be found at the end of the introduction. Captain Morris had taken command of her in St John's in 1793 and under him she seems to have been a happy ship. Aaron Thomas showed that he thought highly of the captain and that he was not unhappy when he observed "But amidst these blessings I remember that I was not a whit happyer then I am at this moment, cooped up with near 300 of His Majesty's *best* subjects, as I am at present".

By the time the *Boston* reached Spithead in 1795 the mutiny on the *Culloden* had already occurred in that port, and the mutiny at the Nore was to follow. In relating anecdotes of his earlier service on the *Suffolk* he referred to some of the causes of discontent, such as low pay and the fact that the living conditions and food of the officers were much better than those provided for the men; but in the main Aaron Thomas seems to have accepted his own conditions as they were.

It will probably be abundantly clear to the professional historian and the naval expert that the editing of the diary has been done by an amateur. I can only plead that the search into the background has been done with enthusiasm and enjoyment. One of my great-great-grandmothers was born at Petty Harbour which is not far from St John's, and is near many places mentioned in the diary. Her husband came from Wincanton and her parents must have known the Newfoundland described by Aaron Thomas. This has added to the fascination.

The diary has been reproduced much as it was originally written. Some phrases have been rearranged so that the text will read more easily but none of the wording has been altered. The erratic spelling and capitalization has been left as it is in the original as this is consistent with other documents of the period. Some tedious passages which had little relation to the voyage have been shortened or removed but to do more would alter the individuality of the work. It has been given the punctuation it lacked. My own remarks have been put in square brackets and the same has been done where occasional words have been added to clarify the sense.

The log of the ship and the muster roll are to be found in the Public Records Office in London. The movements of the ship as recorded in the diary have been checked with these and very little discrepancy has been found. The lines of the ship are at the National Maritime Museum at Greenwich and her history is to be found in several books of naval history. Reading these has made the ships of the Royal Navy and the men who manned them seem like old friends. Many of the leading seamen of that day and later played a part in the history of Newfoundland.

Because Aaron Thomas wrote to a friend who apparently knew the facts of his background he told little of himself except that he was born in Wigmore and was in his thirty-second year at the time of writing. The search for information about the man led to the parish records of Wigmore. These were begun in 1572 and are complete. In them is to be found record of two marriages of interest. The first took place between Aaron Thomas and Mary Pinches on 23 May 1758. The baptisms of seven children of the marriage are shown later. Their third child, Aaron, was baptized on 19 January 1762, which would have made him thirty-two in 1794.

The second marriage took place between Edward Thomas and Elizabeth Pinches. Their son was also named Aaron. His baptism was recorded on 29 October 1769 so he would have been twenty-five in 1794. A problem arose when the muster roll of the *Boston* showed Aaron Thomas as being twenty-five years of age in 1794, despite his own statement. The *Boston*'s muster roll also showed that on 23 March 1794 he had been transferred from the pay lists of H.M.S. *Suffolk*. A search of the muster roll of the *Suffolk* revealed that Aaron Thomas of Wigmore had entered as a Chatham Volunteer in February 1793 when he was thirty. This established him as the son of Aaron and Mary Thomas. I have been unable to ascertain the relationships between the two Pinches and the two Thomases but the families seem to have had a close connection.

Many of the industrial and professional families who became prosperous in England in the latter part of the eighteenth century and early part of the nineteenth were descended from yeomen and the Thomas family seem to fit this pattern. The earlier part of the century had seen more and more land being absorbed into great estates owned by the nobility. It was then farmed by tenant farmers. Aaron Thomas, the father of the diarist, lived in the Bury House, which is still one of the most important farms in Wigmore. He was then a tenant of the Harley family. He must have been a person of some standing as he served as churchwarden for Wigmore in the years 1759 and 1765 and was referred to as Mr Aaron Thomas. His name also appears as Aaron Thomas, yeoman, on an unexecuted lease for land for twenty-one years, dated 1763. He seems to have died in 1767 or 1768, for his name is shown on Church Loan Rates for 1767 and his widow's name for 1768. His name is not among the Wigmore burials so it seems probable that he was buried in his native parish. After that his widow disappeared from the parish. The other family had gone by 1771 but the family connection with Wigmore was not lost.

Aaron Thomas of H.M.S. *Boston*, by his own account, grew up in Ludlow although no record of his residence there has been found; he then went to London and from there, in 1793, to Chatham to enter the Royal Navy. The history of his brothers and their descendants is one of success. From his own rather bitter remarks about friends and financial affairs it seems possible that Aaron was the unsuccessful member of the family in business. He certainly records the fact that he was short of money when he went to join the *Suffolk*. No record of him has been found after his service on the *Boston* and there is no mention of him in his brother's will which was made in 1822. All the rest of the family were mentioned. (See p. xx.)

Possibly the ex-shipmate to whom the diary was addressed was John Price, whose name appears on the muster roll of the *Suffolk*. He too was a Herefordshire seaman. The name Price recurs in the history of the Thomas family and the diarist left the impression that other Herefordshire people would see what he wrote. This, however, is supposition.

The more detailed history of the Thomas family, as I have found it, has been placed at the end of the introduction.

Woven into his accounts of naval life and his adventures in Newfoundland are comments on the political events in Europe and the views of the writer on many subjects. Between 1762 and 1794 England had both gained an empire and lost a large part of it. American Independence had been recognized, and Englishmen's ideas of trade and wealth had changed. Revolution in industry and agriculture had brought about a shift in population as many people moved from the country to growing industrial centres in the towns. Because of scientific progress people were living longer and there was a large increase in the population. Improved roads allowed the ordinary people to travel more easily. Newspapers which had come into being early in the century increased in number and were widely read. These together with pamphlets of American and French origin brought new ideas to men's minds. Many Englishmen had had sympathy with the French revolutionaries before the Reign of Terror. Aaron Thomas had been influenced in his younger days by the witty and colourful Charles Fox. All this is reflected in his writing.

Newfoundland had had a strange history. Aaron Thomas had done his best to inform himself about this new country which he was visiting. It would be interesting to know his source of reading material. By 1794 there were about twenty thousand people resident on the island. Prowse gave the population of St John's and its environs as something less than four thousand. The remaining inhabitants lived in settlements along the coast, which is both beautiful and rugged. They had remained despite overwhelming discouragements and many efforts to remove them.

Shortly after the discovery of Newfoundland by John Cabot the ships of Spanish, French, Portuguese and English were to be found in the bays and harbour of Newfoundland. There was no form of government other than that provided by the captains of ships from the ports of the West of England. They seem to have been the recognized lords of the harbours.

By 1580 there was a great increase in the number of fishing ships which came to Newfoundland from the West of England. This was because of restrictions which prevented them from fishing in Icelandic waters. Queen Elizabeth, who saw the need for good seamen for her fleet, brought about an act which called for four fish days a week and also established a bounty for the fitting out of ships to go to Newfoundland. The English method of curing fish required that stages and stores be built on shore. The crews were well organized and every crew included some women. It is uncertain when it first became the custom to leave some of the crews behind to protect the shore buildings against the raids of rival fishing crews, and the pilfering of the native Beothucks, but these became the first settlers. There were also definite efforts made to colonize the island. In 1610 John Guy established the first colony and he was followed by Sir William Vaughan, Lord Baltimore and others. None of these succeeded but although the original patentees departed some of the colonists remained.

The West Country merchants and their ship captains resented the presence of the settlers or planters, as they were called. Obviously those on the spot could select the best harbours and could start fishing earlier. Much of the failure of the first plantations was probably due to the active opposition of the ship fishermen, who came only for the fishing season.

In 1633 Charles I, through the Star Chamber Court, issued certain laws for the better government of Newfoundland. The exercise of law was put into the hands of the Fishing Admirals. These were the first captains to enter each harbour at the beginning of the season. The second to arrive became vice-admiral, and the third rear-admiral. As many of these men were rough and uneducated, and as they were in the employ of the English merchants, their interests were against those of the settlers. Another law forbade settlement within six miles of the shore, and no resident could occupy a fishing stage before the arrival of the ship fishermen. There was little law and order. In vain the settlers petitioned the British Government for a governor, but the powerful West Country ship owners used their influence to oppose the appointment of one, or of any civil magistrate. Only the convoy captains saw the need to encourage settlement as a check to invasion by the French. It was largely through their protests that despite all opposition Captain Henry Osborne was appointed as the first Governor in 1728. For the next hundred years successive naval commanders were appointed to the position, but as the British squadrons were on the station for only four months of the year the governor was absent for most of the year. Captain Osborne divided the island into districts and appointed magistrates but their authority was contested by the Fishing Admirals who contended that the new system had been introduced by an Order in Council whereas their authority had come from an Act of Parliament.

To add to their other troubles, the settlers suffered from repeated raids from the French, who had a flourishing settlement at Placentia between 1662 and 1762. From this base they attacked St John's and all the other settlements. Unlike the English the French had the full backing of their government.

It was as William Knox said in his evidence before the House of Commons in 1793:

"The island has been considered, in all former times, as a great ship moored near the Banks during the fishing season, for the convenience of English fishermen. The Governor was considered as the ship's captain, and those concerned in the fishery business as his crew, and subject to naval discipline while there."

Towards the end of the eighteenth century a change began with the establishment of a Supreme Court of Civil and Criminal Judicature in 1792. The rule of the Fishing Admirals was at last brought to an end. John Reeves, who was appointed as the first Chief Justice exposed many of the injustices which had afflicted the settlers when he wrote the first important history of Newfoundland. Perhaps Aaron Thomas read it, but at all events he was well informed.

By this time there were well established mercantile interests in Newfoundland. These merchants and the officers of the garrison were the leaders, there was a humbler class of planters or traders who did not fish, but who supplied those who did, and there was a much larger number of fishermen and servants who were usually in their debt. Many of the latter were Irish immigrants who had been brought out as passengers on the English ships which usually called at Irish ports on the outward journey. By the mid eighteenth century approximately half the population was Irish.

In 1794 the inhabitants were once again preparing to defend their homes against possible French invasion. Although France had given up her claim to Canada at the end of the Seven Years War she had retained extensive fishing rights along the shores of Newfoundland. When she declared war on England in 1793 it was feared that she might try to get possession of the island. The British had immediately seized the islands of St Pierre and Miquelon and Aaron Thomas gives a graphic description of conditions there.

The *Boston* and her captain had both been in Newfoundland waters in 1793. The ship had been named by Admiralty Order on 5 November 1761. She had been built by Robert Inwood at Rotherhithe at £10 *7s 6d* a Tun. She was fitted at Deptford as 32 guns, 220 men, and was completed on 12 July 1762. Her dimensions as given on her plans were: length of lower deck 127 ft, of the keel for tonnage 105 ft 1 in, breadth 34 ft, depth of hold 11 ft 9 in and burthen in tons 647 13/94. She remained on the Navy lists until 1809 or later. One source records that she was taken to pieces in 1841.

In 1793 she had been in an indecisive fight with the French frigate *Embuscade* and it was after this that Captain Morris took command of her in St John's. The engagement was described by W. Laird Clownes in *The Royal Navy* (1899):

"In July 1793, Captain George William Augustus Courtenay of the British frigate *Boston* 32, cruising off New York, sent in a challenge to Captain Jean Baptiste Bompard of the French frigate *Embuscade* 34, having first captured, by an adroit stratagem the *Embuscade*'s 1st Lieutenant with a Boat's Crew. Courtenay offered to wait for three days off Sandy Hook and had a written copy of the challenge posted up in the New York Coffee Rooms. On July 30th, a considerable French fleet passed, but the *Boston* kept her station and in the night of the 31st saw a large ship standing towards her. The *Embuscade* had come out to fight. Both ships hoisted their colours at dawn, and soon after 5 closed and began action—the *Boston* with her Starboard and the *Embuscade* with her Starboard broadside. Their evolutions were watched by a great crowd on the New Jersey beach, twelve miles away. In less than an hour the *Boston*'s rigging was so injured that she lost command of her sails, and a little later her main topmast went overboard. At 6.20 Captain Courtenay and the Lieutenant of the Marines were both killed; the two lieutenants borne on the ship's books were both severely wounded; and the mizzen mast was tottering. The crew fell into confusion, but the wounded 1st Lieutenant John Edwards took command and fought the ship. With difficulty the *Boston* avoided an attempt of *Embuscade* to rake her. Her condition was desperate as the wreck of the main topmast hampered the service of her guns, and all her chief officers were killed and wounded. She turned and fled before the wind, followed for some distance by the *Embuscade*, which had, however, been too much injured in masts, sails and rigging to overtake her. After an hour's chase, the Frenchman put about and returned to New York. The *Boston* was much the smaller and weaker ship, and at that time indiscipline had not destroyed the morale of the French Navy."

The *Independent Chronicle* of Boston, 15 August 1793, carried an account of the engagement as told by "a person who was on the *Boston* and has since arrived at the southward": "During the whole engagement a little man was plainly seen, dressed in a short white jacket, walking the quarter deck of the *Embuscade*, with his hands behind his back; now and then, however, taking a pinch of snuff. This was Capt Bompard. He was pointed at by the officers of the *Boston* as a mark for musquetry; but it appears that he escaped unhurt as well as all the officers, we are informed, of the French frigate."

Captain Courtenay had been anxious to engage the *Embuscade* as during her last cruise the French ship had captured or destroyed upwards of sixty British vessels. The *Boston*, after losing sight of *Embuscade*, had a very narrow escape. She was about entering the Delaware to refit in that river when the pilot gave the information that two French frigates were lying at anchor opposite Fort Mud. She discharged her pilot and hauled up for St John's, Newfoundland where she arrived safely on 19 August. There Lieutenant Edwards was given command of the *Pluto* sloop and Captain Morris was appointed to the *Boston.*

James Nicholl Morris (1762 ? –1830) was the son of Captain John Morris. He was commissioned as lieutenant on 14 April 1780 and commander on 21 September 1790. In 1791 he was appointed to the *Pluto* sloop on the Newfoundland station, where on 25 July 1793 he captured the French sloop *Lutine.* He was appointed to the *Boston* on 7 October 1793 which he commanded for the next four years in Newfoundland waters and in the Channel, the Bay of Biscay and the Spanish coast. He was in command of the *Colossus* 74 at the Battle of Trafalgar. She was the sixth ship in line following Collingwood and sustained heavier damage and greater loss of men than any other ship in the fleet. Morris himself was severely wounded in the thigh but remained on deck till the close of the action. He was promoted to the rank of Rear-Admiral of the Blue on 1 August 1811, Rear-Admiral of the White in 1812 and Rear-Admiral of the Red in 1814. He was knighted in 1815 and became a Vice-Admiral in 1819.

Throughout his writing Aaron Thomas could not resist telling anecdotes about people and the most highly coloured stories concern his former captain on the *Suffolk* who later became Admiral of the Blue in 1805. Peter Rainier was the descendant of a Poitevin family, who came to England on the Revocation of the Edict of Nantes. He entered the Navy in 1756 and saw service in the East Indies. He was present at several actions at the siege of Pondicherry and afterwards at the reduction of Manila. In 1764 he was paid off and was then probably employed under the East India Company. In 1768 he was promoted to the rank of lieutenant but saw no service in the Navy till January 1774 when he served in the *Maidstone* in the West Indies. In May 1777 he was promoted to the command of the sloop *Ostrich,* and in her captured a large American privateer after a hard fought action in which he was severely wounded. Approval of his conduct brought him advancement to post rank in 1778 and in 1779 he was appointed to the *Burford* of 74 guns. In her he went to the East Indies and took part in all the operations of the war.

In 1790 he commanded the *Monarch* in the Channel and early in 1793 commissioned the *Suffolk* of 74 guns, in which the following year he went to the East Indies as commodore and commander in chief. He was promoted to the rank of rear-admiral in June 1795, and to that of vice-admiral in 1799. He remained on the East India station as commander in chief till 1804, during which time he assisted at the reduction of Trincomalee and in 1796 took possession of Amboyna and Banda Neira. The admiral's share of the booty laid the foundation of a large fortune. After his retirement from active service he continued to be consulted by the ministry on questions relating to the station.

He died in 1808 leaving by his will one tenth of his property, proved at £250,000, towards the reduction of the National Debt.

Newfoundland became the tenth province of Canada in 1949. This has brought about a rapidly changing way of life. Those whose forebears settled in small bays and harbours are now moving into larger centres so that they may enjoy a more sophisticated way of life. The old customs and forms of speech are disappearing and we are in danger of losing our individuality. Aaron Thomas expected that his notes would be "ramed into some unfathomable hole, where, like the memory of their original owner, they may become a wreck and rot in oblivion". He was not granted his wish to have some part of Newfoundland named after him but perhaps now, one hundred and seventy-three years later, his writing will earn him a place in the literature of the island which was Britain's oldest colony.

I am grateful to Dr A. C. Hunter for his suggestion that the journal should be published and to Mrs J. C. Tonkin of Wigmore who did so much to help in tracing the Thomas family. My thanks are also due to Group Captain W. E. Fisher, Miss Joyce Hall, Mr E. Rowe, Dr L. M. Tuck, Mr Eli Lear, Mr David Webber and Mr E. Sandeman and the staff of the Gosling Memorial Library who helped in a variety of ways.

J.M.M.

The Thomas Family

Aaron Thomas's elder brother John, who was baptized in 1759, had a silversmith's business at 55 St James's Street in London between 1790 and 1814 and after that at 153 New Bond Street. He died on 14 October 1832 at 18 Brompton Crescent in the parish of Kensington. There is a memorial tablet to him in the Wigmore Parish Church. Two of his sons carried on the silversmith's business which may have been continued by their descendants, for it was still in existence there in 1942. The second child was Mary. She became a Mrs Brunton. Aaron was the third member of the family and the next son Thomas died in infancy and was buried at Wigmore. Another brother William, who was baptized in 1764, had an Italian warehouse at 153 New Bond Street between 1802 and 1816, then at 40 Conduit Street until 1819 and at 16 Mount Street between 1820 and 1823. He retired to Eye Cottage, Luston, which is about ten miles from Wigmore. His son, the Rev Aaron Thomas, was instituted as perpetual curate of Leinthall Earles nearby on 30 May 1833 and apparently died as such in 1834. William Thomas of Eye Cottage, gentleman, formerly of New Bond Street, London, Sarah Thomas, his wife and the Rev Aaron Thomas, incumbent of Eyton and Leinthall, are all buried in Orleton churchyard, near Wigmore. The youngest brother Moses, baptized in 1768, was a rate payer at Brewer Street, Golden Square, London in 1822.

John Thomas, the elder brother, appointed as his executors his brothers William and Moses and two of his sons Robert and John William. They were all living when the will was proved in 1832. The will mentions four sons and one daughter, his wife Mary, his sister Mary Brunton, also other members of the Thomas family and a Mr Price of Cumberton, which is in Orleton Parish. Two of John Thomas's sons, Francis Lewis and John William, carried on their father's business; the third son apparently served in the Royal Navy and had his home in Orleton. He died at Ashford Bowdler which is four or five miles from Ludlow and his tombstone is to be found in the churchyard there and reads:

"In memory of Robert Thomas, Commander R.N. who died at Church House, Ashford Bowdler, May 27th 1862 aged 71."

His widow lived until 1889. She was born Elizabeth Price. Another son of John Thomas was Thomas Lane Thomas.

In 1767 old Aaron Thomas of the Bury House had paid 9d for a small house and piece of land in Wigmore. It was lived in by the Edward Thomas family. It was shown on the voter's list of 1839 as being owned by John William Thomas, son of John Thomas, but it seems to have been occupied then by the descendants of Edward Thomas, one of whom married a Price. Although both families had moved away from Wigmore so long ago the family connection with the area was carried on.

One other interesting possibility about the family might be suggested although there has been no opportunity to prove any connection. The Harley family owned much of the land in the area of St Marylebone. Robert Harley, first Earl of Oxford, decided to develop this land in 1717. After the collapse of the South Sea Bubble in 1720, this development ceased for a time and the administration of it was eventually passed over to William Thomas who had long been in the service of the Harley family. In 1721 he was appointed Steward of the Manor of Tyburn and later Treasurer of the Vestry funds and by 1784 Surveyor of the Highways. It seems possible that Aaron Thomas's family tied in with this William Thomas and that they had been brought to Wigmore by the Harleys and then returned to London. The name of Mr Lane in St Marylebone development is prominent and it seems odd that it should be found in the name of John Lane Thomas if there was no connection.

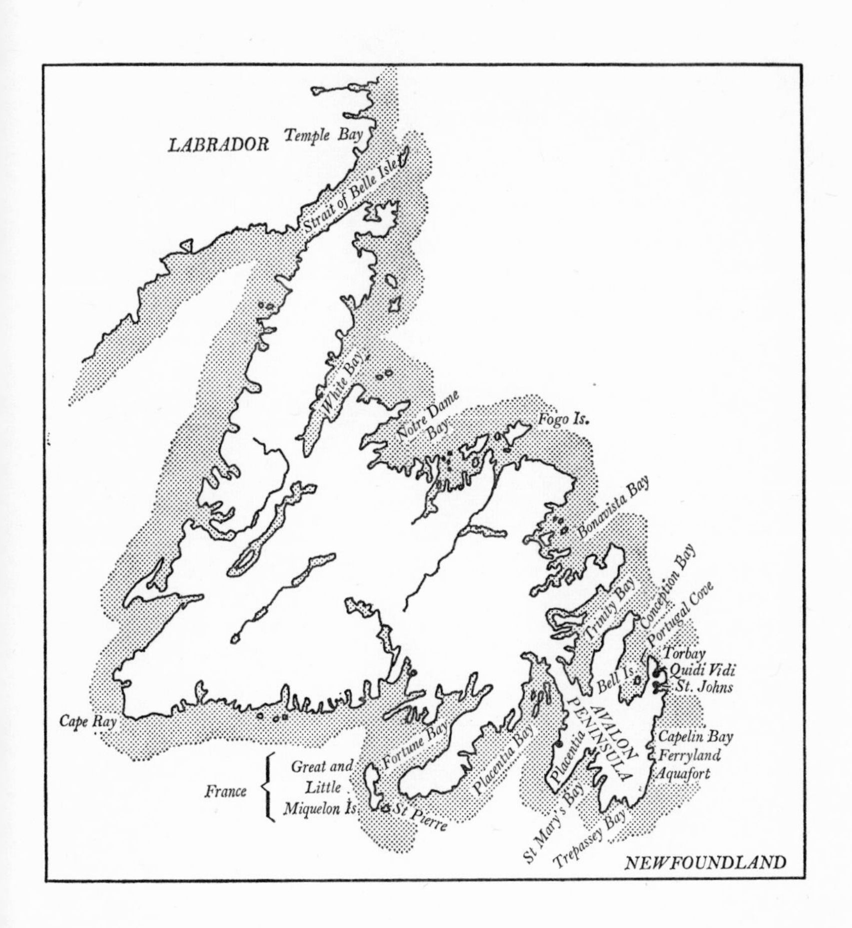
LABRADOR
Temple Bay
Strait of Belle Isle
White Bay
Notre Dame Bay
Fogo Is.
Bonavista Bay
Trinity Bay
Conception Bay
Portugal Cove
Torbay
Quidi Vidi
St. Johns
Bell Is.
AVALON PENINSULA
Placentia
Capelin Bay
Ferryland
Aquafort
Cape Ray
Fortune Bay
Placentia Bay
St Mary's Bay
Trepassey Bay
France
Great and Little Miquelon Is
St Pierre
NEWFOUNDLAND

History of Newfoundland

Containing an Account of its Banks. Fisheries. Climate. Soil. Productions. Lakes. Harbors. Population. Insects. Animals. Charters &c. A copious relations of its first Settlement. And a vast variety of Memoirs of that Country, never before collected, or made known. Some account of the Scilly Isles. Lisbon. and Cadiz in Spain. The whole interspersed with a multiplicity of

Naval Historical
Biographycal Sentimental
Political Geographical
Military. and Moral Sketches

With a great number of new, and singular anecdotes, of Charracters & Places. In which is introduced a Dissertation on Friendship. Written during a Voyage from England, to Newfoundland, and from Newfoundland to England, in the years of 1794 and 1795, Addressed to a Friend.

Preface

In perusing and examining my Manuscript I find various causes for excuse. So multifarious are its defects that a grammatical eye cannot but smile at the constant succession of blunders which every sheet of the pages will present to his view. He will instantly discover the wrong construction of participles, adjectives, pauses and stops, an inaccuracy in writing, and a frequent failure in spelling words of the commonest denote. By way of apology I shall observe that none of these sheets has been rewritten; and altho the want of correction was manifold, yet it neither suited my time nor accorded with my inclinations to give it a revision. Every line was wrote by candlelight, on board the *Boston,* and a part of it when her canvas was afloat in the Wind and the motion she imparted to me might not perhaps be the most lenitive for fostering literary ideas.

Having said thus much of my Farago of Nonsense by way of preface, I cannot resist from making an observation on my Title page. I see it is as full as if the history of the whole world was to follow. Such a multiplicity of matter held out on the Frontispiece and so little to be found within puts me in mind of a Gentleman of fortune who was remarkable fond of his Arms engraved or emblazoned on everything which belonged to him. There was not an iron Pott in his Kitchen, an old Chair in his Garrat, nor a Pane of Glass in all the Windows of his House, but what his Arms were displayed on. So great were his singularitys in this particular, and so strong his attachments to his family Ensign, that he would always have his Armorial Bearings delineated on the glass sights of his Spectacles, and also on the soles of his shoes. "Then," says he, "I can see through and walke on my Arms."

Heraldry antiently was of great use. At the present period I know of no purpose which it is conducive to, unless it be found convenient in exhibiting the folly and nonsense of weak people. In the case of my Manuscript I have made an attempt to display great things on the outside by holding forth a long list of good things and large names, but whoever looks on the inside will feel disappointment. I consider the trappings about these sheets in the same light as I do a valuable diamond ring on a scabby finger.

In some pages I see I have set up for a moralist, and yet if you travel a few yards further you will be convinced it comes from the pen of a licentious fellow. My Morality, I have often been told, would lie in a Sparrow's Egg, and my Religion in the belly of a small Spider; but I have had it often remarked to me that my ribaldry could not be contained in a pair of Blacksmith's Bellows, and that was it completely compressed in a Machine so unwieldy as that the fountain of action would be so well supply'd that the ingress would far exceed the egress.

Thousands of people *think* they possess qualifications which no other person but themselves will admit for a moment. I make this observation to pave the way for my saying that it is possible you may expect I shall want your thanks for the labour which I have been at in this compilation. Be assur'd the case is not so; for as thanks cannot be given without *flattery*, I shall decline all compliments, in the same manner as I would refuse being elected a Knight of a particular Order (instituted by a European Sovereign) with the badge of which they often ask charity.

I have frequently eat a good Dinner without a Table Cloath, and more than once I have dined on an uninhabited island. Near us were Strawberrys, Cherrys, Gooseberrys and other delicious wild fruits. I gathered Strawberrys, but if I wanted Cherrys I had a morass to cross before I came to the wished for place. When I arriv'd here and was desirous of other fruit I had more difficultys to encounter. Every luxurious bit I wanted could not be obtained untill I had surmounted some obstacle. So, in perusing the following sheets, you may trot into a swamp at the outset, but let me recommend you to persevere; the roads may mend, and the weather get better. Before you finish your tour you may meet with something which is pleasing in the way.

Different palates acquire opposite sauces. For my part I am fond of Acids. I beg leave to introduce the following story:

A short time ago I was at Dinner with a Gentleman who requested his servant to give him a glass of Cyder. He drew the cork and a great part of the contents of the bottle, which was

Vinegar, flew into his face. He immediately distorted his Phiz, which exhibited a representation of all the corrosive sours in existence. Then with a piercing voice, as acute as it was shrill, he exclaimed

"Why Sir, it is *Vinegar*!"

To which my companion reply'd, "Oh, you peevish, harsh, austere, tart, verjuice looking rascal! You need not sound your razor grinding pipe, for your frontispiece display'd the completest collection of acids I ever beheld! You vinegar looking rascal! Why your nose seems as keen as the point of a razor, and your teeth as sharp as the points of needles."

To some of the following sheets I apply the above anecdote, where ill humour is carry'd as far as it will go.

On looking over my dissertation on Friendship I see I have pushed my remarks very strong, but I see nothing I would wish to retract. I wrote from the heart, which is the only source where a true notion of its principles can flow from. I certainly consider myself as able to judge on the passions of the human mind. The different situations of life which chance has thrown me in has given me an opportunity of analysing the powers by which Mankind is actuated. The result of my researches I have put on paper in that particular, but whoever casts their Eye on it, I suspect will differ in opinion from me, because few of us will admit our own infirmitys, but endeavour to gloss them over with rough and fine materials, as concenience may offer.

So far I have gone with this kind of preface. I shall proceed no further with apologys as you will, I am sure, admit that you have seen enough from

AARON THOMAS

I

Bound for Newfoundland but forced into Scilly

A short time since I flattered myself in the hope to have sailed in the same Ship as you untill the Olive Branch had declared to all the contending powers that Peace—sweet Peace—had swayed the minds of men and sent you and I to our homes togather. How much I lament the separation from you I shall not here declare, but suffice by saying that Pleasure has an end, and so has Sorrow. So in the present case, the unpleasant sensations arising from my parting from you will give to my mind at times a lassitude and langour which can only be erased by time. I surely am most poignantly stuck in having removed from my presence a person who I had made the honorable and faithful depository of all my remarks.

Having done you justice in this short eulogy, permit me the pleasure of promizing you that my avocations shall be apply'd occasionally in addressing my observations to you. On my return this will be a proof that altho we were separated by the Atlantic Ocean, yet neither time nor place had unhinged the threshold of my recollection to forget the person whose society I shall always remember with esteem and pleasure.

These sheets, which I have address'd to you, you will find very different from a Ship's Journal, having myself little pretensions to Nautical knowledge, yet I am certain you will find much matter, for this I know—let a man with a common capacity be placed in any situation in life and occurrences in great variety will arise for his contemplation and animadversions. For my part I cannot go on Deck and turn my Eyes towards the firmament but what I discover infinite variety—the Sky in various colours, a few minutes more and a revolution takes place which produceth a thousand different shades, pause for yet a few minutes longer and another revolution succeeds, whose variegated hues and golden tinged edges far exceeds the power of the Pencil to delineate or my Pen to describe. Again, I cast my Eye on the rocks with which this Bay abounds and I see nature in a grand and awefull form. If I go on shore and traverse a sandy desert here also is matter for investigation. In short, let the contemplating mind be stationary in a desert or a flower garden and he will find an abundance of matter for investigation.

To inform you that the *Boston* is bound for Newfoundland is a circumstance which I personally acquainted you with at Spithead. We shall wait here for a day or two to collect such Ships as wish to benefit themselves of our protection. After that we shall lie to off Dartmouth to take such Vessels as may be ready from that place; and then we shall proceed on our voyage. I expect to be in England again in November, where I hope to find you, which will greatly add to the satisfaction of again viseting my native Country.

Before I proceed I shall observe that the *Boston*'s orders are to proceed with the Convoy to Newfoundland, which having accomplish'd, she is to cruize on the Banks etc. as intelligence may be received, and then to remain at St John's, Newfoundland untill further orders.

We left Spithead on the 23rd of March, 1794, with a fair wind, for Torbay. We went thro the Needles *[rocks off the westernmost point of the Isle of Wight]* but before we got abreast of Cowes we stuck on a sandbank called the Middle; here we remained for half an hour, as the Tide made we got off without damage.

As we sailed by Hurst Castle and the bold and romantic Cliffs of the Isle of Wight every object occasion'd a different sensation from the impression they gave me when I sailed by them in May last. I had, alas! lost my old faithfull Shipmate. I had a tremor on my mind, as if the atmosphere was ready to crush me to atoms, and every time I looked at the Sun, which that day shone gloriously bright, I thought it warned me of some fatal and important event to myself. This agitation of mind and lowness of spirits continued with me untill my arrival in this Bay when, having been ashore at Brixham a part of two days, my malancholy considerable abated by viseting some of my acquaintances, to some of which you are personally known.

Having last summer, with Lord Howe's Fleet, spent many days in Torbay, I collected a few anecdotes of the places in the environs of this Bay such as I never saw in print. I shall comment on them, premizing first that Torbay is of the utmost consequence to the British Navy, particularly in time of War. Here a large Fleet may ride in perfect safety and proceed to Sea on a particular emergency with more dispatch then from Plymouth or Spithead. Yet at this crisis I cannot but lament the inattention of Government to the shores of this Bay, for at the moment there is not a single piece of Ordnance in the environs of the Bay. It is a circumstance at which I much wonder that the French have not attempted to cut some of our Merchant Ships out when riding here without any of the King's Ships, which frequently is the case. No doubt they are not strangers to the facility with which it may be done.

During the late War the Ministry paid a due attention to this object. They erected Forts and embankments on the Berry Head, Shoalstone Point, Churston Cove and Torquay and also had an encampment the last two summers of the War on the Berry Head. These embankments or ramparts are in perfect order. When they were made great care was taken in their formation, as well as for their preservation, for which purpose I will relate the following little Botanical subject.

We all know that finesse is allowable in War, and that every Engineer should carry on his works with deception and stratagem. The Berry Head and other waste lands in the environs of this Bay are, in most places, cover'd with a Bramble, called in my County (Herefordshire) Gorst. This is a very troublesome tenant, and I have known Two Guineas an Acre given in Radnorshire for clearing the ground of it. Its roots, like the hearts of lovers, are much attached to each other, only with this difference, they combine togather, if left to their own caresses, linked in fond embrace for centurys, whereas the passions of us mortals are like a bubble of Soap blown from a Tobacco Pipe—a puff of wind separates our burning desires and blasteth our joys.

But I had like to forget my little anecote, I must return to my ramparts of earth. These embankments are formed of earth and loose stones. The Officer who superintended the work had Hay Seed and the Seeds of the Gorst sown on the surface of the ramparts. He was led to believe, in just expectation, that the seeds of the Gorst would grow and take root, which would not only add internally to prevent the earth from slipping down, but would add externally to its strength by keeping the green sod togather;

furthermore when these prickly bushes came to maturity their busky heads would give the Redoubt the appearance of a large Bramble and act as a decoy to the enemy. But in this particular the Engineer was disappointed, for the Gorst seeds never took root, the Hay seeds only coming to perfection, it being a property peculiar to this vegitable to flourish spontaneously under the hand of nature alone. The opaque qualitys in this could be render'd of no service.

It being a circumstance of public notoriety that King William landed at Brixham, in this Bay, I shall notice it no further then to observe that the stone on which he put his foot is hid from the public eye, being immured generally with filth and the excrement of Fish. I remember at the Centenary of the landing of King William in 1688 a meeting was held at the Crown and Anchor Tavern on the 4th of November, 1788, by the Constitutional Society, to celibrate the hundredth year of the event. Mr Fox was in the Chair when they passed a resolution to erect a pillar in Runnymead, near Egham, to perpetuate to the world the accomplishment of so great a Revolution. What led me to this remark is that such intelligent Gentlemen as these should forget this Stone of sacred memory after passing the above resolution, by suffering it to remain in its present oozey bed. This is not a little singular and can only be attributed to their not knowing the fact of the existence of this footstep, which lent its assistance to pave the way to so brilliant an epoch in the history of England.

[King William did land here. The Mr Fox referred to was the Whig leader of the Opposition in Parliament. A stone, said to be the one on which William of Orange (later King William) set foot, was preserved on the wharf, and William IV, as Duke of Clarence, visited Brixham in 1828. The stone was moved to the landing place so that he might step on it. This stone is said to be the same one and is placed in the base of one of the lamps on the harbour pier and inscribed "On this stone, and near this spot, William of Orange first set foot on landing in England, the 5th of November, 1688." There is also a statue of William III at the harbour edge.]

Brixham Quay (for the Town is situated about a mile inland) contains about 200 Houses. It has increased in opulence very considerably of late years. Most of its Inhabitants are engaged in the Fishing Trade. Great quantitys of Fish are sent by water to Portsmouth, and from thence by land to London; vast abundance are also sent to Exeter and other inland Towns.

The Berry Head, which forms one of the angles of Torbay, is so well known to Mariners, as well as to yourself, that it will be superfluous in my saying more of it then that it is a headland of considerable height, very rocky, there being not two inches of soil on the top of it. It took its name, the Berry or Bury Head (as I presume) because close to the rock, which is nearly perpendicular, there is water sufficient to float a First Rate. Thus we infer that there is more rock bury'd or berry'd under the water then is above. I have thus noticed the Berry Head to introduce a circumstance in its nature extremely singular.

The Berry Head is solid rock, nearly as hard as granite. A few years ago, as some workmen were employ'd in blowing up a part of this rock, they discover'd, several feet below the surface and in the midst of a solid mass of rock, a tinder box containing a flint and steel which must have lain there for many centurys. How this domestic article deposited itself in this strange situation I must leave you to form your own conjectures on.

Between the Berry Head and Brixham are some traces of a Watch Tower, on a point called Shoalstone Point and near it are the visible remains of a ditch, the works of the Saxons, which runs to Mudd Cove. On this point just spoken of, and below the Watch Tower, is the entrance into a Cavern. Its width will admit six Horses abreast and its height will permit an object twelve feet high to enter, yet this extraordinary opening is so situated amongst hillocks and large broken stones that you may pass within eight yards of it and not perceive it.

I had the curiosity to enter it. On your admission it is light and spacious; having travelled a few yards it becomes dark and narrow. As I kept advancing in this gloomy abode a tremor came upon me which began to stagger my resolution. Every step I took put me in mind of some little sin I had been guilty of. Advancing a little further in this dreary den, this horrid mansion for Reptiles and Hobgoblins, I suddenly, by the extreme solemnity of the place, became possessed of the recollection of all my iniquity and evil acts at once. (Here you will say that my capacity must be pretty large to have in mind such a mass of crimes at once.) For every evil I had committed I fancy'd I saw a grim spectacle ready to chastize my arrogance and strike revenge. Having such a frightfull and numerous army at my front I need not tell you that I wished for a retreat, (a knowledge to effect which must be consider'd as no small military accomplishment in the education of a soldier, as was found a convenient and useful measure more then once amongst the combined Armys on the Continent during the past campaign).* So facing about, I made a precipitate return, resolving in the future to be cautious in entering such an abyss of despair as this.

Returning again, and speaking seriously of this Cavern, it is said that this subterraneous vault has a passage underground to the River Dart, which is a distance of five miles.

In this neighbourhood are more Caverns of this kind, one of which is near Torwood, on the other side of the Bay. But I must abridge my annotations, otherwise I shall not have made the Landsend ere you think I ought to be on my return from Newfoundland.

[The name Berry Head comes from burgh, meaning fort. Cliffs here are about 200 feet high. The headland, some 80 acres of common land covered with furze (gorse, or gorst), is of Devonian limestone in which there are many caves, including Kent's Cavern at Torwood (now part of Torquay). Mudd Cove is probably St Mary's Bay of today, formerly known as Mudstone Sands.]

Churston Cove is remarkable for the singularity of its formation. Situated as it is by the seaside, within the compass of a few yards, nature has made prodigious rocks and mountains which are intersected by valleys, in some places not more then three yards wide, so hemmed in with steep and sudden ascents that their declivitys, in many places, cannot be ascended. Amongst this apparent wreck of nature, of broken hills and rugged rocks, are to be found specimens of the Cornish Diamond *[crystal or transparent quartz]*, some curious stones and petrefactions. To this sublime scene Art has added a Grove of Trees under whose Bows and the adjacent Brambles sport, in frisky wanton-ness, a great number of Rabbits.

The Grand Fleet and others have frequented Torbay much of late and the Bodys of several Sailors have been brought ashore and bury'd here. A great deal might be said of this irreligious practize but it is not a subject for my pen to animadvert on as, for aught I know as little ceremony may attend my own funeral

---

* This refers to the defeat of the British and Austrian armies in the Low Countries by the French.

obsequies as has come to their lot. Sorry should I be to attend the interment of an acquaintance in unconsecrated ground, but how more acuter would the pain be to follow the Body of one whom I revere, like you; but this I know—those poor fellows who lie in Churston Cove will be as ready to answer the *great* call as if their Bodys had been deposited under the sacred roof of Canterbury Cathedral.

Amongst the number of Graves I found here there was one more remarkable than the rest; his companions had bury'd him in an arbor formed by four Buckthorne Trees, whose antling sprays effected a complete canopy. On his Grave they had formed the words W. MAJOR, EDGAR, 1793, in a curious manner with Sea shells and small stones and pebbles. It was wrote somewhat like the following:

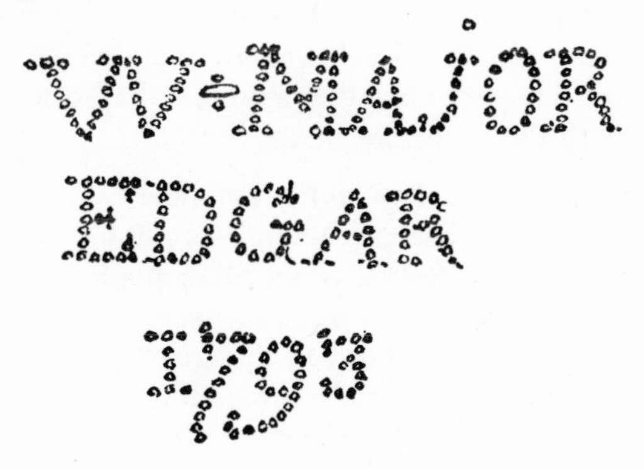

I must confess this little attention to Major's Grave drew from me the tears of sympathy.

"Alas!" thinks I, "Poor Major! Altho no sculptor'd marble or Poetic verses decorate thy bed of clay, yet at this moment thou hast perhaps a mother living, fondly remembering thy boyish frolicks, and only yesterday feeding her mind with the hope of the War soon being at an end, which would bring one of her offspring again to her sight. Perhaps too, Major, thou hadst when living a friend, in whose social company thou couldst not only impart the secrets of thy mind, but enjoy the sparkling glass and the mellow lute. Was he viewing this spot, now humanized by containing thy sacred relicks he would exclaim 'Alas! There poor Major lies.' "

Having paid this tribute of veneration to an unknown Sailor, which is more than the Crew of His Majesty's Ship *Edgar* expected, let me quit the sound of so unpleasant a Knell for another subject of the kind, altho not the same serious nature. But before I proceed on the subject hinted at let me observe that the description given of Churston Cove, when all the objects compressed within so small a compass are consider'd, renders this place a retreat admirable adapted to the purpose of solitary contemplation,—particularly for those Birds of sorrowing notes, such as the Owl, who nightly sends forth her dolefull voice to the surrounding Rocks and Trees. The gloomy and hollow sounds vibrating to the Ear of some chance passenger ceases his tremulous limbs, which he thinks too slowly perform their office. His imagination, momentarily, becomes stationary and some minutes elapses before he thinks he has moved a few yards from the ominous sounds.

The next subject I treat of, altho it has death for its groundwork, yet it very widely differs from anything before spoken of.

As I was one day perambulating amongst the Rocks in Churston Cove I met with the following inscription:

Stop Traveller, pray do not grumble
If on this spot chance should thee tumble
For near these Rocks, tremendous high
Whose rugged forms point to the sky
Yes, be not surprized if in this ground
The Relicks of a Female is found.
For amidst this heap of broken stones
Lies a good natur'd Female's bones.
And as to death all must bow
Know then, this Female is a *Cow.*
So I pray read on, ere thou further trudge
For under this soil lies Mary Fudge*
Then ye horn'd tribe, that chance may here bring
Do o'er her Grave doleful dirges sing,
And let these Rocks and Hills resound,
Echoeing her name to all around,
While Nereids and Satyrs to them relate
The story of poor Mary's fate.
Then round this spot, in herds they'll roam

* I find she was call'd Fudge by the Sailors, from the Butcher who fed her being of that name. [*A.T.*]

And on her Grave they'll drop their foam
As their antling heads with sorrow drop,
Lamenting her unhappy lot.
Yet furthermore I must relate
That this was penn'd by her messmate*
Who of her life's virtues largely shar'd
But by her death they were much marr'd.
Of her good qualitys yet must I tell,
To Cheesecakes, Custards—to all farewell!
Reader, as the truth thou shalt meet,
Know also, she was of Lord Howe's Fleet,
Who when at Sea, Boreas was so rude
As with his winds her to obtrude,
And Neptune too, I think did feast
In always teasing this poor beast.
The Ship was so toss'd Mary could not stand,
She breath'd her last as we made the Land,
For she got some falls, her bones she stove,
And here she lies in Churston Cove. *A.T.*

The lines just recit'd I am well *inform'd* were penn'd by the Captain's Steward, a fellow whose ideas seem not very compatible with his situation. It appears by the inscription that he had a proper value of his messmate's Milky and Creamy qualitys, by writing so long a monody to her memory. Mrs Fudge, no doubt, had often served him in a Rum way,† so it is natural for one toper to lament the death of another.

On the 25th of March, 1794 I had orders to go on business for Captain Morris to the village of Churston. A person went with me whose disposition was not a little volatile. We were landed from the *Boston* at the Cove, and passing by the Graves spoken of earlier our conversation turned upon them as soon as the Eye caught a view of them, on that with pebbles particularly. We walked to Churston Cove. On our arrival there, our missions being separate, we parted under the promize to meet at the Cove at five O'clk, that being the hour a Boat would attend to take us aboard.

---

* Who was Captain Rainier's Steward, on *Suffolk* 74 Guns. [*A.T.*]
† Rum and Milke. [*A.T.*]

I drank Tea with that hospitable and good little lady Mrs Turpin and her Two Daughters, the youngist of which made many kind enquiries after you. *[The records of St Mary the Virgin, Churston Ferrers, show that Benjeman and Jenny Turpin had five daughters. The two youngest were Jenney and Mary Ann.]* As the family is well known to you I need not give the high opinion I entertain of them at this period, having communicated that to you in person after we had been entertained there togather at their house. Suffice me to say that the clotted Cream was not only in excellent order but was also in abundance. It took no small quantity to satiate my unsavoury stomach. After Tea that precious cordial, called by the French Ne De Voya, being handed about, I mistooke Six O'clk for Five. *[This could be Noyau, a brandy flavoured with fruit kernels.]* Being an hour behind my time I was obliged to make a precipitate retreat for the Cove.

On my arrival at the Cove I found our Boat had been there and with my companion was gone on board. This intelligence I learned from his having wrote with pebbles on the grass GONE ON BOARD THE BOSTON. Very well, thinks I, then I shall walk over the Hill to Brixham. So, passing by the Graves for that purpose, on the sod of one I observed, wrote in small stones—

HERE LIES THE BODY OF AARON THOMAS

It immediately struck me that this frail memorial to a living name was the work of my companion while waiting for the Boat.

"Never mind," says I, "Mr C—, your Tomb shall be near mine." So near the adjacent Grave I wrote—

HERE LIES THE BODY OF MAURICE COX ESQR.

For as we were good friends while living I thought it a pity that death should part us; so, out of good nature and real compassion I very obligingly laid my Companion quietly by my side, after which I arose, not from the dead, but from off my Knees and walked from my Tomb to Brixham, leaving only my name behind me. I procured a Boat and got on board my Ship that night.

Having at Brixham purchased fresh Beefe, Mutton, Fowls, Vegitables and a long train of etc., the Boston left Torbay for Newfoundland on Wednesday, March 28th, with a fair wind, taking with us such Ships as were collected in Torbay. The greatest part of this day we lay to off Dartmouth, waiting for such Ships to come out as was ready. We proceeded down the Channel untill the 28th of March when the Wind came right in our teeth, on which day we were forced into Scilly with the whole of our Convoy, intending there to wait untill a fair wind came, which was not for neare three weeks.

[The Captain's log records "Friday, 28th March—Standing into St Mary's Sound." March 29th/April 16th Moored in St Mary's Sound, Scilly.]

II

Stormbound - The Scilly Islands

The Scilly Islands, called by the French Sorlings [*Les Îles Sorlingues*], lie west southwesterly from the Landsend, distant about 9 Leagues. They are a number of islands, interspersed and surrounded by a vast multitude of Rocks. Six of the Islands only are inhabited. [*Only five are now inhabited; Samson was evacuated in 1855.*] In what I have to say of these islands I do not intend to give a history of them, and that for a wise reason—it is beyond my capacity; but what I shall relate will be new and authentic. The historical part will be compressed in a narrow compass and my anecdotes are but few.

The Scilly Isles are of considerable advantage to Great Britain as they look equally into St George's and the English Channels, for which reason most Ships bound from the southward try to make these islands in order to make their course with more precision. They are very convenient for Ships to shelter in from foul winds and bad weather, as we found by experience, for during the three weeks we lay here there was more then one heavy Gale, which had we been at Sea would have not a little discomfited us. Ships bound from the northern States of America frequently call here, it being the first land they make. From a variety of concuring circumstances many Navigators put in here, so that the Sounds and Roads about these Islands are seldom without shipping in them.

The Lighthouse on St Agnes's Isle is of great import to these Islands. It is built of Stone, which is plaster'd with whitewash. It is 51 feet high, the Gallery 4 feet, the Sash lights 12 feet, which makes its height in the whole 65 feet. The lights within the Lanthorne are made to move in such a manner that in the space of one minute you see a glimmering light which gradually increases to a splendid, brilliant and grand luminous light. This revolution takes place in every minute during the night, so that there is no possibility of a mariner taking these lights for those of any other place.

[This lighthouse is no longer in use as such but is a private house. There are now lighthouses on other islands.]

Before the General Deluge, it is said that these islands were situated so near England that the Skull of a Horse would not swim in the channel which separates them; be that as it may, this I must suppose—that the Scilly Isles were formed when Nature was in a grand convulsion, for a more hideous and frightfull collection of Rocks my Eyes never beheld as the view from the summit of Tresco Hill, or the Lighthouse in St Agnes's Island.

I was ashore at St Mary's several times. This is the largest of all the Islands. The principal Town is called St Mary's, alias Hugh Town. It has a small, antient, old Castle in repair, on the summit of a Hill called Castle Hill, alias the Lines.

[St Mary's is the largest island and Hugh Town is today the main area of settlement. The "old castle" is now the Star Castle Hotel, so called from it being built star-shaped. It has been the house of the Governors of the islands.]

It is built only for the use of small Arms. The Castle Hill is completely fortify'd all round with Walls and Redoubts on which are mounted upwards of Sixty pieces of Cannon of different Caliber which defend the Sounds and Roads from any attempt. But Nature, on this head, has been very bountifull for the protection of these Islands for the many Rocks above water, Rocks under water which never appear and which are by far the most numerous, render the navigation amongst the Islands so very dangerous that the Scillonians (as they call themselves) have very little to fear as to a viset from a foreign power.

The men of these Islands are said to be amazing alert with their Oars, and manage a Boat with wonderful dexterity and adroitness. Early initiated, indeed I may say hatched, as they are upon the Ocean, it is not at all surprizing that they should be so very expert in the management of their Prows. *[Scillonian pilot gigs are still famous today for their speed.]*

Ships wishing to put into Scilly, by firing a Gun and hoisting a Weft (which is the signal for a Pilot) will have several Boats put off immediately with Pilots. Amongst these a competition frequently ariseth so as to endanger their own lives in endeavouring who shall reach the object of this contention first, for the sake of the boon given for Piloting the Vessel safely to an anchorage.

To such a height had these contests risen in these rival races that it was found necessary to enact particular rules for the government of these Pilots. These are now not strictly conformed to for you often see these kind of races between the contending partys which, when they get ashore, is the cause of petty quarrels amongst one another.

There is no kind of Manufactory in these Islands. They have all their Goods sent from England. The Inhabitants live by Fishing and Piloting, altho it must be confessed that some of the Fishermen are very well acquainted with the coast of France, particularly Roscoff, a Town in the Bay of Morlaix near the Isle of Bas. This place the French declared a free Port for Brandy, which brought a great influx of English smugglers to it. With Roscoff the Scillonians carry'd on, before the War broke out, considerable traffick, very much no doubt to the increase of His Brittanic Majesty's revenue, and also to the pockets of his faithfull and loyal subjects in these Isles.

[*The smugglers dealt with all the coast of Brittany as far south as La Rochelle and even the Spanish ports. "After 1784, the stationing of a protection vessel in Scilly probably made smuggling more difficult. In 1790, an Act of Parliament allowed the legal costs of cases of smuggling to be met by the Commissioners out of the sale of seizures. After this smuggling gradually declined till its virtual suppression became a source of economic depression in the island." (R. L. Bowley,* The Fortunate Islands.)]

The Town of St Mary's containeth about 150 Houses, all built of Stone, mostly very low. The first time I went ashore, in the Garden of the first House I made at this place I saw a board stuck upon a pole, on which was painted a Bottle and under it was wrote the following inscription:

> Walke round the corner, then you'll see and behold
> The House where good Liquor is sold.

"I see," thinks I to myself, "let me put my head in what corner of the world I will, I find an intaglio thus public and stationary as an incitement to the poor unfortunate devils, whose appetites are full of desires and whose pockets hold only a few pence. Gin and Brandy—oh surely there must be a great profit in the sale of these articles, else Housekeepers would never give themselves so much trouble to expose the commodity they deal in so publicly for sale."

Now I am one of those beings who is persuaded that the immoderate use of strong Liquors is not only a firebrand but the very bane of society. Immoderate use did I say? Yes, I did, and the observation will bear me out. For my part I consider a Dram Shop as a Whirlpool which draws into its vortex everything that is vicious and infamous. Show me a Dram-drinker, and if he is not in his circumstances independent, I am strongly led to suspect that at the same time I see a Thiefe. This perhaps may be judg'd hard reasoning. Admitted—but I see instances innumerable to form this opinion.

The constant use of strong Liquors, even in moderation, is a practize not to be permited. Initiated by degrees, one day after the other, to this beverage, by a few month's custom it becomes a habit which in two or three years becomes a craving after these diabolical drops.

It is admitted, and that but too truly, that most Sailors are given to intoxication. How it is to be accounted for? No other way then this. A Boy of ten years of age is sent by the Marine Society on board a Man of War. With him he takes his morals and his change of Cloaths. On board he gets. Here he is on the Quarter Deck, waiting while the Captain's Clerk takes a description of his person, and his name—in full possession of a large stock of good morals, in a state of innocence, unaccustomed to hear the name of his Maker mentioned but with awe and reverence. An oath had never escaped his Lips and the glass of intoxication the tip of his Tongue had never tasted. In a few minutes he is dismissed the Quarter Deck and turned down in the Waiste. Here he is again a total stranger. He is immediately surrounded by a parcel of Boys (as a parity in years in Lads generally begets acquaintance) into whose society he is infallibly drawn. He becomes a Messmate of some and the companion of them all. These Boys being well versed in the infamous vice of swearing and cursing, their new Messmate, by their example, soon becomes as expert as the best amongst them in a kind of blasphemous language.

But I have yet to account why Sailors, more then any other set of men, are given to intoxication. This I shall attribute to custom. From the long Voyages navigators are necessitated to make and the heat of the climates, their stowage of Beer can only be for a few days. Here ariseth the compulsive needfulness of allowing each man a pint of Wine and half a pint of Rum (mixed with water) per day.

Boys are not allowed spirits in King's Ships, except where the Captain permits it, but they generally get some from the men. I will venture to assert with confidence that a Boy coming on board a Ship who, as I said before, had never tasted the glass of intoxication, if given a glass or two of Wine or a glass of Rum a day for a few months, which being followed up for two or three years, he will be no bad toper as he arrives at maturity nor never refuse a glass when he can get one.

Many things are beneficial when used with temperance and moderation. It may be found necessary to keep the spirits from too low a depression, and here recourse is had to the Bottle to stir up ardour and liveliness, but the same quantity of Wine that would make the blood run warm on the frozen shores of Labrador would make the native of a hott country run mad. But my detestation of a drunkard imperceptibly led me away from my anecdotes of Scilly.

Sunday, April 13th. The most part of this day I spent on shore in St Mary's Isle. It was a beautifull day. I walked most of the Island. Most of the Houses are thatched, I asked the reason. They told me that altho the Isle was more than seven mile round yet the spray of the Sea in rough weather flew over most part of the Island, which falling on the roof of their Houses, were they cover'd with slate or stone, would so corrode them that they would not last two years. *[It is more likely that slate and stone would have been too expensive. These came into use later.]*

I poked my Nose into every Cottage I came athwart, asking the honest owners if they had any Hogs or Poultry to dispose of, which in fact were commoditys I wanted. But the Sounds about these Islands had been so much viseted by Fleets and Convoys that nothing was left for us poor souls in the *Boston* except Eggs.

I find every House here has a Hand Mill, worked by one person, with which they grind their Corn. It is no doubt very convenient for their family use as it stands in the corner of the House and does not take up any more room then a Chair. The poor people live principally on Barley Bread, Fish and Potatoes. The inside of many of their Cotts show visible signs of distress. Under the roofs of some I met with very old people, three who were upwards of Ninety years old. These poor, good-natured, silver-headed persons were born in Scilly, had never been out of it, and had never seen a Coach in their lives, nor a Turnpike Gate. The air here is very healthy, for in general the Inhabitants live to a good old age. I observe the weomen are very beautiful, very ignorant, and was told they are very chaste.

The Hair of the Natives bear a striking affinity to each other. You will not find as in England, Red, Black, Flaxen etc., but they are generally here of the same beautifull colour, which is a fine Auburn, very long and not inclined to curl. I have often thought that you may form some Idea of a person's understanding from the nature and texture of their Hair. For instance a man with a frizzled pate may be taken for an artfull, juggling genius, one with Red Hair to be hasty, hot and impetuous, a man with Black Hair suited to the uncouth and unpolish'd scenes of life, and the man with Flaxen Hair adapted to the purpose of flattery and the softer walkes of society. Were the men of Scilly to be judged of their understanding by the length of their Hair it would be admitted without hesitation that their capacity was extensive and their knowledge deep and unfathomable.

There is no Tree in these Islands higher then a Gooseberry Bush. What few enclosures they have is done with stone walls. The face of the Islands are very rocky, they being interspersed in all directions over with large and small stones and ragged Rocks, so that only patches of land can be cultivated. Here are some romantic scenes well worthy the Pencil of a good Artist. On St Agnes's Isle, as well as St Mary's is a monumental Stone, with many other subjects for the antiquarian inquirer; to such I shall recommend a book, now publishing by subscription, by the Rev'd Mr Trenchard who resided Fourteen years on these Islands, as containing many particulars worthy of being known. [*This probably refers to the Rev John Troutbeck, Chaplain of St Mary's between 1794 and 1808. He published a book "A Survey of the Ancient and Present State of the Scilly Islands" in about 1795.*]

To give you a faint Idea of the hillocks and rocky appearance of places here I have tinted a drawing of a cottage near St Mary's. The stone in the offscape is a monumental memorial to some of their antient Chiefs. I went up to it. It has no inscription on it, it is rough and unpolish'd, about ten feet high, one solid stone. Its circumference is so small that I could clasp it in my arms. The nearer it is to the ground the taperer it gets. [*Probably one of the*

Standing Stones, of Megalithic times; there are several on the island.]

On the Rocks of these Islands there grows Samphire in great abundance. This is an excellent pickle and a small quantity of it, in London, fetches a high price. The access of it here is very easy. The Inhabitants set no value on it, indeed one of the Natives of whom I asked some questions did not even know its name, much less its property. On an island near St Mary's Pier Head, called Ratt Island, I found such great abundance that in an hour I could load a cart with it, but it being sometimes overflowed with the Sea its quality is injured. The best Samphire I ever met with is on the rocks about Dover. It is a quality peculiar to this vegitable that the higher it grows the more pungent it is. Poor people between Folkestone and the Forelands run a great risk of their lives in gathering it. A man had a rope fastened round him and a stick in his hand to poise himself from the Rocks. Two men stand on the edge of the precipice, having made the rope fast to a stake in the ground they then lower the man which is made fast to the other end of the rope as circumstance require. This is the method followed by the people of the Shetland Islands to gather Eggs of Wild Fowl amongst the Rocks. *[Samphire is a fleshy herb of the parsley family, sometimes used as a pickle and for soda in glass.]*

The Duke of Leeds is proprietor of most part of the Scilly Isles. Every Inhabitant enrols his name to take up Arms in case of an attempt of an enemy to land, but I am afraid they would be like Major Sturgeon and put their swords on the wrong side. There is about 50 Invalids doing duty in the Castle and this is all the regular forces now in the Islands.

Was I to attempt a catalogue of all the Shipwrecks that had happened about these Islands the malancholy register would extend a very considerable length. Not a year elapses but two or three are added to the dreadfull list. The most celibrated Shipwreck that ever happened here was that of Sir Cloudsley Shovell, who was lost on the Gilstone Rock in the *Association* Man of War the 22nd October, 1707. His Body was afterwards thrown ashore and bury'd amongst the worthys of his Country in Westminster Abbey, where his Royal Mistress erected a superb monument to Sir Cloudsley's memory. Queen Anne permited the Sculptor in the Monument to represent Sir Cloudsley in a large Wig, lying couchant on a kind of Sopha or large pillow, which he did as large as life. I remember to have seen a criticism on the Tomb in Westminster Abbey, in which the Author was not a little severe on the Sculptor for representing a Shipwrecked Sailor on a Bed of Down. [*Rear-Admiral Sir Cloudesley Shovell lost his life when his flagship "Association" and two others of his squadron were wrecked among the rocks of the Scillies on the night of 22 October 1707 on the way home from the Mediterranean. Addison criticized the monument in Westminster Abbey in an article in the "Spectator" in 1711.*]

Seting one day chatting with Mrs Stevens of old Town in St Mary's, she informed me of a neighbour who had in his possession a Queen Anne's Shilling, which was taken up with a deal of other Silver from the wreck of the *Association.* I went and took a view of it, but it bearing no strong external marks of its being buryed in the deep, I did not buy it, altho he asked only half a Guinea for it, remembering in such matter as that how easy a simple Antiquarian like myself may have his understandings abused by his foisting one Shilling upon me for another. If I could have taken it for a fact I should like to a had the Shilling, for Sir Cloudsley's sake. Some people at Rochester would be pleased to be in possession of this article as Sir Cloudsley was a good benefactor to the City and represented it in Parliament at the time of his death.

In the year 1734 a Dutch East Indiaman was wrecked on these Islands, having on board many Chests of Dollars, and of later date is the loss of the Nancy Packet from the East Indias, with many others. Shipwrecks are so numerous here that it has been recommended to establish a diving society for the recovery of property lost by wrecks on these shores.

Tuesday 15th of April I had the pleasure of sailing in our Jolly Boat up St Mary's Sound. Shut in apparently between Rocks and Islands I could not but admire the romantic and varied forms they assumed as we passed along in our little Bark, particularly the grand appearance of the Man of War Rock, with the foaming waves dashing against its impenetrable sides and the towering rival Rocks of Tresco, between which is the passage into New Grimsby Harbour. They formed a pleasing and awefull view.

We landed at New Grimsby, in which there are only a few scattered Houses. I went here to buy Hogs, of which I bought as many as I was order'd to procure, at the rate of Two pence Farthen a pound, alive. When I got them on board and had one of them killed I found they cost the Captain Four pence Farthen per pound. [*New Grimsby is the present day landing spot for Tresco.*]

I believe I ran my Head into every House in the Isle of Tresco. To everyone I had somewhat to say, and I had to confess they heard my nonsense with patience and good humour. In this particular day's peregrinations I met with several very beautifull girls—one particularly so, according to my Ideas of a fine Weoman. She was employ'd as a servile and was about Seventeen. To grace her handsome face (for which alone I thought Nature had done enough) she had the finest Head of Hair man ever beheld, a beautifull, flowing, Flaxen colour which reached right down to her apron strings. Were some of our London Perfumers to meet this gem, this innocent damsel, this beautifull beauty of all beautys, I am afraid they would tempt her to part with her curly ringlets, for the scarceity of Hair of that colour and length would enable them to offer her a good price for what was properly a commodity of her own growth.

I had a good deal of talk with this home brew'd young female, and heard her artless tales with exstacy. She told me her family history, such as the age of her Father and Mother, her Grandmother's age (which, if I remember right, was upwards of a hundred) but she could not find in the family Bible, for I made her look, how old her Great Grandmother was at the time of her death, altho she said her Mother very well remembered her, as she had been dead only just before she herself enter'd her teens.

"God bless me," thinks I, "this girl, if I can but get her in the humour when I come back from Newfoundland, will make me a good Wife, for if I am allowed to guess at the probable length of her life, by that of her ancestors, she will certainly outlive me. What a charming Idea it is to have a nurse such as this in my illness, and have my temples bathed, when I get old, by this young ravisher."

However I must drop this method of argument and condole for a few seconds with this young female for the loss of a brother of hers who was drowned about Two years ago on the Coast of France. In the Scilly Islands it is difficult to find a family who have not had one of their relations drowned by some accident or another. This arises from the perilous employment of the people, which is generally at Sea in little open Boats, exposed to the waves and tempests, in which they are often caught while Fishing, or passing to Ships in the offing, or in returning to the Islands after they have piloted a Ship out of their Roads.

Altho Tresco is little more than Six mile in circumference, yet in this Island is a fresh water pond a full mile in length, and in it are large Eels and other Fish. [*This probably refers to the Great Pool.*]

I have said before that I bought some Hogs here, one of which was of a person of the name of Ellis of New Grimsby. They had a Son, a Boy of 14, who wished to go to Sea. Wanting a Boy of good morals for the Cabin I gave some encouraging language. I really thought I had met with a prize, for a good Lad is a prize if his morals are really good. When he communicated his wishes to his Mother the Old Lady by no means would consent, altho his Father had no objections. So the Lad I left behind and I return'd to the *Boston*.

I have wrote much without saying a word about a character we had on board the *Boston*, which all this time was at anchor in St Mary's Sound. This is one Hugh Hicks, our Pilot, a man of St Agnes's Island. His Father is Minister of that Island for which he receives a stipend of Three Pounds a year. This, it must be admited, is labouring in the Vineyard of Salvation at no very dear rate. The people here carry on business on the principles of equality. It is not beneath the dignity of the clergy to have the Bible in one hand one day and the next to handle an oar or direct the helm of a Ship and steer her into one of their Roads. The Father of the elder gentleman of whom I am now speaking had a whimsical and truly ludicrous accident happen to him in his life-time.

Hicks was Minister of St Agnes, as well as Father of our Pilot. During his Ministry the Rope of the Bell, which weekly called the Islanders to their devotion, from having stood the bruff of many heavy tugs was worn out and useless. It being difficult to replace it with a new Rope against the next Sabbath, Mr Hicks, with his own hands, made a Rope of Straw, which he attached to the Bell. This Straw Rope hung exposed to all weathers and its end touched the sod of this consecrated ground. A neighbour's Bull, whose constitution being warm, took a roving fitt into his Head and by chance enter'd this repository of the dead. Some evil spirit directed the Bull's mouth to the tuft of grass on which rested the straw Rope. The Bull began eating, and as the gods of discord would have it, got the end of the straw Rope into his mouth. The Bell began to ring. The Bull, not mightily liking his relish of the straw Rope, for it was entwin'd round with tarred twine, shaked his Head. The Bell rung again—the Bull chewed again! The Bell sent forth its dolefull sound, all the Islanders heard it. The Bull guzzled a few inches of the Rope into his throat, the Bell rung again. "Damn your music," thinks the Bull, "I have migrated into the wrong field." He chews—the Bell rings. The Islanders never hearing it but on Sunday (this was Thursday) prepares for Church. The Bull keeps on chewing and the Bell ringing! The Bull finding himself hampered advanced a step, he hold up his head; most unfortunately he swallows all the slack of the Rope into his enormous paunch. Fire and Fury! The very joists which support the Belfry shake with his struggles. His foaming mouth is discolour'd and tinged with his blood, there is no disgorging the entangled bait without casting up bowels and all! The Bull becomes faint after being so long pined, he moves his head now and then and the Bell rings.

A Dog, perchance passing by and smelling the blood of the Bull, must needs go and see what was the matter. At the sight of the Dog the Bull kept shaking his head, he thinking no doubt that the Dog came there on purpose to deride him. From the continuance and constant shaking of the Bull's head at the Dog there was a constant ring of the Bell. The irregular, violent, and different sounds which the Bell now sent forth made the Islanders think that the Parson was in a great hurry or that Providence had benefited them by wrecking a large Fleet on their Island (with due diffidence I make this remark). In this glorious hope the men run with their glasses to the highest hill to behold the fruitfull harvest. But the Golden view was all delusion, for on the minutest inspection with their best glasses amongst the Rocks no dismasted Ship, no Mast forced from its hull, nor even a solitary cask was to be seen floating amongst the Breakers.

Others of the Islanders, suspecting that the Lighthouse was on fire, run to give their assistance, but finding all right there had again to guess at the cause of the alarm. At last the principal part of the people meeting near the summit of the hill, they communicated their suspicions to each other that they must a slept for three or four days, that this was Sunday and the Parson being angry by tolling the Bell so long and no one attending was the cause of his Ringing with such violence. So the men, who had just before ascended the Hill with the *charitable* hope of partaking of the spoils of a Shipwreckt Mariner, descended the same hill, in the same hour, their faces clad in sorrowfull looks, to the Church to pray for all those who travel by Water and Land. Some of the *Saints*, having reached the Churchyard, what was their surprize to find that all this commotion, this tumult, this alternative of hope and fear, this confusion which had taken place in this little republic of honest men was occasion'd by a four legged animal! A poor beast who had met with as strange accident as ever befell a traveller of his specie before.

Mr Hicks was absent a fishing when this catastrophe happened to his Rope of Straw, but the noise that this singular event kicked up in the Islands may, without difficulty, be conceived, for altho some part of it I have cloathed and dressed out yet the circumstances of the Bull ringing the Bell by eating a part of the straw Rope is a fact not to be contradicted. I have omited to state, as some assert, that old Hicks, the Clergyman, threatened the owner of the Bull with an action for trespass.

One thing I have yet to observe of the men of Scilly, which shows the effect custom has upon us, not only on our minds and manners, but even on our shape. This is exemplify'd in men who from their youth are almost continually sitting—so the men of Scilly, from being from childhood the greatest part of their time seting in their Boats, they have uncouth and ill shaped Legs, their knees bend outwards and their whole gait when walking portends to a seting position.

The shores of the Scilly Islands abound with rare and very curious Shells. Some are highly polish'd, of the colour of Terra de Sina [*Sienna*], others are striped alternately with Blue, Laylock [*lilac*] and White, perfectly transparent, and many on taking off the outer shell show a translucency and clearness equal to mother of Pearl for brightness and fineness. Having before, in London at Sales, seen specimens of these beautifull productions of Nature, I availed myself of the opportunity which now offer'd, and desired the Bumboat people which attended the *Boston* to bring me some of these Shells. I procured about half a Bushell, which were brought to me by three or four different people, for which I gave Sixpence to each person, for they are in great abundance. I pleaded that I was an unfortunate antiquarian, a bit of a Botanist and something of a Physicist, but had not found out the Philosopher's Stone in all my researches, that my head was loaded with desires after these and the antique matters, but that most unhappyly my pockets were so light that I had it not in my power to give them heavyer proofs of their deserts in endeavouring to please me then by offering them Sixpence each. This scanty pittance they, with seeming thanks, accepted. I at the same time observed that for such charitable acts they would, no doubt, be rewarded in the world to come.

These people telling others the market they had for the Shells, few came off but brought some of these curiositys with them. No other person in the *Boston* having a taste after such articles, I soon became loaded with more than I wanted, but a man bringing a specimen of some Shells which I had not seen before I desired him to bring about a pint of them the next day. Some other Islanders being by at that time, overheard our talk. The next morning *all* of them brought each a lot of these Shells. I could only buy of one, the others prest me to take theirs and give them Sixpence, which was the same as I had given the other lot, but I would not buy any more. This caused a violent quarrel between these people, they insisting to share the Sixpence between them all, altho there were four of them. They became so inflamed at each other that my Cabin, in which they all were, was so heated by their hot words that I begged that they would desist untill they got on shore when they would benefit of the cool and open air to settle the point of issue in, also they might call the Steward of the Island *[who acted for the Duke of Leeds, as Bailiff]* who would act as arbiter and settle the dispute without necessitating the party complaining to have recourse to the Court of Justice.

One thing I discover'd, which did not a little surprize me. While the *Boston* lay in the Sound the Islanders daily brought off Eggs, Milk, etc. to sell. These they sold at an exorbitant price to the Ship's company,—for instance a bottle of milk, which cost one Penny ashore, when these people brought it on board they would charge four Pence for a single bottle, and other articles in the same manner. Hicks, our Pilot, used to tell the Islanders as they came on board, how the things were wanting and what price to ask. He himself, at the same time, would take a profit, altho in the daily habit of receiving favours from Gentlemen in the Ship he returned the compliment in this knavish way.

I have now completed all I have to say of the Scilly Islands, and I shall tell you that the wind coming fair we sailed thro Broad Sound, followed by our Convoy, which consisted of Seventy-five

Vessels of all descriptions, which were bound for Newfoundland, Nova Scotia etc. on Thursday, 17th of April.

[The log records "Thursday, April 17th standing through Broad Sound".]

III

The Atlantic Crossing

Early in the morning, after we had been at Sea a few hours, Five Ships hove in sight. We made the private signals, which they did not understand. We cleared Ship for Action and bore down upon them. They hove to and we sent an Officer aboard. They turned out to be Five Vessels from the *Havanah*, which had run without Convoy and got thus far safe. We took one Seaman out of one, who wished to enter, who was a few weeks before wrecked in the *Converte* Frigate on her passage home from the West Indias.

The next day we fell in with a Fleet of Dutch Merchantmen from the West Indias under Convoy of the *Argo*, a Dutch Frigate 36 Guns. She gave the British Flag the usual salute and the *Boston* return'd the compliment. It blew a Gale of Wind from this day untill Sunday evening when it moderated. The *Mary Ann*, a Brigg, one of our Convoy, spoke us at the close of the evening and told us she had sprung a Leek and was then in such a situation that she was afraid to bear away for Ireland, not expecting to swim for many hours. Captain Morris told the Brigg to keep in company and to hoist lights in case the Leek increased.

Easter Monday, 21st April, 1794—Cape Spear in Newfoundland bearing S 71—11 W Distant 448 Leagues, the *Mary Ann* of Dartmouth foundered and sunk within pistol shot of us; all her hands were saved. In the night she had dropped astern of the *Boston*. As soon as it was light she made signals of distress. We hove to and presently the *Mary Ann* came alongside. Her Hold was full of water, her Pumps were choaked up and rendered useless. There was a heavy swell running, she rolled prodigeously and every Sea that came was expected to send her to the fathomless deep. At this critical period, to the unhappy crew and Passengers on board now held in suspense between life and death, our Boats were hoisted out and manned (at the risk of the lives of our people who manned them) and set off for the Ship which was now laboring hard. Altho the *Mary Ann* was within Musket shot of us yet the Boats were frequently lost by the Eye from the Quarter Deck. But the Boats reached them safe, and in two or three trips brought forty-one of her hands on board out of seventy-four, the others having been put on board a Brigg which hove to to assist. Not twenty minutes after all her hands had left her she fell broadside and filled, then righted, Pitched, and went down. So you see what a miraculous escape these sojourners had from a watery grave. Most of them lost everything except what they stood in, few could save a change of Linen. There were many Passengers on board, men who engaged themselves in the Fishing season at Newfoundland for a certain price. The principal part of these men came from Newton Bushell in Devonshire, and its environs. Some of them, who are expert in the Art of Fishing, get thirty Pounds for their services for the season, others, taken from the Plow tail will get Ten Pounds, and sixteen for the season. They are carry'd free of expense. They will all return, if they like, to England by November or December. Most of them pay their own charges back, which perhaps they get for a few Shillings.

[The Captain's log on the 21st records "Picked up men from Mary Ann of Dartmouth", and the muster roll shows "Supernumeries 36".]

It is surprizing the great number of people who go to Newfoundland annually from Devonshire and Dorsetshire. Newton Bushell *[now a part of Newton Abbot]* and Poole are the principal Marts where people are hired for this employ. As I suspect when I arrive at Newfoundland I shall have occasion to speak at large on this branch of English Trade, for the present I shall forego any further observations and revert to the *Mary Ann*, which had just foundered, and her people which were brought on board the *Boston*.

Amongst them was one Thomas Pasmore, a painter by trade. This poor fellow was born at Morchatt Bishop, near Crediton in Devonshire. When brought on board the *Boston* he was so overcome with fright and terror at the dangerous situation from which he had just emerged that he was unable to speak. He was emigrating from his native Country for the inclement climate of Nova Scotia, where, he told me, he had a brother, a Watchmaker at Halifax, to see whom he had narrowly escaped with his own life.

I remember observing, when the *Mary Ann* went down, that some Ducks (which had been liberated from their confinement on the Ship before the disastrous event took place) on their being launched into the great boundless Poole, seemed to enjoy, what they thought, the happy change. They indicated the pleasure they felt by shaking their tails and flirting the briney fluid over their feather'd backs. I fancy the pleasant sensations would be of short duration as they would not find a homely barn, nor a friendly hand to shelter them from the nightly fogs, nor to relieve their natural wants, but it would soon be all poverty and wild dispair on the watery main.

No occurrence of moment arose worth relating untill the 24th, on which day one Edward Maddison, a Seaman, jumped overboard and was drowned. For some days before this man had, at times, shown symptoms of a disorder'd mind. Some of the Officers earlier in the day, had given him some slight correction, as he was playing a deceptive part, after which Maddison had told them he would jump overboard. On this particular day Maddison was acting monkey tricks. An Officer went to him, and in gentle terms begged he would desist, but it was to no avail. The Officer spoke in harsher terms. Says Maddison "I'll jump overboard". "Do," says the Officer—and I gad, the poor fellow was as good as his word, for he run to the Gangway and overboard he threw himself. The Ship immediately backed her sails and a Boat was hoisted out as the man kept swimming, but before the Boat could get to him he sunk and was never seen again. *[The Captain's log on April 25th recorded that E. Maddison (Seaman) fell over the gunwale and was drowned.]*

We had another accident of this kind, altho different in its circumstances, on the first of May, Cape Spear bearing S 78 32 N Distant 389 Leagues, when a Man belonging to the Gunner's Crew fell overboard and was drowned. We had been making a Signal to our Convoy with a Gun when this Man got on the outside to reload. While he was sponging the Gun the Ship took a heavy roll, he fell off and was lost. This poor man was an honest fellow and well esteem'd in the Ship. He had, at the time we left England, a wife living in the Moor House, at Shire Moor near North Shields. *[This man's name was George Knight.]*

The next day, May the Second, I saw a brace of Birds called Irish Lords. How they came by this ludicrous name I cannot learn, they always being found some hundreds of Leagues from the Land, unless they were Christianed by some witty Irish Mariner out of compliment to the Lords of his Land who, like these Birds, emigrate from their soil as soon as the Royal Sign Manuel has dubbed them Right Honorable Peer, to fish for good things in the neighbourhood of St James.

[Some Irish absentee landlords lived in England while extracting large rents from the peasant tenantry in Ireland. The Court of St James's was a special attraction.]

On Saturday 10th of May, Cape Spear N 21 10 N Distance 219 Leagues, it being perfect calm, the Ship traversed all around the Compass. The Ship's Company was exercised at the Great Guns. At performing the evolutions an accident happened to the Ship's Cook and a man of the name of Scoffield, which nearly cost them their lives. They were firing with tubes, one of which hung fire. The Cook was priming again when the Powder Horn, which was in his hand, caught fire and burst. The explosion shattered his hand in a violent manner, it set fire to the cloathes of Scoffield who was standing by and burnt his face and hands in such a manner that it was feared he would never recover his Eyesight again. The Cook was scorched in a terrible manner, and the quantity of blood which issued from his hand was astonishing.

We had met with much bad weather and contrary winds but had experienced no Gale so violent as befell us on Tuesday, May 13th. This was the most boisterous and tempestuous day I had met with during my short acquaintance with maritime affairs. The briney Ocean dashed in furious combat against the potent winds, both seeming momentarily to lay aside their dispute and combine in terrible junction to strike a vehement revenge, a mortal or destructive blow to the daring Mariner for thus presuming to traverse the unfathomable, watery empire. The Sea this day may with truth be said to run mountains high, the long tremendous swells, formed into Mountains, often broke over the *Boston*'s Gangway, while the Gunwhale on the Larboard side lay under water. Some vessels of our Convoy not half a mile from us buryed for some minutes from our sight.

As we made no very great progress on our Voyage, Captain Morris found it necessary to be carefull of our expenditure of water, and as on this day flour and plumbs were served to the Ship's

Company to make Pudings of, orders were given that the men must go to the Scuttle Butt on the Quarter Deck for water, and there mix their Pudings to prevent a waste of water. Accordingly Nine or Ten goes to the Quarter Deck, each holding their flour with their two hands. The very instant they got on deck the furious winds, without regard to age or youth, forc'd, in one moment, the Hatts from the heads of both old and young. These were kept by the wind bouyant in the air. The men stood amazed and could not take their eyes from this phenomenon. At this critical moment the Purser (who is a very innocent and harmless man) came on the Deck and seeing the attention of all looking at this flight of old hatts says, with great earnestness, to the men at the Wheel:

"God bless me," pointing to the flying hatts, "there is a flight of Birds, I wonder what is their names?"

"Old Hatts," replys the men.

"Oh! God bless me!" says the Purser, "I'm glad I came on Deck, which was to look at an Island of Ice (there being one in sight) but in addition to that curiosity I have seen this strange tribe of the feather'd creation."

Then, turning about, he dived below (where he was always to be found in bad weather seting in his cabin in the dark for, being a good economist, candles to him was a heavy object). Into the Gun Room he gets, where the Surgeon was seting with a good fire in his front and Doctor Marshall's Treatise for his instruction in his hands. This good bonny Scot or Officer, which you please, being in Men of War equally as *active* as the greatest drone in the Ship (the business being entirely done by Surgeon's Mates). The Surgeons themselves rarely know more of the men's diseases than what they take from the Sick List or the verbal word of their Mates, they, poor souls, being employ'd in the more *important* concern of catering for the Wardroom or Gun Room Mess. So altho the Purser bolted into the Gun Room and aloud declared that there was to be seen from the Deck a flight of very curious birds called Old Hatts, yet he could not prevail on a single Idler to start from his seat. So much for my Old Hatts.

In the above story I see I have made use of the word phenomenon. This brings to my recollection a circumstance which occur'd in the *Suffolk* when I was in her last year. In that Ship I had the *honour* of serving His Majesty fourteen months in a double capacity,—honourable I say because I had the honour of serving the most *honourable* subject His Majesty had in the Ship,* as well as occasionally lending power and strength in chastizing any attempt made by a hostile band. For my assistance to this Honourable Personage for fourteen months I was rewarded with a sum not sufficient to reimburse me in money I had laid out for newspapers and writing paper. Leaving this worthy, silverheaded Personage to be rewarded as he rewarded others, I come to a dissertation on the words Phenomenon and extraordinary.

I received orders (not directions) to extract Yeast or Barm to raise Bread with, from Captain R[*ainier*]. This is in part done by a Chymical process, which process it was known I was acquainted with, in drawing it from Potatoes. I proceeded, and from the Potatoes I produced Yeast that rose Bread as light as can be seen in any Baker's Shop in London.

Showing the article, and describing some of its propertys to the Captain "Sir," says I, "it is a perfect Phenomenon to observe the singular motions of the Yeast."

"Damn your Phenomenons or Phenomenas," says the Captain, "cannot you use the word extraordinary?"

"To be sure, Sir," says I, "but there is so much more music in Phenomenon then there is in the word extraordinary."

"Damn you, and your Music too!" says the old boy—and then marched out of the Cabin in a surly humour.

I shall now return to the tempestuous 13th of May and give you a Catalogue of the accidents of the day which fell within my notice. These being of no serious nature the perusal of them will not create much anxiety.

Early in the morning I was alarmed at the general cry of "Surgeon's Mate, Surgeon's Mate". On enquiry I found that every Sea that struck the *Boston*, she shipped Tons of water in the Galley. The Cook's Boy was half suffocated by a Sea as he lay in his Hammock there. The Body was brought and laid upon the Booms, to be out of reach of the water. On viewing his body he appeared lifeless. It was recommended to try the rules laid down by the Humane Society, but no one on board understanding an Iota of the practize, nor no book to be found containing them in any of our little Librarys, we were forced to the old custom of

* Captain Peter Rainier was Captain of H.M.S. *Suffolk*, 74 Guns. See p. XVIII.

Salting the Body. Six or eight hands began rubbing the Boy from foot to head with salt, from the friction of which signs of returning life soon appeared, and at last our endeavours were crowned with success. During this business I fancy we had instilled into him as much salt as would cure half a dozen good oxen at the Red House. True it is I am certain that no piece of salted junk ever came better salted from the Victualling office for the use of His Majesty's Seamen then this Boy was, and had he died, for aught I know, his carcase was so well pickled that it would a kept as long as the Mummeys of the ancient Egyptians.

I observe that this poor Boy, only a day or two after the accident, was dry'd and shrivelled up in a surprizing manner owing, I presume, to the salted state of his body, so that we found it necessary to steep him in Sea water daily, up to his chin, to draw the briney particles from him. This the poor Lad readily submited to, to preserve (as he said) his youthfull look. But there is another misfortune attending him, which I hope to cure him of in a few days time, otherwise it will be a serious circumstance to the Ship's Company, and that is the great drought which attends him. If he goes on drinking the same quantity of water for six months as has been sufficient to suffice him for these two days back, by the period above stated he will have swallowed as much water as would float a Ship of the Line.

The Waiste of the Ship this day was nearly up to our Knees in water. As she rolled the water would gush from under the Sheep Pens in Midships with such force that it put me in mind of London Bridge, thro the centre Arch of which the water, on ebb Tide, flows with great impetuosity.

I saw the Carpenter battening down the hatchways, in doing of which he broke the handle of his hammer.

"The devil take the handle of this hammer," says he, "I wish the Hoggs had eaten thee when thou wast an Acorn." I thought this an admirable method of expressing our displeasure at the failure of a piece of this specie of wood, which is the most illustrious Tree of the English Forests.

We had a Black Catt in the Ship. She, not knowing where to keep her feet dry, jumped into a Midshipman's Hammock as soon as he turn'd out. Shortly after, a man goes unknowingly and lasheth the Hammock up, with the Catt in it—the consequence was suffocation. Towards the close of the evening the Midshipman turns in, and by chance the dead Catt was tumbled under one end of his Pillow; there was then a horrible stink, but between Decks in a Ship is not always a good place for a delicate nose. For my own part, I smelt the delicious fragrancy after the Midshipman had been in about an hour. This diabolical funk being stationary, he called for men to look around. "For," says he, "there is a foul stink indeed, somewhere in your quarter".

They looked, but their eyes could not perceive what their noses so strongly tasted. As the people passed his Hammock, "My God!" says they, "here is a fine fogo, this is a Funk Island to be sure, this odor can never be the produce of Pease and Salt Pork alone, that's a fact, for this fragrant, sweet scent must be brew'd from all the filth in Europe."

"I certainly shall be poison'd before morning," says the Midshipman, "For God's sake look again." In the saying of this he had raised his head from his pillow, then laying it down again on the hidden treasure, he unknowingly forced the *musk* from its lodgement, which instantly perfumed the adjacent regions with a stronger fragrance than had been experienced before.

"You have now found it," says he, "have you not?"

"No, Master, nothing but a more spicy smell, don't you smell it very strong now?"

"*Now!* smell very strong indeed it doth, it far exceedeth the effluvia that can arise from the junction of all the morbid carcases in the habitable world," says the Midshipman.

This focus of funk and filth was endur'd all night, for it was not till the morning after the Gale that they discover'd the cause. The Midshipman, who was but a Boy, was often jeered about this horrible Hogoo, which was such a nuisance for a whole night, to 300 of His Majesty's best subjects.

Amongst other fatallitys of *great* moment a part of the Captain's Dinner met with a disastrous event. The Captain's Cook was preparing some Mock Turtle, which he had strongly impregnated with some good Old Madeira (which had smelt the climates of the East), delicious Veal, Gravy and plenty of Herbs. As the Cook was holding, at an unseasonable moment, the Saucepan of Mock Turtle to season it higher with Kian, a Sea forced its way thro the Starboard bow Port. This floated Six Pigs, Two Harness Casks full of

Pork, a Tub of Tar (into which the Pigs were thrown), the Butcher, and terrible to relate—the Cook, with the Turtle in his hand! The Six Pigs were floated in the Tub of Tar to the Gangway, when a Lee lurch taking the Ship, they were jerked, Tar and all, into the Cable Tier, into which place they had no sooner arrived then they were run with vehemence amongst the Quartermasters, who were then at Dinner. The Pigs, being cover'd with Tar, the men took them for Porpoises or Sea Devils which the Sea had washed amongst them. They were soon convinced to the contrary by their grunting, and falling foul of the Pease which the men were eating for Dinner. As to the Harness Casks, they were floated aft with such rapidity and violence that they broke down a part of the Bulke head of the Captain's Cabin.

The Butcher, at the time the Sea came athwart his posteriors, was spitting a Leg of Mutton. Up to his middle in water, the torrent forced him aft. At the same moment a large dripping pan was bouyant at his breech. He held the Spit erect, the rapid stream carry'd him along with the Dripping Pan at his tail.

"Behold Neptune," says a Seaman, "with his proper accompaniments." "There goes a Charioteer." Says a third "What a glorious ride has the old God of the Sea got."

By this time the Butcher, with his Shell, was drifted against the Captain's Cabin, a part of the Bulke head of which being made of Canvas he thrust his Trident, alias the Spit, thro with such violence that the Mutton also made its appearance. This very narrowly missed the head of the Captain's Servant who was then in the act of stooping to pick up an Azimuth Compass, which was dislodged from its place by the shock the Ship had receiv'd from the resistless surge. By the singular motion of the *Boston* (the Butcher having still the Spit through the Canvas), she received a Lee lurch, which forced the point of the Spit thro the Picture of Captain Courtenay [*a former Captain of the* Boston; *see p. xvi*] which hung on the Starboard side of the Mizzen Mast, and shattered the Glass into atoms and spoiled the Portrait, the Spit having enter'd the head part a little above the Nose.

The Cook, on the water striking him, let go the Saucepan in which was the Turtle. The saucepan floated, and poising itself, by dint of good fortune, on the abatement of the Flood rested, not like the Ark on Mount Ararat, but on the topsy turvey end of a match Tub, its savory contents being safe. The three Pigs, which had escaped drowning in this second deluge were directed to the Mock Turtle at the same time; each being so forcibly tempted to ravish its contents all three thrust their heads in at the same moment with surprizing force; its circle being small, and the rim of the Saucepan of such narrow extent, that after they had filled their mouths with this delicious food they were unable to *swallow* any by reason of the rim of the saucepan being so extremely tight on their throats that their swallows were entirely stopped up. Each tried to force a passage down his windpipe—but in vain. They presently gave a Grunt, now and then interspersed with a gentle squeak, as if smelling to the nosegay in rival pleasure. As the rim of the Saucepan held them so tight by the Neck neither of them could recede. But a few minutes had elapsed before they burst out in the most clamorous and turbulent and vehement out-cry three Pigs ever made. The violence of the *motions* was equally as violent as their *noise*, each trying to extricate himself from his entanglement without effect. This horrible *harmony* continued, in dreadfull trio, for some time to the no small pleasure of such of the men as had met no serious accident themselves. The three Pigs, with their heads in the Saucepan, still kept up an awfull and terrible noise, each pulling a *different* way. At last, as if by general consent, they all gave a grand pull in a *contrary* direction, from the force of which the Saucepan *burst* asunder, altho made of Iron, and the Mock Turtle was lost.

This was not the only mishap that befell our Dinner. The Leg of Mutton, when brought to the Table, was found to be so basted with Tar that it was perfectly spoiled and unfit for use, to the no small disappointment of a Midshipman who had not partaken of fresh meat for several weeks before.

Having so far disposed of My Catalogue, I shall relate an Anecdote of a Right Honorable person, Brother to a Peer of the Realm, who is a Midshipman of our Ship. This is the Honorable Robert D*[igby]* who is now about twenty-two years of age, and measures in height I fancy near four feet, six inches high. On this ever memorable 13th of May this young Gentleman had the Fore-noon watch. The noise of the wind on Deck was so violent that the Officers with difficulty could hear each other speak, to add to which the cold was intense, and the spray of the Sea, flying over the Ship's Quarters, made remaining on Deck not very comfortable.

This young Gentleman wished to find an Asylum in his watch on Deck, more sheltered, for which purpose he came under the Half-deck; but here finding the water at times breast high, and not very cheering, he hit upon a perfectly new and original stratagem to keep his little Legs and small body out of the water, which was as follows:

Under the Half-deck hung the Captain's Cloak Bag; this, he privately conveyed to the Cable Teir, in which place, at this time, was only one Quartermaster. The Right Honorable Gentleman requested the Quartermaster to put him in the Cloak Bag, tye it up, carry him in it under the Half Deck, and deposit it on the Nail where it always hung. For the boon of a little Grog, the Quartermaster readyly fell into his Ideas. He deposited the young Gentleman in the Bag, which he conveyed to and *hung on the Nail* under the Half Deck. Hugging himself in a position not unlike that of an Ostrich in the Shell, he wisely supposed he was as secure from injury as the Portraits of his Ancestors at Sherborne Castle. Indeed, from the extreme duty of the Ship, having the night before had no rest, he was soon rocked into a deep sleep. The Bag hung and swang about by the motion of the Ship with the little Gentleman in it, with all the equipoises of mathematical skill, thus proudly in embryo enjoying a banquet of Momuses.

[Momus, son of Nox, was the ancient god of ridicule but is not infrequently confused with his brother Somnus, god of sleep.]

When all hands were Piped to Dinner his Messmates could not find him. Supper came—he was not to be found, Bedtime came, his watch on Deck came, the night passed away and the morning came—but he was not to be found! Various were the conjectures of what had become of him. He was searched for fore and aft, but in vain. His Messmates, with long faces, a sorrowful exterior, with an interior of an opposite quality, who had fed his little vanity, made enquiries amidst observations mingled with regret and unfeigned Grief—but all search was in vain; he was not to be found.

About Six O'clk the next morning this young Gentleman was discover'd by the following accident. The Ship had rolled prodigeously all night. The Lanyard which was reeved thro the top of the Bag and hung on the Nail, by friction, with the motion of the Ship, was nearly separated—just before Six O'clk the Lanyard or Cord broke in two. *Down fell the Bag*, the Honorable Gentleman and all. Here was a discovery!

As soon as the Bag fell on the Deck he cry'd aloud for Help, Help, Help! The men run to the place where the voice issued from when, strange to relate, was turned out of a Cloak Bag the Right Honorable Robert D[*igby*] Son of a Baron of the British Empire and Brother to an English Earl, who had taken refuge in a base article, made of common canvas and tarred twine, to the great disgrace of the people of England, who held a proper abhorrence of a single act like this, tending to the French system of equality.

I remember the morning before this event happened this young intended legislator was discanting at large on the ancient English Agrarian Law, as also on that of Gravelling [*gavelkind, i.e. land tenure*]; but I do not presume to say that any mention was made of dislike of them, altho by them younger brothers were provided for in a *better* way then they are by the present English Laws, as far as relates to the sons and daughters.

While the storm was raging this day in frantic fury I was stood under the Half Deck, conversing with a person on the nature and propertys of winds. I find it is a received opinion that the swiftness of the wind, in a storm, is between fifty and sixty miles an hour. During this conversation, to prevent myself from falling, I held fast to an Iron Stanchion. In the middle of my dissertation the Ship shipped a tremendous Sea. A ton of water I believe came down, a full hundredweight I am sure; fell to my share. I was obliged to make a precipitate retreat, leaving my Lecturer to take care of himself, who had not much less than two hundredweight of water on his head and shoulders. This would suffice to stop the mouth of any orator the world ever produced, for a short period, be his Lungs ever so healthy or his voice ever so strong.

After the close of the day when the weather became more moderate I saw those Meteors, often spoken of by seafaring people. They are called Corposants, and are a volatile kind of Meteors, or Ignis Fatuus [*literally "foolish fire": phosphorescent light*]. They are often seen in tempestuous weather about the Sails and Rigging of Ships. They are most frequent in heavy rains and sometimes appear like a Rainbow at the extremity of the Sails, at other times they appear faint, like a Candle. They are produced by some Sulphurous and Bituminous matter which, being forced down against the Sails, show a luminous light. From these strange appearances Seamen infer that storms come from sulphurous spirits, which rarifying the air, put into motion and cause these terrible contests on the Ocean called Hurricanes. Some account for these Meteors in a different way by saying that they arise from the Spawn of the Fish which riding on the Sea are struck with great violence by the Bows of the Ship. This separates them into millions of particles which fly amongst the Sails, and these compress'd into small bodys produce the phenomena or phantom described.

Wednesday the 14th of May, Cape Spear distant 182 Leagues. In consequence of the tempestuous weather of yesterday the Brigg *Commerce* of Poole foundered and sunk. Her Crew was saved by the *Industry,* of the same place. In the Gale yesterday she lost all her Masts, and had not a spar left on board. This was the second Ship we lost of our Convoy.

We had now been twenty-eight days from Scilly, and the passage began to get tedious. I had much time to spare and a contemplative recollection of a studious turn. . .

In the thirty-ninth year of her reign Queen Elizabeth enacted a statute . . . obnoxious to English freedom . . . that was levelled at the most useful subjects her Majesty had, viz. soldiers and Sailors. She declared that if any Soldier or Mariner was found wandering about the Kingdom, without having in their possession a testimonial, they shall be judged to have comited a felony and shall suffer death, unless one honest Freeholder will take him into his service for one year. When the caprice of man is consider'd it must be allow'd that this Law bore very hard on the unfortunate Subject, as it cannot but be observ'd by those who have travelled in the Inland Countys of England how, even in these polish'd times, with what contempt a poor Soldier is treated with. As for Sailors, who so nobly brave the dangers of the deep, they are, I am convinced, in Inland Countys, consider'd in a more despicable light than the Soldiers. To elucidate which I will relate the following:

In November, 1792, I was on business at Wheatley, Oxfordshire. I called at a House call'd the Chequers, then kept by a man of the name of Hartford. While I stopped there a man in the habit of a Sailor came and asked for a night's Lodgings. He was told by the Landlord that their beds were full. The Sailor went away. I knew their beds were not full and asked Hartford his reason why he refused him.

"In truth," says he "I make it a rule never to lodge Sailors, for I consider them as thieves."

"The devil you do," quoth I, "if you were to make such an observation as that in the environs of Portsmouth Point God help you, for I am sure I could not, was I with you. What! Do you consider them all as thieves, Mr Hartford? Why, I think a true Sailor as honest a character as any Churchwardens or Overseers in all England. An honest Tar! Why they are the grand springs of the bulwarks of Britain, a set of men who despise danger, are generous to their enemys, and the only contention which a Sailor aims at, when on board, is that none shall exceed him in his alertness."

To all this Hartford reply'd "It is a foolish opinion we have got, but none of us country people feel a partiality for them."

May 20th brought us early in the morning into sounding which indicated our being on the famous Banks of Newfoundland, therefore not a great many Leagues from the desir'd Harbor of St John's, to which place the *Boston* was bound. As a proof to determine where we was our Ship was enveloped in one of those fogs which eternally hover over the Banks. Fog guns were constantly fir'd, and a horn continually kept sounding to warn other Vessels of our situation. A European, who has never been in this part of America, can have but a faint Idea of these Fogs. You frequently can see but a few yards before you, and by getting on Deck for two hours you will get wet to the skin. The Ship's Riging and yard collect great quantitys of these particles, which fall on Deck in drops which would cover a half Crown piece. These Fogs are no less injurious to the health of the human specie than they are to the Sails and Riging of the Ship, for a Ship employed on the Newfoundland Station receives more damage to her running Riging etc. in one month then she would was she employ'd in the Channel service at home in England in Three Months; but as I promize myself to make further observation on Fogs after my arrival in Newfoundland for the present I shall drop the subject, and that for a very cold one—it being to speak of Islands of Ice.

[The log of 21 May records "Fresh departure from supposed place on Bank".]

This day, for the first time in my life, I saw one of these awefull and massive bulkes, an Island of Ice. The Fog was very thick and it was not more than half a mile from us. The *Boston* was going at the rate of Six Knots an hour, it passed us on the Larboard side. I could not but look at it with horror and amazement, to see such an enormous mass floating in the midst of the Ocean. Its hideous appearance would make the stoutest resolution shrink when it is recollected for a moment that a part of this frightfull structure, had the *Boston* struck on it, would a been sufficient to a consign'd her to a watery Tomb.

These Islands of Ice (for in the course of the day we saw several others) assume a thousand different shapes. Some appear like pyramids, others represent Towers and broken Walls with Forts and Spires, the next you will see will look like a Dome with a City in ruins, others appear again like a half Arch, and some are so singularly formed as to look like a Bust. I declare one I saw had a strong resemblance to our famous orator Charles Fox.

When I first saw this representation of Charley—so snow white! "Why," thinks I, "to be sure that must be a marble Bust of Mr Fox, which a few years ago was presented to the Empress of Russia, and which Her Majesty was transporting from Petersburgh down the Gulph of Finland to Warsaw, by way of the River Vistula, to be placed in the Diet Chamber there, in order to assist her gracious Highness in her *pious* designs on the people of Poland. Perhaps by the interposition of a higher power the Vessel, in which the Bust was, became a prey to the waves and was wreck'd. The precious treasure did not sink but floated into the Baltic where it got frostbitten and congeal'd with Ice and spent several months thus stationary without moving from his *post*. At last, by the warmth of the luminous Sun, a separation took place between him and his cold associates, and the Bust of Charles Fox remain'd attach'd to an Island of Ice which, by strange conjuncture of motion, floated down the Sound of Copenhagen, Bergen and the Faroe Islands and so into the great Atlantic Ocean. But how far, or in what manner, my good friend Mr Fox means to travel or disentangle himself cannot be in my province to determine."

[Catherine II the Great of Russia did set up a bronze bust of Charles James Fox, whom as an Enlightened Despot she professed to admire, among those of ancient philosophers in her gallery at Tsarskoye Selo. This fact evidently lies behind Aaron Thomas's fantasy.]

Seriously speaking, I this day saw various pieces of Ice so placed and formed that they put me in mind of a London Common Stage Waggon with Six Horses. I endeavour'd to persuade myself that

I was drinking English Ale at the Pack Horse on Turnham Green, in a parlour fronting the Highroad as the Cavalcade passes. But Alas! I was not on Terra Firma, nor at Kensington neither, but a many hundred miles from England, my native Country. *[Turnham Green, Middlesex, is about two miles west of the London borough of Kensington.]*

These Islands of Ice, altho seen floating here in the month of May, are not masses of Ice frozen last Winter, but were frozen about a year ago in the Greenland Sea or the Labrador Coast, which on the Sun assuming its powers, separates these immense Seas of Ice into large fields and islands and is then drifted about by the winds and the currents for fifteen or sixteen months before the Sun totally dissolves them, during which time some of them are found 300 Leagues from the place of the formation.

I know a Gentleman who was within two miles of one of these enormous Islands when it broke in two, and he says that the noise that it made was louder then that occasion'd by a Frigate firing a whole broadside at once. There is frequently found on these Islands Foxes, Sea Lions and Seals, which chance had fixed on this Ice when it separated from the continent (if I may be allow'd the expression). The Lions live on the Seals and a Bird called Ice Birds. The Lion, being the colour of the Ice, he lies down, the Birds light on him in great numbers and become an easy prey. They are about the size of Crows, all white, except their Bills and Feet which are yellow. I shall drop these frozen subjects for one of an opposite quality, to speake of a Lad whose constitution in particulars, resembles a Sallamander.

[The sea lion (Eumetopias Jubata) is not indigenous to the North Atlantic. Since the animal in question was "the colour of ice" A.T. may have been referring to the polar bear.]

This Boy's name was Phillip Knight *[confirmed by the muster roll]*. He was possessed of the evil propensity, when asleep, of crying "Fire". He got so much in this evil habit that sometimes at night he would alarm the Ship. He was convict'd and thrash'd for the offence more than once. It would not do! This evening, as soon as it was dark Knight, who was my Cabin Boy, left the Berth, went under the Half Deck and cry'd "Fire!"—Captain Morris heard the voice and order'd the offender found out. This was no difficult matter. Knight was to receive a flagellation on the bare posteriors, in the morning, of a dozen lashes. We had a Painter in the Ship who understood the rudiments of Drawing. Now this poor Boy Knight had some pretensions of Wit, which I fancy he had in some degree collected by living at different Public Houses in London in the quality of a Pott Boy.

Early the next morning he goes to the Painter and prevail'd upon him to delineate on his bare Bum the representation of an old Weoman's face!—This was comply'd with and finish'd in a stile that would not disgrace the antechamber of the Royal Academy. Nine O'clk came and Mr Knight was made fast to the Gun. His Breeches were taken down!—and behold the old Weoman's face! He entreat'd for forgiveness but all in vain, stroke fell after stroke. He threw his body in as many positions as an Eel, the Cat o nine Tails was by no means an agreeable application!—At last he cryed aloud "O! For God's sake pity a poor Old Weoman! How can you Gentlemen stand by laughing, and see a poor Old Weoman, with only one Tooth in her Mouth, beat about the head in this manner?"

This was no bad hit of the Boy's, but he must receive his Dozen, no abatement could be made. He happen'd to have a remarkable large button on his Breeches, and this button was apply'd exactly to the touch hole of the Gun during the ceremony. By the great and furious motion of his body the button struck fire against the opposite metal! and absolutely fired off the Cannon, which was loaded with a Twelve pound Ball! Luckily it did no injury to none of the Convoy, but the consequence was the immediate liberation of the Culprit, whose hair was singed off his pate by the flash in the pan.

The circumstance of firing the Gun in this manner was the subject of much conversation in the *Boston*. I myself made more than one experiment on the body of the Boy. I found the composition of his body strongly impregnated with metallic matter!—Very likely you will be much surprized at this assertion, but it is no metaphysical observation, being well known in the Chymistry world!

The above anecdote I quote to introduce the surprizing qualitys of my Shipmate Knight. He was very useful to me on the following occasions:

Having no Chaffing Dish on board, he was a good substitute, by holding the Tea Kettle in his hand he would keep it boiling for any length of time. Again, if I had a Bullock's Heart or a Broil for Dinner, let him keep his fingers to the edge of the plate and that alone would keep it hot! His presence in the Cabin at Dinner time answer'd the purpose of Tin Covers. We generally put him under the centre of the Dining Table; the genial heat arising from this precious Carcase kept the Dishes in a state of warmth far surpassing any forced temperature. I once sent him ashore for some Eggs. He filled a small Basket full and one Egg he brought on board in his fist. I went to use it, but found it hard boiled! I question'd him on the subject, when it was found that by holding it in his hand one hour and twenty minutes the heat from his hand acted on the Egg in the same manner as if the Egg had been immersed for five minutes in boiling water. The Captain's Taylor found him very usefull in keeping his Goose Iron hot, and was he to work in a Blacksmith's Shop his presence at the anvil must be very desirous as the Iron would never cool while he was near.

There is always a Compass kept in the Captain's Cabin. This was frequently found to vary from that in the Binnacle. It was displac'd, from the supposition of its imperfection, but the new comer was as full of variations as the former; but the true cause was not known untill the affair of Knight's fiery composition was discover'd. He was often requir'd to be in the Cabin on domestic concerns, and the more he approach'd the Compass the more he led the Needle astray by his sulphurous qualitys. The result of all this was not very favourable to Knight, he being order'd to do duty in the Galley as the Captain's Cook's Mate, the Ships Company giving him the appelation of the Sallamander, which name he will retain no doubt as long as the *Boston* is in commission. [*According to the log Knight was later drowned, by falling off the cable whilst clearing a hawser when in port.*]

Friday May 23rd. After passing a number of Islands of Ice we came in sight of Land, soon after we could plainly descry Fort Amherst and Signal Hill, between which the Harbour of St John's lay. We fir'd two Guns as a Signal for a friend which the Fort answer'd, and at about Seven O'clk in the evening we dropped anchor in what is called the Narrows. Soon after Captain Morris was viseted by the Commandant and the principal Officer of the Garrison, who came to congratulate him on his safe arrival and to learn what was going forwards at the Fountain head of Politics—London—that grand Emporium of the British Empire.

Reverting to our Voyage, I find from persons better inform'd then myself that we had a bad passage, having been from Spithead sixty-two days, which is a long period when it is known that the voyage is sometimes made in a month. During the night all hands were employ'd in warping the Ship thro the Narrows.

[This date is confirmed by log.]

IV

St John's to Portugal Cove by Indian Path

On *Saturday, 24th of May*, the *Boston* was safe moor'd in the Harbour of St John's. This is a safe capacious Harbour, about a mile and a half long and at the Broadest part not more than a mile across. It is shelter'd from all winds by great and stupendous Hills. The Mountain on the South side is a grand and magnanimous one rising suddenly several hundred feet above the surface of the water. Its towering sides and rocky projections here and there giving berth to Spruce Trees. I have been this morning steadfastly looking at this Mountain, and observe from its loftyness that the whole Harbour of St John's is in shadow from it. There is a few Flakes at the bottom of it, which give it a very pretty appearance. [*For a description of fish flakes see pp. 181–2.*]

Sunday 25th May I was ashore at St John's, and being some part of the day alone I could not resist reflection. Here I am, in full possession of all the little wants that could make some men happy. But alas! It was not so with me—I was not happy!—The Rocks, the Barren Hills, the Lakes, the Spruce Trees, the new specie of Birds, the Flowering Shrubs and the Indian Tea had lost its effects on my imagination!—and for loss of what? Why the presence of one object then in England! Could that been had, the Flowers how sweet, the Rocks how romantic, the notes of the feather'd tribe how melodious, the Lakes how transparent—and even the Barren Hills themselves would appear fertile and green! To you, my good friend, I confess this fault for the last time. I shall no longer continue in this strain. From the human specie I shall proceed to treat on a different kind, I mean Dogs—in this Country a most useful animal indeed.

The celebrity of Newfoundland Dogs in England is so notorious that the value of them there needs no comment, but their usefulness in Britain cannot be put in competition with the great utility they are to the people of this cold Country. In this Empire of Frost and Snow great quantitys of wood must be used by the Inhabitants whose winter here is from October to April!—or May! In this Country as soon as the Snow falls it freezes. The people then cut their wood for firing, for Fish Flakes and for Building etc., etc. This wood is sometimes cut seven or ten miles in the woods and is drawn home by Dogs. They have gearing the same as Horses; the wood is put into Sledges which they draw, and sometimes they drag a single stick only, attended by one man who wears frost shoes. This labour of Dogs is daily thro the winter and a hard service it is.

These Animals here bear a more hardier aspect in general to what their same specie do in England, so much so that on a superficial view their kind does not appear the same. Their difference ariseth thus—in Newfoundland the Dogs commonly are their own caterers. They chiefly live on Fish and many of these sturdy race fish for themselves. It is no very uncommon thing to see one of these Dogs catch a Fish. Bitter hunger is their monitor and as it presses upon them they go to the waterside and set on a Rock, keeping as good a lookout as ever Cat did for a Mouse. The instant a Fish appears they plunge into the water and seldom come up without their prey. This is a wonderful property in these Animals, but it is as true as it is singular, for when Newfoundland was first discover'd these Dogs were found in a wild state, none of the savage Indians did they associate with. They kept in herds or companys the same as Bears and Wolves do now. In winter they lived by hunting and killing Foxes, Beavers etc., and when these failed them they had recourse to the watery element, which never refused them relief, for if the neighbouring Seas were frozen over they would perambulate on the Ice on which they would find Sea Lions, Seals and other animals that became an easy prey when attack'd by a formidable host of these Dogs.

In Summertime they follow'd the same business of Hunting and when the woods deny'd them food the Sea Shore became their rendezvous. Here they catched Fish to suffice their wants and when nature was satisfy'd they betook themselves again to their haunts in the woods, where they had nothing to fear from rivals, going generally in such numerous herds that flocks of Wolves would shun them. I am told that in winter these Dogs were the greatest enemys to themselves, for when on the Barrens their food began to get short they would, as their appetites increas'd, set up a dismal howl, and this noise of theirs would continue untill they arriv'd at the Sea Shore. Before they reached the Beach they might a travelled several miles, but before they began their march they collect'd in great numbers, four of five hundred in a drove. Everyone of these would give his yell, and the horrible Harmony produc'd by this tumultous assemblage must, no doubt, strike terror into every Animal within the limit of the frightfull sound. Thus Beasts, who otherwise might have become their prey had they travelled orderly and quietly like peacefull citizens, made all the haste in their power to escape from so piercing a clangour. These Dogs, in Summer, lead the perfect life of an Idler. They do no kind of work whatever. These poor Creatures, lean and meagre, all day lye like lifeless carcases in the Sun; when night comes they prowl about under the Fish Flakes in great numbers, quarrelling and fighting with all the stragglers of their own species that they meet, and yet they seem now so much degenerated from their antient character that nothing now remains of their former good qualitys, except that of Diving and their strength and agility for drawing wood, for they are at this period as great a brood of cowards as any of that kind of specie. I doubt not but that one single English Bull Dog would put to flight a Posse of twenty or thirty of them.

One of these Newfoundland Dogs, after he had been constantly worked in the woods during the winter, then slain, is not bad eating. The Hams, salted and smoked with Juniper Berrys and branches of Raspberrys and the Indian Tea, in point of flavor, is superior to the celebrated Hams of Bayonne in Gascony. Dog Hams are a new article in the Epicure's Catalogues. Had you sent to the Cock, in Cornhill for a Ham, and had they sent you this specie, you and your friend would a put it down as fine Westphalia as ever was eat.

Thus far, my good Fellow, I have got to the 25th of May. I have wrote 194 Pages filled with something, whether entertaining or informing you will judge. This I know, I have had some trouble in putting my Ideas on paper. I have related passages and circumstances as they have arose, at all times of which I have had you in mind. Do you know that as I am writing these Sheets and my Pen is forming these letters I fancy I am telling a Tale? I think I am relating the Chit Chat of the day to you! I seting on one side of the Table, and you on the other—but what is my mortification, on raising my head, that I do not behold you! The mellow sound and friendly tone of your voice does not vibrate from my Ear to the vital parts of my understanding. To my observations I get no remarks of yours. Alas! I have not the pleasure of your presence, but still while my mind is plunged in deep thoughts I always fancy I am in your Society! Under such Ideas my mind dictates to my Pen first that the story I am relating is to you seting at the other end of the Table. On more mature consideration I know that you are some thousands of miles asunder. But still my hope doth not fail me but what your Eyes will, sometime or other, be laid on this paper.

In regard to the future plan of these Sheets I find my mind varys. I thought to give my remarks daily as they arose, but this I perceive is liable to objections for I mean to speak on the Charters and Laws of Newfoundland, the Fisherys, Soil, Religion, natural Curiositys, Rivers, Lakes, Fogs, wild Animals, Bays, Harbours and Creeks, Birds, Trees, Inhabitants, Climate, and Military Government. These various subjects will come better under one general head than if scatter'd about in different pages. Altho I am, at this moment, in possession of a tolerable fund of general information of the Produce and Geography of this Island yet I shall not blend them togather in one single mass but speak of each distinctly, particularizing only to you the days I viseted a fresh Harbour, a place new to me, and the days the *Boston* sail'd on a Cruize.

I dined one day with Sir Herbert Calvert (he being dead above 300 years ago), in the month of January on Green Pease and Stewed Cucumbers brought to perfection in a Hott House in this world of Frost and Snows, drank Tea at Governor Guy's, danced at the *Princess of Bonavista*, supt at Lord Baltimore's and slept in the same Room, and in the same Bed on which His Lordship first rested his Bones on after his Voyage from England. I shall not tell you how I slept each night, altho I may sometimes tell you what my thoughts were. The Pillow, to a person in possession of a clear conscience, is a temporal paradize for Meditation, the morning Ideas being like a Rivulet of water which has for its Bed a marble bottom, with veins of Porphyry, Onyx and other precious stones.

The water of a river which proudly flows in such a valuable channel cannot but be clear, transparent and fine. So the person who goes to Bed free from the fumes of Wine riseth in the morning with a mind perspicuous and clear as a glass of Rock Water; you may shake it but it will not be discolor'd. But the man who goes to repose intoxicated, in the morning is similar to a Glass of water with sediments at the bottom, the instant it becomes disturb'd it becomes discolor'd, thick, muddy and is of no use but to throw on the Dunghill.

But I have wander'd from my subject. The *Princess of Bonavista* has just hoist'd out a Signal to know if I have nothing more to say concerning Lord Baltimore's Bed. In answer I say "No!" The *great* will but little engage my Pen, except it be in giving names of those who first got Grants of Newfoundland. I travell in a very humble sphere and my Pen, which is a French one, has a very strong dislike to the word LORDS! I humour him all I can, but you see what a scratch he makes on the last page where I had twice wrote the word LORD! Why this is very strange! I absolutely can no more manage my Pen with my finger and thumb than I can manage the Helm of the Brittania in a Gale of Wind. Oh! I see my Pen has become more flexible and tractable. It writes LORD as pliant as it doth CITIZEN! He and I, altho we are in St John's harbour fancy ourselves at Sea. He is in a perfect good humour. I suppose it is for the *Princess of Bonavista*'s sake, who is our Commander, but the ill natur'd gods have led her to be so angry with me that she has hail'd the *Boston* and vowed she will "*speak* us" if she has not a catagorical answer about Lord Baltimore's Bed, and that the answer before given is dissatisfactory.

What do you think "speaking us" means in nautical terms? In sea phrase speaking means the inoffensive, harmless, pacific and friendly design of firing a cannon loaded with Shot at you—Hit or miss. But if the Shot falls on your Ship and *kills a man* the Laws of England take no cognizance of the Act, for it is defended by two powerful and potent words in the Navy, which his Majesty allows as a great and mighty Shield for his Naval Officers to act under in cases of extreme emergency. The one is obedience, the other necessity. But as there is no premeditated design to kill, but only to ask some question of the Ship, it has become a custom if she doth not bring to after a Gun is fir'd, to send a Shot at her as the final Courier. If blood is spilt it is consider'd as their fault for not earlyer manifesting obedience to the Laws of the Land. His Majesty's Service requires *obedience* from all his subjects in every part of the world, on the high Seas particularly. I believe our Law Books do not furnish a case where the Commander of one of His Majesty's Vessels have been punish'd or fined where a catastrophe of so malancholy a nature has occur'd.

I am not afraid of being suspected as a Lawyer, having met with but scanty pittance of the good things resulting from the Law. In no time of my life was there such a general outcry against Lawyers as there was last winter. The sarcasms thrown on that body was not a little severe, how true I know nothing about, but what will suffice for myself to judge from that there is wrong somewhere is the immense fortunes made by Lawyers. There is not a County in England, as a Traveller passeth along, but what he beholds some stately Dome or lofty Turrets, and on asking who that House belongs to we are answer'd "To Counselor Rap, the King's Servant at *Law*", "The late Attorney General, the Master at Rolls, Lord Chief Justice Blubber, Mr Barron Shark, Young Mr Flake, the Son of the Late Justice Flake", or "it was built by Queen Anne's Auditor, or the Solicitor General to George the First" etc. etc.

Tuesday, June 3rd, I went to Portugal Cove in Conception Bay. Having heard of the singularity of the Indian Paths I wish'd to weary my bones in exploring one of them, being pretty well inform'd that there was no danger to be apprehend'd from Wild Beasts or Savage Indians. The distance from St John's to Portugal Cove is suppos'd to be fourteen miles. I had engag'd one Thomas Murphy, a poor, honest old Irishman, who knew the Path perfectly well, having been in the Country for Twenty Years, as my Pilot. The morning was fine. For three miles the road is perfectly good, having been made within these two years, by subscription of the principal Inhabitants of St John's, to a place call'd the Tilt House. This is nothing more than a miserable Hut, put togather at the expense of Captain Skinner, the Chief Engineer of Newfoundland, as a Rendezvous for Gentlemen and Ladys who go a Tilting in the winter on the ice on a Pond about three miles further in the woods call'd Twenty Mile Pond. The Partys, who bring their own provisions and Liquors, find in this Hut a good fire. The mouth of the Chimney is so wide that a Dorchester Butt may be lower'd down it with ease, and yet it is not more then fifteen feet from the top to the bottom, so there is no danger of being incomoded by the Smoke.

[In the Colonial Records of October 1792 there is a letter from W. J. Epps requesting the Governor's approval of the intention of a committee of the inhabitants of St John's to make a road to Portugal Cove for which a subscription had been entered into. The Governor signified his approbation and requested the names of the committee.]

After we passed this House the Trees are fell'd so as in winter to make the way easy to Twenty Mile Pond, but your passage is over Bogs and stumps of Trees, which render travelling horrible at any time but when the face of the earth is several feet cover'd with Frost and Snow, which generally is the case in this Country from October to May.

Twenty Mile Pond, so call'd from its being that space in circumference, from its magnitude properly is a Lake. To this Lake, as soon as ice sets in, the Inhabitants of St John's repair, drawn in Sledges by one or two Horses or by Dogs. Lapped up in Furrs and warm Cloathing they bid defiance to the piercing winds. On their arrival they spur on their Charioteers, and with all the swiftness of Nimrod, totally laying aside all apprehensions of danger, they skim o'er the glittering surface with all the security of a Bird. Very seldom is there any accident happens. The ice being several feet in thickness would bear up many Tons weight, so that there is no peril or hazard to be entertain'd, which makes this kind of exercise not only very amusing but desirable in point of health. This pleasing Sport is call'd Tilting. It is common for the people here to say—"Mrs Drowsing is gone tilting!" or "Ensign Splatterdash and Captain Cobwebb are going on a Tilting Party tomorrow. Will you make one of the number?" All the waters of the Lake are a mass of ice. It is of a body so thick that it will bear up Mount Etna itself; and all the Islands in the Mediterranean Sea thrown into its Volcano into the bargain.

From this short description of the winter amuzements in Newfoundland I need make but little further comment to show with what avidity the fair Sex pursue Tilting!—The ice here answers the same purpose as the Pump Room at Bath, or Hyde Park and Kensington Gardens to the Citizens of London and Westminster. The men on the ice show their agillity and courage to the fair ones by their Dogs and Chevals, in the manage of which much dexterity is display'd. So in return the Ladys will not be wanting to exhibit marks of heroism to the Hero of their fancy.

You will say that I have made but poor progress towards my Journey to Portugal Cove. I must tell you that Twenty Mile Pond is directly in my way there, and in winter the way is right athwart it, but it being now *Spring*! here (altho in June) I am obliged to make a circumambulate route along its Banks. But I cannot enhance the value of this Lake by saying how delightfull its borders and its Shores how green, for altho I have travelled near five miles by its sides, and sometimes not then ten yards from its border, yet I have not been able, more then four or five times to get only, as the Limners *[artists]* say, but a Bird's Eye view of it. This circumscribed view ariseth from the natural propensity wood has, in this Country in growing in vast abundance on the Borders of Lakes; as Rooks delight in Ruins, so wood here delights in the environs of water, particularly if there should be a gentle ascent, for there you will find it so thick that a Hare would find it a difficult business to penetrate Spruce and other woods growing in such quantity about this spot. Was a man dropped from the Clouds he would find himself as closely wedg'd in as ever an individual was amongst the crowd on a birthday at St James', without any possibility of escaping or extricating himself, unless assisted by Hatchets and Pioneers. *[Royal birthdays at the Court of St James's were occasions of crowded festivities.]*

When I was walking by the side of this Lake the Sun was very powerfull and hott. Surrounded on all sides by Spruce Trees and young shoots the Sun had such force, and the fumes of the Spruce was as potent all the way I passed as if I had held my nose over a jar of the essence of that article. The smell was by no means disagreeable, but I got overpower'd with the heat. My head ached, and being in other respects much fatigu'd, I, and my Companion Murphy sat down to rest ourselves at a small opening we found, which led to the Lake, and was the winter path across the Lake to St John's. We refreshed ourselves with Biscuits and water, having in our sight a very considerable body of water of Twenty Mile Pond in which were Fish in great variety. On its shores and little Islands Birds unknown in England, and on its banks has trod Bears, Wolves, Beavers, Otters and other animals whose presence would not be very pleasing, altho the Beaver would delight the Eye and mind as we studyed his industrious qualitys. We saw none of these creatures, but Murphy told me that about eighteen years ago, within a mile of that spott, he fell in with a Flock of Wolves, but the Wolves had their apprehensions!—as well as Murphy had his fears! Each took a contrary road, so they soon got rid of each other. I told him I thought he had better a left that story untill our return, but he assur'd me that there was no danger of a viset from them as they now never came out of the Interior of the Country. [*See note p.* 73.]

Our stay here was about an hour. I wish I had had your company. We only had a view of water and Trees. The Spruce Tree is the most prevalent wood of this Country. I think that this is not an improper season to enumerate to you the many usefull purposes to which the Spruce Tree is apply'd by the people of Newfoundland. It answers for a great many purposes; of it they have no Domestic article but what the Spruce has some concern. The following is a list of the principal uses to which this Tree is applicable in Newfoundland:

Yeast, to raise Bread with
Essence of Spruce, the common drink here
Building Houses
Bark, to cover their Houses with
Firing
Building Fish Flakes
Preserve the Sails of their Vessels
Oars, for their Boats
Masts and Yards for Ships
Cattle browse on its tender Branches
Making Pudings with

The above is a hasty list of the precious, good qualitys of the Spruce Tree. There are a number of subordinate, serviceable ends which the Inhabitants apply it to. I shall speak somewhat particular of the qualitys before spoken of.

From the Spruce is obtain'd an East [yeast] or Barm that riseth Bread as well as any yeast that can be procur'd from Malt. I, myself, have try'd it and the Bread was as light and as snow white as any Bread I ever saw. The people of this Country use Spruce yeast and nothing else to raise their Bread with.

I now come to a grand and important article, not only in Newfoundland, but in the habitable world!—It is Spruce Beer! In this

Country it is the principal beverage of the people. From the Spruce Tree is procur'd the essence of Spruce, with which the Beer is brew'd. The process of making the essence is very simple, nothing more than putting a few Gallons of water in an Iron Pott on the fire, and into this Pott keep throwing the branches of the Spruce Tree. It must be kept constantly boiling and when arriv'd to the consistency of Cream one half pint of it will be a quantity sufficient for thirty Gallons of Beer.

In England I have made this Beer. I there used to get a pott of essence containing five Ounces, thirty Gallons of water, 12 lbs Mollasses and one pound of Ginger, these put togather in a moderate heat, and work the same as you do Ale, fine it with Isinglass and bottled off in Stone Bottles. In warm weather, in two or three days, it will be *highly up*, as the London Dealers in that article say in their advertisements.

The discovery of Spruce Beer is recent. Its History may be easyly traced. Forty years ago it was a Liquid unknown in England, and for twenty years after that it was used only as a Medicine on the Continent of North America. In Nova Scotia, where the tree grows so stately that it is consider'd as the King of the Forest, the soil being deep, the use and beneficial quality of Spruce Beer is of anterior date. In the Province of Georgia in 1732, when General Oglethorpe* was there I find mention of Spruce Beer, but it in general was treated with the same insignificance as Birch Beer is at this day amongst the English. The short passage from America to Newfoundland occasion'd an early common intercourse; what was known in this Country was soon known in the other. As soon as Spruce Beer was known in America it was adopt'd in Newfoundland.

I find a number of instances in Newfoundland of persons going into the Woods and being lost. At first it was suppos'd that they fell prey to wild Beasts, but from a variety of concuring circumstances it was found that they had become a prey to the scorching heats of the Sun. From the use of Rum the spirits became languid in the Woods, and from a state of sprightliness and activity the person by degrees was lulled into torpidness. Once in this situation he was to *[r]*refacted by the Sun and absolutely burned to death.

---

* General James Edward Oglethorpe was the leader of a company who brought settlers to Georgia in 1732 and the next year founded Savannah.

The summers here are more sultry then in England. Since the use of Spruce Beer has been known none of these fatallitys has happen'd. A man goes in the hottest weather into the Woods with his Axe, his costrill* of Spruce Beer and his face greased with Pork to keep off the Muscatoos. He here works the whole day taking seasonable supplys of Spruce and at night he returns in the full possession of health to his family.

The wonderfull efficacy of Spruce Beer cannot be better given then in observing its effects in the following relation. If you go to Bed in a state of inebriation (which I hope never is the case) and when you rise in the morning in possession of a *good* headache, take a copious glass of Spruce Beer you may depend upon it that your pain will soon be reliev'd and order and regularity restored to your brain. In expressing my opinion I cannot say enough of Spruce Beer. The man, who for a short time useth this beverage only, will find himself in possession of a collective memory, his facultys vigorous and strong, a mind Cool and Easy and an understanding comprehensive, capacious and intelligent. This is a strange observation, but the man that reads this and will try the experiment will find in the end that I have stated a fact. Did the Spruce Tree vegitate and flourish to the same degree in the environs of Mecca as it doth in the North I am afraid some of the Pilgrims would stop short of the House of God and pay their devotions to this Tree, even in the sight of the famous Black Stone in the Walls of Kaba or the House of God. But Kaba is not my subject, nor the East, nor Mecca neither, but the virtue of a Tree of a spiracal form call'd Spruce.

Spruce Beer is deem'd by Physical men the best Antiscorbutic in existence. This was fully prov'd by the British Army serving in America in the late unfortunate War. It was there the common drink of the English Legions who, early in the unhappy contest, found its effacious effects, hence rose a knowledge of Spruce Beer in England. It was introduced at a period at the Tables of the Great as a luxury. After a few months it was made by Dealers and sold by them at the enormous price of one Guinea per dozen quart Bottles altho it did not at the time stand them in three half pence per bottle. This was in the year 1779. An article so profitable could not but occasion competition. In 1781 it was sold for ten Shillings

* Costrel—A flask or bottle with ears, to be suspended on the person.

per dozen. Every year reduc'd the price and in 1778 it was sold for Three Shillings per Dozen only, and on my leaving London at the outbreak of the present unpleasant War in 1793 I believe there was not Half a Dozen Shops which made the Spruce Beer for Sale, it being found from the bursting of Bottles and other attendant accidents not worthwhile to make it.

There is a Merchant at Quebec, of the name of Taylor, who had a Patent for the sale of Essence of Spruce. He consign'd this article to a person of the name of Bridge of Bread Street, London. They distributed great quantitys of it at a very considerable advantage to themselves. They kept up the price while the Patent was in force, but on the time expiring it became so cheap that few Dealers are to be found.

The next purpose to which the Spruce Trees is usefull here is for building and covering their Dwellings with. All the Houses in Newfoundland are built of Spruce. With the Bark of the Tree all the Houses are cover'd except a few in St John's and Placentia. For firing Spruce is the common article. It also serves for the necessary purpose of Fish Flakes, both in building and covering, which yearly want repair. The Spruce growing handy, it is got with little trouble.

In every Harbour, Creek and Cove there is what may be called a Parish Pott, this holds about 20 Gallons, and it is filled with water and Spruce Bark, which is boiled togather; they then dip the netts of the Fishermen in to it, and the Sails of their Boats to which it is a great preservative. This Pott is generally the property of one person, and it is seldom that you will find more than one of these Potts in a Creek or Cove. For dipping a set of Boat Sails they pay 3/6d. I am told the Owners have made Fifteen Pounds in one season by Dipping! This is all clear profit, the Bark and firing not costing anything. I mention this circumstance of dipping to show in this particular the property of the Spruce Tree.

It will be needless to mention that all the Boats, Oars etc, are made of Spruce. In this Country the Spruce Tree doth not grow to that magnitude to be of strength or length sufficient for Masts or Yards for Ships of War, the soil being light; but in Nova Scotia the Spruce Tree raiseth its head higher, the soil there being deeper the Tree takes firmer root, and it aspires to a considerable degree of superiority in consequence, so much so that the Dock Yards of Portsmouth and Plymouth might be supply'd from the Forests of that Country with Masts and Yards.

The last observation, for the present, I have to make on the Spruce is that when Cattle are turn'd into the woods they browse on its young branches, their Milke then has the flavor of Spruce. I have tasted butter made by the fair hands of Mrs Skinner, the Wife of the Chiefe Engineer, which has been so strongly impregnated with Spruce that even the *nose* would taste the flavor.

The natives have a method of mixing fine Pudings in this Country, Spruce is an ingredient, a certain proportion of Flour, Eggs, and the blossoms of Dandelion are the principal consonant parts. They are very light. I have not yet tasted one so I cannot give an opinion.

I think you will suppose it high time to enquire after my Pilot Murphy. I left him seting down on the borders of Twenty Mile Pond amusing himself in contemplation of Spruce, if he did not it was his own fault having plenty before his Eyes.

I shall resume my journey and quit Twenty Mile Pond, endeavouring as well as I can to give you an Idea of an Indian Path in Newfoundland. This path to Portugal Cove is, I am told, a fair specimen of the generality of them in this Country.

Newfoundland being in all parts intersected with Bogs, Barrens, Lakes, Morasses, Hills, Rivulets and Woods we find all places are plaster'd or thickly scatter'd with stones of all shapes and of all sizes. Over a Country on which Nature is suppos'd to have dealt with so sparing a hand travelling must needs be difficult and fatiguing. Indian Paths are only for persons on foot and are so narrow as not to admit two persons abreast. You enter one of these Paths, about half a yard wide, hemmed in on each side by invulnerable woods. You have to step on stones, some as big as the axel tree of a Waggon, others less,—you pass on for a few yards and then you come to a Bog. You have to tread on a long narrow pole, on a broken root, a stone, a bundle of brush wood, a tuft of Moss, or cling to the branches of a Tree while some of its lower decayed stumps serves to put your feet on to creep from tree to tree. If any of these auxillarys fail down you come in the Swamp.

After you have got over a Bog you commonly have a gentle ascent to get up, the surface of which is a continual Spring, the water oozing out from amongst the broken stones and stumps so as to create a moisture very unpleasant to walke over. On descending this slope you always find a small Rivulet to wade through, unless you choose to venture your limbs in crossing by stepping from one stumbling block to another. The path is sometime three or four miles right down one of these water courses, where the Hillocks and stones are as uneven that they have a strong resemblance to an old stone House tumbled down, and you are trampling over the Ruins. A part of the road is sometimes a soft path, this is over a Swamp entirely cover'd with long Moss; to the Eye it appears free from wet but the instant you put your foot on it you sink up to your ankle in Slush and Moss. Whoever has penetrated into the interior of the Country when it is free from Frost and Snow will find the foregoing picture fairly drawn. My companion Murphy inform'd me that it was a common adage in Newfoundland —Always in travelling to be last in the Bog and first in the Wood. The triteness of the observation I think so forcible that it needs no comment.

I shall conclude my account of Indian Paths by stating that about four years ago the Purser of the *Rose* Frigate, then on this Station, being at Bay of Bulls, a distance of about twenty miles from St John's, came to a resolution to walk it. He did so, but under circumstances not a little laughable, for he lost his Shoes, tore the Skirts of his Coat off, and what was worse then all, rended his Breeches in such a manner as decency forbid him entering St John's untill after night had sett in. Indeed the Path which Murphy and myself this day traversed often exhibited the Strap or the sole of a Shoe, which no doubt were left behind from the goodness of the understanding that subsist between them and their owners.

Reverting to Murphy and myself—when I was within five miles of my journey's end, from the badness of the Path and the excessive heat of the Sun, I found much difficulty in proceeding! Every half mile Murphy, who led the way, would turn round to encourage my pace. Presently I heard a Cock crow, which forebode being near the Residence of something that was human. Never to me was the voice of the Cock more gratefull. Had three Nightingales set up a Trio the most melodious, at that moment their Serenade would a had no effect on my Ear.

Being arriv'd within sight of the Houses, and well knowing that my frame bore external marks of fatigue and weariness, I could not but figure to myself the inward satisfaction that I felt in the hope that on putting my head into the Public House, where Murphy had assur'd me there was a good one, I should discover in the face and actions of my Landlady all those little domestic feelings and attention which would elevate and counterpoise the trifling toils I had met with. I fondly fancy'd that in my Landlady's countenance I should trace all the Graces, the Smiles, the cheering looks and the comforting Language which I once experienced so gaily, cheerily, merrily, sprightly and readily from the Mistress of the Flower de Luce Hotel or Half Way House between St Omer and Bologne, in France.

I bent my course towards the House with such presentiments. Acknowledge I must that my appearance did not command respect. Unfortunately I had left part of my Shoes on the road, stockings I had none on, having Muscatoo Trousers. A Stick I had in my hand that would vie, in point of size, to the Ensign Staff of a First Rate. Shanco, alias Murphy, was equip'd in stile corresponding in the Habiliments of a Knight's Esquire. I soon got sight of a Weoman. As soon as I perceiv'd that she was retreating to the House I dropp'd my Staff. Who should this be but Mrs Harty, or Hartley, my Landlady.

I enter'd the House, but alas, all indifference! All was unconcern and cold negligence. No soothing look, consoling speech or motion made that indicated the smallest desire to please. The Lady offer'd me no domestic office by action or word, she handed me no chair, she did not say "Sir you seem tired, will you not set down? How far have you walk'd?—The Sun is very powerful!" I thought of my good Landlady at the Hotel of the Flowers de Luce in France. What a contrast between the two! I thought what a Blessing is a good natur'd Weoman. I asked for some water to wash my feet in. Mrs Harty show'd me a little Prill that run within a few yards of the door. To it I went and perform'd the job. I return'd to the House, put on clean stockings and shoes which I had brought with me. I felt myself, in a short time, reviv'd, was vigorous, things had assum'd a new appearance. The Landlady's disposition also had assum'd a new temperature.

I observ'd she had a Pott boiling on the fire. I told her I was hungry and wanted something to eat. I ask'd what was in the Pott. It appear'd to me as if they were not over willing I should know the Contents. I took the Lid off and suppos'd there was a Ham in, and so there was—and a Brace too. It contain'd the hind part of a Seal which was catch'd that morning in Conception Bay. It was taken out of the Pott, I eat some of it and can pronounce it, according to my Palate, not bad eating, altho it is consider'd in general on an average with Dog's Flesh. The natives never use it when they can purchase Salt Pork.

Having satiated my hunger for the first time with the flesh of Seal and spoken some extravagent and hard strain'd compliments in favour of Mrs Harty's conciliating manners, Sociability, elegant Deportment, versatility in conversation and the praiseworthy decorum and *reserve* with which she at first observ'd Strangers—by this kind of dissimulation I worked into her confidence. I now and then got a Laugh from her. She let me in to a little of her History by degrees. I at last discover'd that Newfoundland was her Birthplace, so she of course fell under the appellation of an Indian Weoman.

I now was in Portugal Cove, Conception Bay, on the Northern Shores of Newfoundland. The Portuguese Adventurer who discover'd this Country first made the Land which forms the angles of this Bay. He enter'd the Bay, which he named Conception, as conception is the Mother of all things. He coasted round this spacious Bay and landed on this spot, which he named Portugal Cove in compliment to the Country which foster'd him in his discoverys. There are several small Islands in this Bay only one of which is inhabited. This is call'd Bell Isle, and is reckon'd to be the fertilest spot to be met with on the northern Coast.

Lobsters are in such plenty at this place that they are used for Bait to catch the Codd Fish with. About Sunset I went out in a small Boat to inform myself of the fact. The result was far beyond my expectation. I was not in the Boat more then Half an Hour, during which time one man hooked fifty-nine Lobsters.

There is some Art in Lobster catching. The man stands erect in the Bows of the Boat, with a slender Pole fourteen or fifteen feet long in his hand, at the end of it is an Iron Hook. He keeps his Eye steadfastly on the water. The instant he gets the sight of a Lobster he darts the pole at it and with surprizing dexterity hooks it under the Tail. As soon as the Fish is tickled he bends his Tail, fatally for himself! which presseth as a Ring around the Hook, and it is the only assistance wanting to haull him into the Boat. Mornings and evenings is the time for catching Lobsters, when there is no Swell or Sea, they then come out of their holes to feed. The Boats which go after them move slowly on the water's surface. They very seldom miss one they aim at. It is not a little astonishing the good propertys which custom gives us; I was very much struck with its effects this day, observing that the man who was catching the Lobsters had got several into the Boat. For my part I had not fixed my eyes on one before he had got it half out of the water. That I might have a fair chance I laid my frame in the Fore part of the Boat and my head suspended over the Bows. The man's Legs were across my neck, so that I was nearer the water more then four feet then he was. But all this would not do, I could not see one, altho he was hooking them in as fast as he could. I consider myself as in possession of a pair of good Eyes and the apparent advantage he had over me in point of seeing arose entirely from custom.

Before night I return'd to Mrs Harty's and had all the Lobsters piled in a Heap at the Door, meaning to have some of them for Supper. A large Pott was put on the Fire and two or three dozen Lobsters were put to death in a few minutes. As they were boil'd they were put outside the Door to cool. We had one heap of Boil'd Lobsters and one heap of live Lobsters. We employ'd ourselves in cracking and picking the boiled Fish outside the Door, when a scene was produc'd that put me in mind of the General Deluge. No sooner had we begun picking the Fish then we were surrounded by Fowl, Cows, Ducks, Goats, Geese, Cats, Horses, Calves, Pigs, tame Sea Gulls, Sheep and Dogs, in short all the Specie of every kind which is domestic in Newfoundland. When I threw the Claw of a Lobster a Cat, a Goat and a Hog would start after it; generally the Cat was successful. When the body of the Fish was checked off the Fowls, the Cows, and the Gulls and the Sheep would join in pursuit. I saw a Horse, a Calf and a Dog smelling the same flesh, each in perfect good humour.

The scene, as singular as it was extraordinary, I could not but view with exstacy and surprize. It impress'd on my mind the certainty that by early initiating, animals of various kinds may be brought to eat of one common beverage. The Shores of Newfoundland being the grandest mart in the known world for Fish it is the cheapest food in the Country. The Inhabitants give it to their domestic animals and they all eat it. But I shall not quit this representation before the Ark as yet. Seeing a Beast of every kind so very intent after his provender I thought we might turn their application and diligence in some measure to our recreation and mirth.

In our posse was a white Horse, uncommon docile and quiet.

Amongst us was a black Cat as calm and pacific or as violent and furious as you please. Our live Lobsters were still vigorous and strong. We began our frolic (Mrs Harty joining in) by hanging the Horse's mane and Tail full of Lobsters; the hair not being capable of receiving the impression of pain the Horse stood his ground. We then seiz'd the Cat and put no less then four large, *live Lobsters* on her *Tail*. The moment the Claws embrac'd her Tail her tumultous outcry put some of our Companions to flight. We found means to convey the Cat on the Horses back. The instant she felt her paws in a spongy substance she stuck her elastic fangs up to the hilt in the Horse's back. His posterior was towards the Door. At this very crisis the Horse sent forth a volume of wind that would vie with the Mounts of Vesuvius and Etna. The noise of this volcano was not a little dreadfull. I had some fear that the House would be blown down in the storm as the eruption did not cease for some minutes, the Horse keeping kicking and thundering, the Cat clawing and squawling. However, at last the Horse took to its heels with the Cat on its back, crying and scratching every step the poor animal took, increasing his terror and scarefaction.

When the Horse took his flight he bent his course amongst ragged Rocks and broken stones. I was under considerable anxiety for his neck, but when the convulsion of laughter was a little moderated the people assur'd me that there was no cause for alarm as he was possess'd of the facultys of a Norwegian Goat and would climb with the same facility as a Wild Catt.

The appearance of this Horse was so whimsical and odd that its erasure is not easily taken from the mind. Figure to yourself a white Horse, his Mane and Tail platted with Lobsters. This is not only a new but elegant Trapping for Chargers. It would excite no small degree of merryment to the passing crowd at Charing Cross to see one of His Majesty's cream color'd Horses led out of the Mews ornament'd with these polish'd Fish.

It is reported here that the Duke of York has receiv'd a grand defeat from the French Republican Army in the neighbourhood of Tourcoing, and that he was obliged to save himself by flight, without a single attendant, and was forc'd to swim on Horseback across the River Lis, to prevent his falling into enemy hands. If this intelligence is true I am very sorry for it, for His Highness must for a certainty be in a great hurry. I am afraid when he plunged into the water there was no danger of his *stock* of provisions sinking with him. Now must not the surprize of this Noble Personage be great when his courser was emerging from the River, on the opposite side, to behold his Mane and Tail cloathed with that delicate Shell Fish—Lobsters! This, to the Commander of an Army retreating without his baggage, must be as seasonable a relief as the Manna was to the Sojourners in the Wilderness.

[A British army under the command of the Duke of York had been sent to Flanders in 1793. It failed to take Dunkirk and was defeated at Hondschoot.]

But to return to Portugal Cove. The Horse and Catt being out of sight the bustle they had occasion'd was more moderated. Our animals, which were more then two of every kind, return'd to the door of the Ark with freedom and security. I saw no symptoms of jealousy amongst our Republican threshold—everyone did as he liked, the Cow eat with the Sea Gull and the Fowls eat with the Goat. All was harmony and contentment. I saw but little contention about eminence or pre-eminence. Everyone had his share of Lobster. The Cow was milk'd as she stood mumbling over the shell of a Lobster. This scene continued till sable night drew her shadowy curtain over this part of the Globe and warned us that each must retire to his resting place. But before I retreat within doors I must indulge myself in an Idea about the Ark and Mount Arraret.

Amongst the record in sacred writ how tremendous was God's declaration to Noah when he announc'd the dreadfull intelligence that the end of Man was come. What must be the sensations of Noah when the potent Governor of the Universe declared "The end of all flesh is come before me, for the earth is filled with violence through them, and behold I will destroy them with the Earth!" At the close of the scene before me I could not refrain from musing o'er Noah and his household. Poor man! He had a mighty business on his shoulders. No mortal, before or since, had more tempers to conciliate than he, however he acquit'd himself with eclat. But in this concern he was assist'd in the infinite power of God.

As night set in we quited this Lobster scene and retir'd into the House. I consol'd myself under the Idea of having a good Supper of Lobsters, but on making enquiry I found that there was neither Oil nor Vinegar in Portugal Cove. Without one or the other this Fish, in my opinion, is not worth eating. Here was nothing to be got but Pork and Biscuits. Tir'd with the fatigue and adventures of the day (as I am sure you must be with the repetition of them) I went to Bed, which was not a bad one, altho much cannot be said of its trappings which was nothing more than the Sail of an old Boat hung round in elegant disorder. It was daubed here and there with a plaster of Pitch which, to my terrify'd mind, represented some diabolical ruffian with a Sabre in his hand, ready to run me through the body the instant I closed my Eyes in sleep. Another daub was splatter'd somewhat like a Castle; this I thought was enchant'd of course. It being a double Bed room my fears were soon dissipated by the entrance of a young man who was going to occupy the *blankets* which lay on the Bedstead at the opposite side of the chamber. I asked a multitude of questions. At first he answer'd freely, shortly he got a little smack of the Acid, and presently he grew full as sour as Burgundy Vinegar. I talked the young Dog to sleep; but he, in his slumbers, was as troublesome to me as I was to him a few minutes before. In the morning I asked him where he was born and he reply'd at Harbour Grace and that he was a Fisherman. I told him that altho he was from Harbour Grace yet he was a graceless dog. I believe had I used a small quantity of flattery I could have induced him to sojourn with me, as a Volunteer on board the *Boston*.

Wednesday 4th June. As I was turning out of Bed my foot I catched on a ragged part of my bed furniture; this discompos'd the order of the Sail Cloath so much that a volume of dust was put in motion in an instant. With the dust also fell a volume of Entick's Dictionary. I wonder'd what brought that there, knowing that none of the Family could *read*, therefore could have no use for a pocket vocabulary. I carry'd it to Mrs Harty who said it was a Prayer Book. I had joked and laughed at her a good deal the previous evening. I thought she was now speaking ironically.

"I know," she rejoin'd, "It is no vortex, but my husband's little Prayer Book, who is now Fishing for Salmon at the mouth of the Little Codd Roy River."

I have said much on adventures at Portugal Cove without saying a word on its situation etc. Here are about Twenty Fishermen's Hutts, a Fish Room and a Fish Flake. It has a Waterfall with a pole over it for a bridge. The Cove is hung with large Rocks or Mountains. Amongst the Hutts are scatter'd a number of small Hillocks and broken stones. This Sketch [*reproduced on the jacket of this book*] was taken in a Boat about half a mile from the shore.

[*Judge Prowse, in his "History of Newfoundland", gives the number of families resident in Portugal Cove during the winter of 1794 as 34 and the total population as 200, of these 33 were men, 27 women and the remainder were children. Today it is a fishing village with a population of* 1040. *It is the terminal for the ferry to Bell Island. At that time there were thirteen families resident on Bell Island. Large iron ore mines were operated at Bell Island and the town there grew to a population of thirteen thousand. These mines have recently closed down and many of the residents are moving away. Despite modern innovations the description of Portugal Cove as a place of rocks and hills close to the sea still rings true and there are still people of the name of Harty living there.*]

Before I made my final exit from the place I breakfasted with Mrs Harty on Indian Tea, the growth of Newfoundland. This is not a bad article. I shall have occasion to speak of this Herb hereafter. I observ'd they gave their fishing people this Tea for Breakfast, which was put in a Pott with water and Molasses. All was boil'd togather and given them with Fish and Biscuits. This is the common people's Breakfast and Supper in Newfoundland.

Altho I pertook at this House of Salt Pork, hard dry biscuits and the most homely fare yet Mrs Harty was not behind hand in point of charges. In this respect she vied with Houses of capital resort in London. I have dined on Veal Cutlets at Saunders in the Strand, supt on Beefe Steaks at Garrick's Head in Bow Street, when to the Theatre at Covent Garden, and my expenses would be on a par with the amount here for one night's entertainment.

About 7 O'Clk in the morning I bid adieu to Madam Harty and Portugal Cove. Murphy and myself set off for St John's in good spirits. We trod our old path o'er stumps, Poles, planks, Moss, stones, slush, Bogs, Rivulets, Ravines, water courses, Hills and Dales, and none knew what else—except those who have frequent'd this desolate path. When Murphy met with an old acquaintance—I mean a stone over which, the day before, either he or I had tumbled over, or a Bog, he would cry out "Here Mr Thomas, here is the Bog Hole where your foot stuck in yesterday, take care for it is the very Slough of Despair itself."

It is the custom of modern writer and travellers to introduce Biographical Sketches of their underlings, come they under the denomination of Pilots, Guides, Pioneers or Guards etc. I shall follow the rule of my predecessors in order to make myself look big amongst those who have not the *good fortune* to know me. Murphy's history is but short, I shall compress it within a few lines. He tells me, and that very truly I make no doubt, that he emigrated from Ireland, where he was born, with the hope of bettering his fortune; that he has been in this Country for several years, has met with woefull disappointments, and for the last ten years has entirely abandon'd his original design viz—that of bettering his fortune, that the Fish every year seems scarcer, and that the fourth of June had arriv'd, the Fishing Season half over and he had not been able to get a berth in a Fishing Vessel. I told him that my own Motto was Never Despair—and recommended its adoption by him.

We kept walking and chatting along the Indian Path on our return untill we came near Twenty Mile Pond. I heard a violent chirping of a great number of Birds nearly over our heads amongst the Spruce Trees. I noticed this to Murphy who rapp'd out an Oath and swore that the noise of the Birds indicated the presence of some strange Animal, adding with dreadfull energy—"This is the very spot where I met the Flock of Wolves I spoke of yesterday!"

"God be mercifull to me," thinks I, "What! have my Parents bred me up with tender solicitude to these years, to become at last food for wild Beasts!"

This is not a time for hesitation. Each had a large Spruce stick in his hand, we had no fire arms. I would, at that moment, gladly a parted with *some* of my Limbs to have a vital part of my body in *safe* security, my whole frame was nearly deliquated. Unfortunately I was in the front, there was no room for two abreast as the path was so narrow. Presently a little animal darted across the path about five yards before me.

"There goes one, Murphy," I bawl'd out as loud as I could vociferate, but he did not see it. Immediately, turning my eyes on the other side of the path I saw an animal looking most steadfastly at us, and not more then four yards from my face, setting on a projecting spray of Spruce Tree. I lost not a moment in showing the animal to my *Friend* (at this crisis I thought Murphy's company more valuable than the society of any soul I ever associated with). The very instant he saw the Creature, most loudly he exclaim'd "Put yourself in a posture of defence! It is a wild Catt."

Before the words were well out of his mouth the creature retreated. She cantered backwards and forwards two or three times within our sight, as if wanting to cross the path after its Mate.

The heads of these Catts are exactly like the tame ones, their bodys are larger. They were of a dark brown colour, the tips of the ears red. The body and tail the shape and motion of a Greyhound. They never attack the human specie unless they are fell in with near the abode of their young, when they will exhibit the most daring resolution. Not one Dog in a thousand will face them. The moment they espy a Dog they draw their four feet togather that they will not cover a Crown Piece, when they are in this position their aspect is hedious and frightfull. If a Dog approaches within six yard of them they are sure to fly at him; they light on the head and the poor Dog is instantly blinded. These Catts have a property of a very singular nature in their Tail, at the end of which is a Nail as pointed as a needle. This is a formidable weapon and they have the same power of using it as the Scorpion has his Tail. I am told that it moves in a socket. If so it is elastic, and truly unfortunate must the animal be whom a Wild Catt falls on, for while she holds fast with her paws she is digging away with her Tail, and death must infallibly be the issue of her perseverance. These Catts have the same agility amongst the Trees as Squirrels have. They eat the Eggs of Birds, live on Berrys etc. There are a great number of them in Newfoundland. [*This "wild cat" was undoubtedly a marten.* (Martes americana strata). *These are now quite rare on the island and they are only found among mature spruces. The peculiar tail is a myth. The Newfoundland wolf* (Canis lepus beothucus) *has been described as a distinct sub-species. That they were common at one time is amply shown in older books on Newfoundland. The last known specimen was shot on the Topsails in 1911.*]

When Murphy and I arriv'd at the further end of the Lake we were overtaken by four Fishermen going to St John's with Salmon from Portugal Cove. They set down to rest and Murphy intimated his desire to get home early, as he expected a Merchant to call him who would perhaps give him a Berth. I understood him. The remainder of the road being good I could as well walke with the Fishermen as with him—we parted. These men had Twenty-eight Salmon to carry between them, some of which weigh'd ten or twelve pounds. The day being hot their fatigue was not a little. On their arrival they would find but poor compensation as perhaps all the Salmon would not sell for fourteen Shilling. They learn'd that I belonged to His Majesty's Ship the *Boston* which was a serious concern to one of them, for my society impress'd upon his weak intellect the certainty of being Impress'd into the King's Service. He absolutely avail'd himself of running into the woods with the Salmon on his back, supposing I had sent Murphy forwards for the purpose of bringing a Gang of the *Boston*'s people to force them on board the Frigate. In the evening I return'd safely and free from hurt, by no means displeased with my Tour to Portugal Cove.

Boston. St John's Harbour, 10th June 1794.

Last night the Houses of this place were illuminated on account of the capture of the Island of Guadulupe by the British Forces.

[In 1793 a large contingent of British forces had been sent to the West Indies. English planters had made great fortunes and Pitt was anxious to acquire the French West Indian Islands for the British Empire. A lack of knowledge of conditions in the West Indies made such a campaign a very difficult undertaking. Disease killed thousands of British troops. Little was added to the Empire and 40,000 troops lost their lives. The dreadful loss crippled England's effort in Europe.]

The mouth of this harbour is at this time almost blocked up with Islands of Ice. One of them is very large; from the top of it I see a torrent of water gushing down occasion'd by the Sun, it being now midday it has much force. The Ice is melting very fast. Had I this ponderous Bulke of Ice on Tower Hill a multitude would be soon collected as large as that assembl'd at the execution of the Scotch Lords. The base of this Island covers a greater space then the Tower itself, and in point of height the Ice is most lofty. *[A.T. was presumably recalling the executions following the 1745 uprising, Lords Kilmarnock and Balmerino in August 1746 and Lord Lovat in 1747.]*

Altho this is the middle of Summer in England, yet we had here last night a severe Frost, so intense that had it been with you—farewell to all your Fruits and Vegitables! The weather was this morning as cold as ever I felt it in January in Britain. As soon as the Sun makes its appearance the cold is dissipat'd and its luminous rays are gratefull and pleasing. This time of the year is call'd *Spring*—in Newfoundland. The Vegitable Kingdom is just peeping from its winter habitation and the cultivated spots are assuming their livery of green; the Sun instills his genial qualitys into plants and herbs in a very bountifull manner here, they grow more in one week then they do in England in three. The summers being short, the Sun is very powerfull and everything is brought to perfection in a short space of time.

The only vegitable which at present can be procur'd here is Dandelion, which grows wild. I have a salad of it most days. It grows plentifully in England and is there generally known by the vulgar name of piss Beds. It is a yellow flower, and in shape is exactly like the blossom of Marygolds.

The old custom of mine of never passing a Churchyard without viseting the repository of the dead has not lost its force on me here in America. At St John's is a Church, built of wood, where the worship of God is perform'd according to the tenets of the Church of England. I have been in the Cemetery of this building and the following is the fruit of my researches:

Epitaphs in the Churchyard of St John's, in the Island of Newfoundland.

Sacred to the memory of Robert Hodge of Brixham, nigh to Dartmouth, in England, who in the great dutys of life was a sincere Christian and a true friend.

If Christian virtues ever claim a tear
In pity, Reader, kindly drop it here
A faithfull husband here lamented sleeps
A faithfull Wife, his earthly absence weeps.
To her, and their dear offspring, be it given
With Christ our Saviour, all to meet in Heaven.

On John Heard, aged seven years.

Saints, at your Heavenly Father's word
Give up your comfort to the Lord.
He shall restore what you resign
To grant you blessings more divine.

Here lies the remains of Michael Gill Esq., Judge of the Admiralty of this Island, and for a number of years Justice of the Peace. He was an indulgent Father and a tender Husband. This tomb is inscrib'd to his memory by his disconsolate Widow and Son. He was born at Charlestown in America in 1699 and died at St John's, Newfoundland 8th March, 1772.

These three Memorials were the only epitaphs worth transcribing.

[*These memorials are no longer to be seen in St John's, nor do there seem to be any Parish Records of that period. Presumably they were in a Burial Ground no longer in existence. The first Church at St John's was built around 1700 within the precincts of Fort William. This gradually fell into a state of disrepair. In 1720 a larger wooden church was built near the site of the present Cathedral; by 1759 this had also fallen into a state of decay and a new and finer edifice was built to replace it. In the Colonial Records of 1790 and 1792 there are several letters concerning the state of repair of the then existing church, which Captain Skinner, the Chief Engineer, was requested to inspect. A letter to the Rev John Harries of St John's dated 25 September 1792 acquaints him that in consequence of the dangerous state of the Church, Divine Service might be performed in the Court House during the winter months or until the Church is repaired and that directions would be given to the enlargement of the Burial Ground, the present one being full. Captain Skinner, in conjunction with the Rev Mr Harries, was instructed to fix on the proper piece of ground for the Burial of the Dead. A new Church was eventually built in 1800. John Heard was probably the son of John Heard, blockmaker, who was listed as a householder in St John's on a census list for 1796.*

Michael Gill was the son of Captain Michael Gill whose name first appeared in Newfoundland shipping lists in 1698 when his 40 ton vessel brought salt, pork and cyder from New England. Captain Gill seems to have traded mostly with Bonavista, which place he defended against the French in 1705. His sons Michael and Nicholas came to Newfoundland and both rose to hold many important positions. As Judge of the Admiralty Court Michael Gill seldom gave judgement against a merchant.]

V

Capelin Bay

Thursday 27th June. The *Boston* sailed from St John's yesterday morning and after a pleasant run anchor'd in this Bay this afternoon. We are on a Coasting Cruize, Captain Morris meaning to viset St Pierre (lately taken from the French) and some of the principal out-harbours. [*All ports of Newfoundland outside St John's are referred to as outports or outharbours.*] I understand our stay here will be for a few days, therefore I shall class my remarks under one date, even if I stop here for a month. On our Passage to this Bay the Sea afforded to our sight some very extraordinary phenomenas of Nature, so plentifull were the Islands of Ice on this Coast at this time that I counted Twenty-Nine in view at one time. [*The log of June 26th–29th—"Moored in Capilin Bay".*]

Capelin Bay is more properly a Harbour, being a mile and a half in length and not more than a quarter of a mile across in any part. Its mouth is defended from the Sea by two very small Islands called Stone and Goose Islands, there is deep water and a very good Anchoring Ground. It is esteem'd a safe Harbour. In this Bay is a little Inlet called Brewing Cove, so call'd because Men of War, who come to anchor in this Bay, brew their Spruce Beer in this Cove. Here is a small Hutt erected to shelter the men from the rain. The Rocks are very romantic, at a distance from the Hutt is a Cascade. The Spruce Beer, when brew'd, is laid on the ground in Casks to work. The Ship's Boats then take it on board for use. I have made use of my Pencil to represent a scene to you, in viewing of which I had much satisfaction. [*This is missing.*]

About a mile from Capelin Bay is Ferryland where there is a considerable Settlement. Near two hundred Houses and Hutts constitutes the place. Here are some good Stores and much Trade is carry'd on in Fish. There is a Harbour of difficult access; before it lyes Ferryland Head and the Isle of Boise.

In Queen Anne's reign the Fishermen and Planters of this and the neighbouring Bays sent home to England complaints of a want of protection, as the French had, at that period, settlements on the Southern Shores of Newfoundland. To these complaints the then Ministry in England paid attention. Colonel Charles Lilly, an Engineer, was dispatch'd to survey this part of the Coast and he arriv'd in Capelin Bay in Her Majesty's Ship *Burlington* the 1st September, in the year 1771. He went to work, finished his Survey, return'd to England and reported that Her Majesty's subjects at Ferryland had not the share of protection which was enjoy'd by the Harbours and Bays in the environs of St John's; that the population and the quantity of Fish cured at Ferryland entitl'd them to look to Her Majesty for the means of defence and protection. In consequence of these representations a Fort was order'd to be built, according to the opinion and Plan of Colonel Lilly, on the Isle of Boise, which would command the entrance into Capelin Bay, Ferryland Harbour, Aquafort and Crow Sound. This Fort was completed, and mounted seven Guns. From it was never fired an angry shot. It is now in Ruins, and the Guns cover'd with rubbish and weeds.

[Parts of cannon and ruins of fortifications are still to be seen on the Isle of Bois which has been variously spelt Buoys, Buoyes or Boise in older books. In one case it was referred to as Little Bog Island. There are records of it having been unsuccessfully attacked by the French in 1708. In 1753 it was granted to Robert Carter of Ferryland who later maintained the garrison there.]

I was walking one day on Ferryland Head, looking towards the Sea. I saw a thick vapor or mist rise in a narrow compass out of the Ocean near the shore. I thought it was the smoke which issued from a Gun when fired, only it rose in a larger column. I instantly pointed it out to the person who was with me who immediately said "It is a Whale blowing". This is the first time I ever saw a motion of one of these creatures. Presently we saw the fluke of his Tail and the enormous Fins on his back. He kept rolling and blowing about in chase of a Fish called Capelin *[Caplin (Mallotus Villosus)]*.

Capelin is a small fish but larger than an Anchovie. It is of considerable importance to the Fishery of this Country. What I have to say of Capelin is of so strange a nature that I am very much afraid you will doubt my veracity. As the old saying goes "Seeing is believing". Had not my own Eyes been witness I do not think I should a given credit to the History of them, even when related by a person of respectability. Luckily at this very crisis is the time of their being in season. There is, at this instant, such Tons of them togather all around the Beaches of this Coast that you may fill a Boat in a few minutes. They go in Shoals, and appear first on the Northern Shores, moving regularly and slowly towards the Southward. This progress takes about six weeks in performing. At the time they are on the North Shore there is not a single Capelin on the South Shore, and visa versa, but when they are on the South Shores there is not a single fish on the North Shore. This pilgrimage they make every year at this period, and a Pilgrimage of Martyrdom it may be called for them, for millions and thousands of millions never return, and yet more die thro their own stupidity then lose their lives by the Nett, the Whale, the Grampus [*Black Fish or Pothead Whale*] and all their living enemys put togather. It happens thus—They go in great numbers so innumerable as the Leaves of the Trees in an immense Forest. They frequent sandy beaches and sandy banks. I, myself, have been in a Boat amongst a shoal of them. If you put a Basket out you will draw it in full. I have put my hand over the Boat's side and have grasped five of these fish in my hand at one time. Whales are very fond of these fish and will follow a Shoal of them till his hunger is satiated; he always finds them near the shore. They always, on being pursued, make very foolishly for it. Those nearest the Whale force the others forwards, so that if those which are in the front wished to retreat it would be impossible, the Whale is in their rear. They run for the Beach with great swiftness, the whale following with equal velocity. In the instant they approach the sandy Beach tons of them are thrown on shore and there perish. If there is a large Swell or Surf the havock amongst them is still greater. In these kinds of pursuit the Whale, in his eagerness, is often thrown ashore with them.

In Ferryland Harbour on a calm day when there is no Surf or swell, the water being only gently agitated, every little roll left a number of Capelin on the sand to perish. The shores, wherever these fish viset, are strew'd with their bodys. In Coves, Creeks and places which are desolate or uninhabited the Bears, Wolves, Foxes and other wild Animals come out of the woods and feast on dead

Capelin. These fish are delicate eating, particularly the female, which has a roe nearly as large as the rest of her Body. The Male and Female differ materially in appearance and do not look like the same specie. They viset the shoal waters and sands at this season for the purpose of depositing their Spawn, which is here brought to maturity. They afterwards retire to deep waters and remain unobserv'd by the human race untill this season returns again. I am told that one of these Females will produce, in one season, upwards of five thousand young. Such astonishing fecundity amongst such thousands of millions, I should think, would fill a Bay as extensive as the Bay of Biscay is with Capelin in a few seasons. But in overhauling the Capelin which was brought on board the *Boston* I observed that for one female there were two hundred males. The difference in numbers of the sexes is too curious and too voluminous to elucidate. I shall suffice myself in saying that had the Lioness and the Deer the same degree of fecundity as the Rabbit and the Capelin the world would soon be over-run with the former.

The Capelin, no doubt, destroy numbers amongst themselves, the Whale makes considerable havock for he will hold Two Barrels full of them in his mouth before he swallows one fish. Tons and tons of them are thrown ashore every year and very amazing quantitys are taken for Bait for catching the Codd with, as well as dry'd and eaten by the people. From so many fatallitys and enemys to this specie you may infer the prodigeous slaughter amongst them, yet every year they return in undiminish'd numbers, as silly as boldness and ignorance can animate, to the very spot where their predecessors perish'd.

I consider the Capelin Fish as a blessing to Newfoundland. While they are in season the Fishing Boats get fresh Capelin every night for Bait, in the morning the people proceed to the Fishing Bank. They throw out their hooks and lines baited with fresh Capelin, the Codd Fish being fond of them bite avariciously and plenty is generally the attendant of this temptation.

Vast quantitys of Capelin are salted and dry'd to be used as Bait at other times, as well as for food for the Winter. Having enumerated the desirable possession of these fish you must admit the mercifull divinity of God in causing such resort to these valuable little creatures to the shores of this desolate and barren Land.

Capelin Bay is so call'd because Capelin frequent that Bay more then any other. While the *Boston* lay in this Bay a Boat used to go twice a day to get Capelin for the Ship's Company. It seldom took more then an hour, when they would return with as many Bushells as was wanting. On the Capelin quitting the Shores the Providence of God is shown in a very exalted manner to the shores of this land, for after them come a wonderfull resort of Fish call'd Squids, which serves as Bait. But I shall speak of them hereafter, as well as the fish which follows the Squids.

Captain Morris daily used to let the launch go fishing for Codd for the Ship's Company. I have seen them return with more then one hundred Codd, some weighing Sixteen and Seventeen pounds, all of which were serv'd out to the different Messes.

[*Caplin appear on the shores of Newfoundland earlier to the south than to the north, but they occur inshore to the north and south simultaneously; the overlapping of the caplin seasons in these areas may be reduced if the season inshore is particularly short in a given year. Although caplin near a beach may on some occasions be chased ashore by some predator species of fish or mammal, by far the more dominant reason for "going ashore" is that it is on the beaches, in the intertidal zone and just below it, that the spawning act takes place. The fertilized eggs remain in the interstices of the gravel till they are hatched some two weeks or more later.*

Mature male and female caplin do differ in appearance, for the males which are considerably larger in size have also rather prominent spawning ridges (the fuzz along the sides of the body). It was thought for a long time that all the caplin die after spawning, but there is some evidence that some females do recover to spawn again. It seems likely that all males and most females do actually die after spawning. The figure of five thousand young is probably rather low. Egg counts show that the numbers may vary from about 15,000 to about 52,000.

Caplin Bay is now known as Calvert.]

VI

St Pierre's

July 2nd, 1794. We left Capelin Bay on Monday 30th June and anchor'd in the Road before the Town in the Island of St Pierres, or St Peters, this afternoon. [*The log records: "July 1st—in sight of land. Working into St Pierres. July 3/11: Moored in St Peters Road."*]

On the point off Ferryland is a remarkable Rock call'd Hares' Ears, so named its appearance having an affinity to the Ears of that Animal. Between Cape Broyle and Cape Race are these singular, mountainous rocks call'd the Butter Potts. They are situated on the edge of a Mountain about five miles inland and extend in length, I suppose, three miles. There are a number of these huge Rocks, and their sponsors Christianed them Butter Potts from their resemblance to the domestic utensil. They are very remarkable Sea marks and are so high that they are seen from Trinity and Conception Bays which are on the Northern Shores. [*These are hills which rise abruptly to a height of about 1,000 feet and they are some nine miles inland from Ferryland. Here, for many years, a group of deserters and other outlaws had a hideout. They were led by an ex-naval man called Peter Kerrivan and were known as Kerrivan's Gang. They lived off the land and occasionally raided the settlements. Despite naval expeditions organized to capture them they flourished for many years in the latter part of the eighteenth century. Once four were captured and they were hung from the yard arm of a British frigate in Ferryland Harbour.*]

When we were within nine Leagues of this Island Captain Morris, at day break, found himself near a Brigg, steering a Course for America. A Shot was fired to bring her to, merely to ask if the land then in sight was not St Peter's. An Iota of an Idea never enter'd the head of a soul on board that anything French was in her. On hailing her we were answer'd by a *Frenchman*, in broken English, that they were bound from Fortune Bay to Spain, but had put into St Peters for Wood and Water. A man answering in a French accent naturally gave us doubt. A Boat was sent on board and in her was found seven Frenchmen, one Italian, and one Englishman who was born at Taunton, in Somersetshire. These people, the preceding night, had cut her out of St Peter's Road and were making their escape to some part of the American States. The Frenchmen were Prisoners of War, being included in the capitulation of St Peter's when it surrender'd to the British Forces. They were all brought on board our Ship and put in Irons. The Brigg we took with us back to St Peter's, she being a Lawfull Prize, and was afterwards sold for five hundred and two Pounds. Her name was the *Providence*, of Dartmouth in England, whereof was Master John Hilling Godfrey of Newton Bushell, in Devonshire.

The island of St Peter's with that of Miquelon was taken from the French Republic the beginning of this War by the *Alligator*, Frigate, and a detachment of three hundred men under the Command of General Ogilvie, from Halifax. The French had here at the time about 60 Soldiers, kept in this place, according to the Treatys with Great Britain, for the sole purpose of enforcing the police. These, with about four hundred miserable Fishing people, surrender'd at discretion. These Islands, in all the late Wars with France, have been taken by the English, and as constantly restor'd by the English to the French, as shelter for their Fishermen. You will find their name in almost every Treaty for these one hundred years back. The fortifications here do not deserve that name. It is perfectly barren, not a Tree grows on the Island.

[According to James's "Naval History", the first act of hostility in this quarter (the Newfoundland Station) was the capture of the small fishing islands of St Pierre and Miquelon, which had been taken from the French in 1778, and were injudiciously restored to them by the treaty of 1783.

Aware of the importance of these fishery islands, the British Government, in a few days after war had been declared, dispatched orders to Halifax, Nova Scotia for their immediate seizure. After a show of strength by Brigadier-General Ogilvie, with naval co-operation, the French commandant, M. Danseville, surrendered the islands.]

The Town of St Peter's contains more than one hundred Houses, all built with wood and boards brought from the American States. A number of the Inhabitants, Prisoners of War, have been sent to

Nova Scotia. Their Houses are now empty, but they took much pains to break every pane of Glass in their Windows before they quited St Peter's for fear the English should be benefit'd if they left any in perfect state behind. The whole of the Inhabitants are to be sent away in a month's time, and then the Town is to be burnt down and everything destroy'd, after which the English Soldiers will evacuate the place.

I am ashore here a great deal. There are a number of fine Weomen among the French. They powder, dress and all are as smart as any of the fair ones I have seen at St Omer and Amiens.

On Monday, July 7th I spent one of the most precious days as yet I ever met with, valuable because in a few hours my eyes beheld more foreign objects and singular animals in the Creation then was ever compress'd in a much longer space, at any time in my life.

Captain Morris, with a party of Officers of the Fourth Regiment of Foot, then doing duty at St Peter's, and Captain Skinner of the Royal Artillery, who is Chief Engineer of Newfoundland and was with us on the *Boston* the whole of this Cruize, had made a party to go to the Island of Miquelon and take a Cold Collation with them. I was of the party. Port, Lisbon Wine, Porter, Spruce Beer, a Ham, Tongues etc., a Gun for every man, was put into the Boat. Deeply laden with precious lumber she shov'd off with a fair wind for the Island of Great Miquelon, distant about twelve miles. It was a very fine morning. Our little Barque pass'd between the Islands of Great and Petit Columbier, leaving the Isle de Verte, alias Green Island, on our Starboard hand. We met with multitudes of Sea Birds flying over our heads, and quantitys on the water. They were all of a new kind to me. I shall speak particularly of them on our return.

We got thus far when the wind dy'd away, the men were oblig'd to take to their Oars, the original plan was given up and a viset to the Isle of Langli, alias Little Miquelon, was substituted in its place. We alter'd our course and soon got into the Straits which separates St Pierres from Langli; here were two large Whales playing on the surface of the water. We presently saw a large Bird not unlike the size of a Goose, I find it is call'd a Loon. Captain Skinner fir'd at it but the Bird dived, and rose again at some distance. We follow'd and fir'd at it several times but unless it is hit on the head it cannot be killed. We failed in our design on the poor animal and the pursuit had run [*us*] some distance out of our way.

[*The Loon may have been a common loon or loo* (*Gavia immer*) *which the writer later called "lewes". Looneries is a European term for the cliff colonies of the alcids, especially murres.*

The Coast of Langli Isle appear'd rocky and inaccessible except at one place which seemed to form a small Beach or Cove, we steer'd for it. On our arrival it was supposed it would answer the purpose, as about five yards from high water mark there was a kind of Gutter or shelving Rock by which the height of the Island might be gained and our provisions carry'd up with safety. The Cove was no larger then twice the length of our Boat, there was no doubt but our Boat would lye here in perfect security during our stay on Shore. After so close a scrutiny by Captain Morris, whose eye is as keen and his head as clear as any Gentleman in the Navy, he gave orders to land. We all got out, and in two minutes after, a Surf so violent set in as to endanger the Boat! Fortunately an Anchor was in the Boat. The Boat's Crew, with much dexterity, shov'd off, let go the Anchor, veer'd out a small Hawser which kept her in perfect safety. By giving her more Hawser she backed alongside a broken Rock on which we creeped, got into our Boat again and immediately pushed off.

The Surf setting in the instant we land'd gave rise to a variety of comments, amongst others it was debated what name to give the Cove. It was propos'd each Gentleman should give it a name applicable to the circumstances which had befell us in the Cove, and that which was judg'd most suitable by the majority of voices should be adopt'd. Surprize Cove, Sudden Cove, Unawares Cove and Cove Perplexity were immediately named. Unawares and Perplexity were immediately rejected. The opponency lay between Sudden and Surprize! Captain Brown gave a long Lecture to show that the words Surprize and Sudden were of the same derivation, and that their meaning was undisputably similar! But Ensign Foster, of the 4th Regiment, held out for Sudden, and declar'd that the words Sudden and Surprize were distinct, and never would be consider'd homogenous, as for instance if a man goes on unlaw-full business and is sure within himself that the eye of no human soul observes him, but if a man comes up and detects him in the act of his depredations—that is Surprize, for during the time that he is performing this forbidden deed his mind is in agitation. The horrors of punishment cannot escape his head, and the moment he discovers the fangs of the Law has grabbed him he is, that very instance, in perfect and complete surprize, and this surprize is made entire and full merely because the act was unfair, bad and contrary to Justice. Now if a man in broad daylight, goes upon an unlawfull concern, and the opposite to the common Rules and Manners befalls him—that comes within the denomination of Sudden, strange, singular and extraordinary. [*Suppose*] near my House there is a Brook through which I generally ride my Horse, and I have occasion to cross it, and no Rain has fallen near my Residence lately. I mount my Nag, but on my crossing to the water's side I see that the waters have overflow'd their usual bounds and I cannot get to the opposite side without risking my life, I am not *surprized*, for I well know that Rain has fallen at the source of the River, or at some distance on its Banks, above this passage. I then say—This is a sudden Rise, or an unexpected swell, and in regard to this Cove I say it was a sudden Surf but not a Surprizing Surf, I therefore give it as my opinion that it be called Sudden Cove.

Captain Morris interfered by observing that a method struck him which would end all dispute, and to his proposal he was confident there would be no dissenting voice. This was to call it Sudden Surprize Cove, which would be adopting the Ideas of the two principal Orators. This was a happy hit, all fell into agreement. Captain Morris was to be Godfather; a Bottle of Wine was handed to him to throw gently into the Cove for the use of the Christianing. But it occur'd that the Wine was precious and probably might be wanting for a more *charitable purpose*. The Firing of a Volley of small Arms would be a Momento more suitable then dashing a Bottle of Wine to Atoms. All hands handled their Arms ready to Fire. Captain Skinner made an Oration fitted for the *solemn* occasion, giving Neptune the reason why it was called Sudden Surprize Cove, he finish'd with the following Stanza. At the word SAKE the discharge of Musketry was to take place:

You Sudden Surprize Cove
In you our Boat was nearly stove,
Thy hollow Caverns for once shall shake
In firing a Volley for thy sake.

The instant the word sake had been repeated a General Salute took place. The noise amongst the Rocks was prodigeous but we made a capital discovery, a most singular scene immediately made its appearance. On the Guns firing a number of Birds flew out of the Cliffs and crevices, quickly took wing and escap'd over our heads. They were the size of a Blackbird, the shape of a Pigeon, had white under their Wings, their Tails tipt with white, red Feet, and other parts of the Back. They are call'd Sea Pigeons and are very numerous, frequenting uninhabited rocky and desolate shores. They are very fond of high Rocks where the water issues in a manner like Tears. Every twenty yards on this side of the Island the water oozeth out in this gentle manner and is almost one continual weeping Spring. Those parts of the Rock which are always wet have a blackish look and when the Birds are not on the wing they appear quite black themselves, so that it is a difficult thing to see them, unless they walke when on the Rocks, which but seldom they do. From this circumstance some of the Gentlemen were for renewing the Dispute about the Cove and said it would not be improper if it was call'd Disturb or Pigeon Cove. [*The Sea Pigeon is almost certainly the black guillemot* (*Cepphus grylle*) *which has a white wing patch, not white under the wing, nor in breeding plumage are their tails tipped with white. This species, in winter plumage, is nearly white so that leeway can be allowed for his description of it.*]

Our Boat kept rowing under the Rocks along the Coast in hopes to find a landing place. We espy'd an Eagle seting on a dead Stump, on the very summit of an exceeding high Rock. He was fired at but the shot did not tell. The Bird seem'd to treat the report, and the noise of the shot against the stones, with perfect *contempt*, as it did not take to wing for a full half minute after the Gun was fired. It then gave a piercing, sharp, shrill note, left its Perch, took a small circuit, and return'd to the old, dead, white Stump from which it first took its flight. Moving slowly on, within a few yards of the first Eagle, we saw another; nearly the same circumstances attended this as had just passed with that before. We killed neither of them. Their heads are white, their Bills yellow, all their bodys of a chocolate colour. There are a number of them on this desert Coast. I observ'd these Birds were always seen on an old Stump or a dead Stick, situated on the edge of the highest part of this rocky Coast. Their appearance, Voice, Gait and manners are consonant to the solitary, lonely, dismal and retir'd life they lead. Like a Hermit they do not associate with their own specie unless it is one month of the year, which is the season of propagation. *[These were probably Northern Bald Eagles locally called Grepes. They are known residents of the south coast.]*

We had not coasted two miles from Sudden Surprize Cove before we came to a promontory, or point of Land, of a very singular appearance. The Rocks were very high, there was a split in them of width sufficient to admit our Boat thro; join'd to this Point was a low Rock on which was a rude Cross, some religious Relick I presume. The whole had a striking effect. The representation given you of it here has not done it Justice. *[Not now in the book.]* After we had view'd it for some minutes it was pronounc'd Cape Split, from the opening or crack on its side. Perhaps this place had been named before, if so it was unknown to any of us. Some of the Party were for calling it Cape Crack, Cape Split or Cape Eagle, from the Eagles that were seen near it, and others said that Cape Cross or Cape Catholic would not be amiss, from the Roman Relick standing on the Rock. This led to a short digression on Religion in which it was maintain'd that it was the duty of all Protestants to eraze every vestage of popery, but this Idea was scorned by all present and Cape Split was the title we left it.

While in this Boat this day it is surprizing how big I thought *myself*. Columbus, I fancy'd, was a mere Pedestrian to *us*. Here we were, giving names to Coves and Capes, which I could not but think belonged to some vast unknown region. Louis the Fourteenth never was so *big*, in his own mind, as I was. But I wanted, like all Travellers, to give my name to some Bay, Cape or Rock. I had some thoughts of asking for an Island, or a *Continent*, but I suspected there were so many Adventurers who wanted to hand their names down to posterity, and whose pretensions were superior to mine, that I despair'd of ever seeing in the Charts of this part of the world a Rock called Thomas's Rock.

After we had doubled Cape Split we got into a large Bay, the angles of which is the north point of Great Miquelon and Cape Split. As we coasted along there was plenty of Christianing. At last I espy'd a small Cove and begged it might be call'd Cove Thomas. There was in sight at the same time an Island of Ice. I was told my vanity should be gratify'd—and then, pointing to the Ice, all hands were desir'd to enter that in their Journals by the name of Thomas's Island. I could not consider this as a last acquisi-

A frigate (*centre*) circa *1762, similar to H.M.S.* Boston. *Detail from a painting of* Ships entering Harwich *by C. Brooking*

St John's, Newfoundland, by R. P. Brenton, 1798

The upper end of the Harbour of St John's, circa 1790

tion to my fame, but answer'd it would resemble my own Temper —spotless and inoffensive, and as to its durability, it would be like my own frame subject to change and final dissolution.

The Isles of Langli and Great Miquelon are joined togather by a Sand Bank which, at low water, is dry. A little to the left of this Beach we landed our Stores on a fine sandy shore. A few yards from our landing place was a gentle bank to ascend, which having gained there is a plain grassy spot. Here it was determined to Dine. The provisions were carry'd up by our people, and the Wine safely lodged. Alongside of us was a Rivulet of fresh water. The Sun at this time was uncommon hot, and the Muscatoos and flys very troublesome. On examining the spot around us I found there was plenty of Strawberrys, large and quite ripe. There was also, in vast abundance, Raspberrys, Gooseberrys, Currants and other wild Fruit in great quantitys, but not yet at maturity. Our Cold Collation was eat off Scallop Shells, the Table Cloath was the Boat's Foresail; the machine to drink out of was a West India Cronk [*conch?*] Shell. All our little materials were applicable to our aquatic entertainment. Our stay here was for about two hours, before we embark'd a general Salute took place. For my own part I left it with regret. The whole Island seem'd to abound with the fruits spoken of above; within a few yards of our Dining place a capital Dessert of Strawberrys were soon gather'd, and Raspberrys and Gooseberrys were in astonishing quantitys but, possessing all these delicious fruits, in other respects the Island is barren. It is not inhabited, there is not a House on all the Island, it has no Bay, Harbour or Creek which a small Shallop can enter.

Proceeding on our return to St Pierres we saw two Seals, their heads just above the water. Captain Skinner fired at one of them but missed it, the animal immediately sunk. There is numbers of them on this Coast and they are frequently seen on a sunshiny day seting on the Rocks, in which situation they are often kill'd by Bears and Wolves, who seize them before they can make their escape.

While I was on the water, on our route home, I could not refrain from reflecting on Geography and Nautical Science. One thing struck me. I have seen Cape Lookout in America, Languard Fort at the extremity of the Bermuda Isles, Middleburg in Holland. The engraver in delineating small Charts finds no trifling inconvenience on the score of long names and I believe in our little

Voyage of this day this difficulty was no part of our consideration.

As we approached the Isle of Grand Columbier the quantity of Birds which were on the wing absolutely was so great that they cast an extensive Shadow on the Ocean. The water also had multitudes of them riding on it. The Island itself was positively so cover'd with them that I may say with truth there was thousands and thousands of them. We rode close to the Shore where they sat with great boldness, as thick as they could well stand. We fired shot amongst them and killed several. At the report of the Gun they took wing, which crowded the air in such a manner as to resemble the space before the entrance to a Hive of Bees. These Birds were all of one kind and are called Puffins or Sea Parrots. Their heads are exactly alike Parrots in point of shape, much about their size, the bodys of them black and white. The head and the beak are the principal beautys of these Birds; the beak is trisecious, and colour'd in shades in perfect unison to the national Cockade of France—blue, white and red. They are amphibious, living on the water by day and on Shore by night. They make holes in the ground like Rabbits, in which they breed. People who go after their Eggs take Pick-axes and Spades to get at their nests, this is called Puffin digging. But they generally choose such a bold shore for their rendezvous that there is no getting at them. If there is one of them in a hole it is dangerous to put the hand in unless you have a very thick glove on as they bite very severe.

Grand Columbier, on which these Birds are, is a small Island, its circumference not being more then two miles. It is separated from St Pierre's by a narrow Channel about the width of the Thames at Somerset House. View'd from the water it has a majestic and noble appearance, raising itself to a magnanimous height regularly to one point on the Summit of which is a freshwater Lake. Altho it is inaccessible in all places except one yet its acclivitys is nearly cover'd with verdure which gives it a show of a splendid grandeur seldom to be met with in these barren regions.

On our return to the Ship, from the report we had made of these Birds, Lieutenants Varlo* and Macradie obtain'd leave to go the

---

* Ensign Varlo of the King's Own Regiment, whose name is to be found in the Colonial Records. John Macredie was then 3rd Lieutenant on the *Boston*.

next day, and reconnoitre the Island and endeavour to catch some of them. They set out with two Boys, night came but they were not return'd. It was feared some accident had befell them. A Boat was sent in search. As the Boat approach'd the Island they fired a Gun, which was the Signal agreed upon in case anything happened. A Gun was presently fired on the Island as an answer that they heard them. After waiting some time the Lieutenants and boys descended the mountain and with difficulty got into the Boat which was sent after them. It appears that they made an attempt to come off but the Surf was so violent that they had lost their Boat; they then ascend'd the mountain, lighted a fire, and made an agreement to keep Watch by turns all night. They were thus situated when our Boat came so seasonably to their relief.

The Governor of St Pierres, Major Thorne of the 4th Regiment, gave a Dinner to the Officers of the *Boston* in the late French Governor's House in the Town of St Pierre's, and as there are some singularitys attending it I noted a few of them down. *[This account of the dinner party was copied from the original by Judge Prowse and was included in his "History of Newfoundland" as a footnote in his chapter on St Pierre and Miquelon.]*

It being understood that it was intended, by the British Government, to Evacuate, and afterwards burn St Pierres so of course every Officer here kept up but as small a stock of necessarys as the nature of their situation would admit. Amongst other articles which muster'd short was Wine Glasses. Every House in which Inhabitants were left (for many of the French had been sent to Halifax) were viseted to produce these usefull Vessels for this grand occasion. The day came, Dinner was served to about 30 persons. The Wine went round to a late hour. Jollity, Gaiety, Merriment and good humour were predominant in the countenance of all. God Save Great George our King was repeated a number of times, expressions of attachment and Loyalty were carry'd to the extreme (altho by and by Two of the Party, not quite a Thousand Years ago, had nearly been thrown out of a window for favouring somewhat of Republicanism). But to do the business in a more exalted manner all hands must needs mount the Table to drink Success to the *Boston*. The Table was so cover'd with Decanters, Glasses, Bottles, Fruit Plates, Knives, Punch Bowls etc., etc. that it was with difficulty a foot could be shoved on. But as there is few enterprizes but what the British Army and Navy will overcome, so in this particular all impediments were soon overcome, and the Table was soon cover'd with the Officers of the Navy and Army. —Success to the *Boston*, was given,—and just as each man's Glass came to his mouth,— Down comes the Table, with a terrible crash,—as if all the Masts of the *Boston* had gone overboard at once! Here was curious Sprawling amongst broken Glasses, Platters and Bottles. By the same heavy stroke all the Lights in the room were extinguished, so that the Caterstrophe was the more darker and lamentable. *Each man*, not being perfectly *himself*, and having the stump of a broken Glass in his hand, he run it against his neighbour's face, maiming and wounding one another. Some of them thought they had been suddenly assail'd by the Enemy, and that a shot from a Cannon had upset the Table, for they cryed aloud—To Arms, To Arms. I Gad, thinks I, you are at Arms, at Legs and faces too, for Old Nick himself would not wish to be in the midst of ye.

When Candles came I looked at them and saw this heap of superior beings struggling in friendly Agitation to regain their Legs. But to see a Red Coat and a Blue Coat alternately, moving and tumbling about in a cluster I could not but compare them to a pile of Lobsters, some alive and some boiled. Propper assistance having arrived, and the Party regained their Legs I need not comment on the friendly Look given to one another! Two Companys of Light Infantry came in and moved the broken remnants. The wreck was soon cleared, but to the great discomfiture of all not a whole Glass remain'd!—I mean, not only in the Governor's House, but not in all the Island—Bowls, Bottles and all shared the same fate.

It was getting a late hour; it was propos'd, by way of finale, that the whole company should march (as well as they could) in procession, Drums and Fifes at their head, round the Room and Hall. In the Hall the Band of the Regiment had been playing all evening. They had been supply'd plentifully with Liquor, and as the Bottles were empty'd they put them under the Table. The Procession came, unawares, upon the Band, they suddenly moved the Table for them to pass, but in the hurry the Candles fell down, it became dark. The Table was withdrawn, but the empty Bottles remained *Point Blank* in the way of the Procession. Captain Johnson was the first!—Right in he goes among the Bottles, he trod upon ten or twelve, but like a true Hero he did not notice them, but advanced. The rest of the Gentlemen followed, in *tolerable* order, cracking the Flint, cutting their Shoes, cursing the Bottles as they burst, and asking if they were full or empty. One or two of the Rear fell amongst them but no serious mischiefe happened.

St Pierres was the Head Quarters of the 4th Regiment. All their Band was here, which was a capital one. It played all evening at intervals, Drums and Fifes. Our Officers, on the morrow said they were Drumed Drunk. On our return to the Ship, which was late at night, the Band played for us to the water's edge. Some were so inebriated as to get up to their Arms in water, in mistaking the Boat. We got on board all safe, with the satisfaction of having left not one single Wine Glass within the Governor's Jurisdiction, nor one solitary Bottle of Wine in Major Thorn's Cellar.

There is an Island call'd Dog Island opposite St Pierres. There is six or seven Houses on it. The inhabitants, on the capture of the place, were sent to Halifax. Our Ship's Crew were sent on Shore here for recreation, it not being thought prudent for them to go to St Pierres for fear they should in any way insult the French people. A number of our people being on shore on Dog Island one day, they set fire to a Shell of a House. There was more smoke then fire. It gave some alarm at St Pierres and some trouble was taken on board the *Boston* to find out the Author of the conflagration, but to no effect, Mr Nobody had done it.

Some spots of the Island was fertile, and it being abandon'd, the Produce of the Earth became the property of the public. We avail'd ourselves of this circumstance. Being in want of Hay for our Livestock on board we cut a quantity of Grass, made the Hay on shore, stow'd it in the Ship. It was a serviceable and very usefull article.

There was a young Whale cast on shore, in chasing of Capelin I presume, on the Beach of this Island. I went and saw him. It had lain there for a fortnight and was in a state of putrefaction; it weigh'd, I suppose, about Two Tons. The fat of one side had been cut and carryed away. There were six men from St Pierres came, while I was there, they put Ropes about it in the hopes of turning the Whale to cutt the fat from the other side, but after bousing for a long time, their strength, and mine added, could not turn the ponderous Whale. I cut off some of his flesh, and altho it was corrupt, yet it retained a smell strongly appertaining to that of fresh Beefe. The flesh of the Whale, in this part of the world, is often eaten. The Gills of the Whale is what is used in England for Whale Bone. I cut off a part of the Gills of this Whale, which was more then 24 inches long. I thought it a great Curiosity, the external part being cover'd with cream coloured Hairs. The root of the Bones represented fine workmanship and was flexible, and in colour was Ivory. I afterwards lost this curious piece by puting it on the Booms to air. It was thrown overboard and lost by accident.

In the Islands of St Pierres and Miquelon, when captured by the English, was about 400 Fishermen and Fifty Soldiers. The French Inhabitants from Miquelon were brought to St Pierres where all remain Prisoners of War at large, except those which have been sent to Halifax. Every Offensive instrument is taken from them. They are allow'd to Fish, for which they receive 2/6 for every Hundredweight.

The French Governor has erected an Edifice here, it being a regular Building, two Wings to correspond, a Courtyard, a Facade and Domestic Offices of every description, ornamented with Military Trophys and War like instruments. Over the door, within the Courtyard, was the late King of France's Arms, two Flags with the Flower de Luce extending in folds on each side. Since Royalty was abolish'd in France the Republicans at St Pierres have, with a Chisel, cut all the Flower de Luces in the King's Arms and on the two Flags. This shows the temper of the French in this part of the Globe.

The French people have had notice to hold themselves in readyness to embark and as they can carry little of their Household Furniture with them articles of bulke are to be bought here at present for half their value. I have purchas'd a Bed for fifteen Shillings. One of the same quality, in London, I have paid fifty Shillings for.

The domestic Scenes of distress amongst the poor French were many and afflicting. Grown old on the Island they got a comfortable living Fishing—and thus aged and infirm, numbers were forc'd to go God knows where to spend the remainder of their days in a strange Land. I met with an instance of two Sisters, each about Fifty. The one was sent to Halifax, the other was going to Guernsey in a Cartel Ship. How it happen'd that they were separated I know not. They had a Goat to sell, with a young Kid, and as Captain

Morris wanted one I bought this of the two Sisters. I paid her for it, and as one of our men was leading the Goat away the poor Weoman came to the door, looked after the Animal, clasped her hands, cry'd most bitterly, and exclaim'd "O! my Poor Goat!" I return'd to her, and by soothing looks and pacific words endeavour'd to assuage of mind. She said she was to embark, on the morrow, in a Vessel, then in the Roads, for Guernsey, and she could not keep her Goat no longer. She was inexorable, the loss of her Goat she deplored in the most afflicting terms; a Monarch hurl'd from his Throne could not a felt his misfortunes more acute then this poor French Female did the loss of her Goat. A few days before she was part'd from her Sister, and now from her Goat; her days of Sorrow were come. She should never see Happyness again. I left her, in some degree of comfort, by assuring her that I would make her case known to Captain Morris whose Humanity, I was sure, would prompt him to an early opportunity of interceding with the Governor to get her destination alter'd for Halifax, when she would be restor'd to the society of her Sister.

I met with a number of other sorrowfull Tales from French Housekeepers, all regretting and expressing wretchedness of mind at leaving a spot where they had earn'd their Daily Bread. Now, by calamitys of War having, as they said, lost their all, *[they]* were as ready to begin the world again as they were on the day of their Birth.

[St Pierre was restored to France again in 1802 by the peace of Amiens but as war broke out again in the following year it was again taken possession of by the British. It was not until 22 June 1816 that the colonists returned to their old home. One hundred and fifty old families were returned to the island by two frigates and since then many French fishermen have come to it. The present population is about 5,000].

With Mankind in general I could not but deplore the fate of Wars, the misery it occasions, the changes it makes, the Villages that are deserted, the Towns that are dismantl'd, the Churches that are despoiled, the Fields that are uncultivated, the Commerce that is destroy'd, the Family that loses its Father, the Wives that loseth their Husbands, the Sisters that loseth their Brothers, the Mother that loseth her Sons, the children that become Orphans, the Manufactorys that are at a stand, and the thousands of Boys who go harmless, inoffensive and innocent from their Homes, but return to their native places Vagabonds and strolling Thieves—at best with a disposition full of Idleness and Sloth, even afterwards leading a roving, beggarly life tippling in Ale Houses.

Before I leave St Pierres I have something to say of our Pilot. He was a Frenchman. His name is Barrere, but I do not know that he claims any relationship to the National Legislator. This I know, he was one of the noisyest, impudent fellows I almost ever met with. The number of tricks he play'd on board, was I to relate them, would take more time then suits my conveniency. He had no scruple to declare his Republican principles, and said if he was sent to France he should be put to death, for some of his fellow Prisoners would inform the Committee of Public Safety that he had Pilot'd the King of England's Vessels into the Road of St Pierres, and the Gilloutine sure was to be his Reward if he went to France. I explained to him the nature of Greenwich Hospital as being a comfortable Retreat for disabled Seamen and men worn out in Sea Service. He said there was no other Pilot at St Pierres but himself, and the *Boston* was the third English Ship of War which he had Pilot'd safe into St Peter's Road, and that he would much rather go to Greenwich then to Paris. He said that he was entitled to a Reward from the English King. He run from me to the Captain on the Quarter Deck, with hat in hand. He desir'd Captain Morris would enter him as a *volunteer* for Greenwich Hospital. On the morning of our leaving St Pierres, after he had pilot'd us out and he was about quiting the Ship, he came to me and said Captain Morris had order'd him a Bottle of Wine. I told one of my Cabin Boys to give him a Bottle of Lisbon Wine, they gave him a Bottle to take ashore. Off he sets with it into his Boat, but some days later I discover'd that instead of a Bottle of Lisbon Wine they had given him a Bottle of Spruce Beer. I thought it no bad joke, and could not blame them, but I am sure that when he drew the Cork he would damn the English generosity.

VII

Placentia Bay

11th July, 1794. We left the island of St Pierres this morning at eight O'Clk, with a fair wind and a stiff Breeze and anchor'd in this Harbour at seven O'Clk, having run not less then ten or eleven Knots, or miles an hour, and this is esteem'd by Nautical men a very quick Passage. We passed within a League of Cape Chapeau Rouge, or the Mountains of the Red Hatt. It is the most remarkable Cape in all Newfoundland and is an immense heap of ragged, craggy Rocks placed one upon the other. When viewed from the sea every Fathom of your move gives it a new shape. Its appearance is said to be most striking when Fog is hovering about it. It appears like a Dutchman without Legs, afterwards like a Hatt, then a Lion Rampant, a Bust, a broken Turret, a rough Dome and lastly a broken, irregular, craggy, inaccessible Mountain. This Cape is the Southern angle of Great St Laurence's Harbour.

[*Log 12/14 July—"At anchor in Placentia Road."*]

Placentia Bay is one of the largest Bays in this Country. From St Mary's Bay to Cape Chapeau Rouge (which are the two angles) is twelve Leagues athwart. The Length of the Bay is more considerable. The Harbours, Creeks, Coves and Inlets in it are many. There are also several Islands, St Mary's Keys, Galloping Andrew and some other Rock which makes the Navigation dangerous here, as the Bay is commonly cover'd in Fog.

His Majesty's Cutter, call'd the *Placentia*, was run upon a Rock in this Bay last winter and lost, in the Fog. The Cutter was beat to pieces but happyly all the Crew got ashore and were saved. The Harbour of Placentia is not a remarkable good one, but there is an Arm where Vessels may ride in perfect safety; but the ingress and egress is so difficult that few Ships go into this Arm unless they are going to stop here for some weeks.

The Town of Placentia is a Settlement, in importance, next to

St John's. There are about 200 Houses or Hutts huddled togather, built on a kind of Sand Beach, which is nearly surrounded by water. The Inhabitants in Placentia mostly come from Waterford in Ireland. The face of the Country about this place is unusually Mountainous and Rocky. The Town, at the back of it, has a narrow Arm of Water which is overhung by a hideous Precipice. Salmon, very delicious in flavour, and equal (tho small) to any in the world, are caught here in great multitudes. Here is a small Fort with about twenty Artillery men. I saw two of these Soldiers return one morning from drawing their Nett. They had haul'd in forty-six Salmon at one draught, which was Provision for the Garrison (if it might be so called) to suffice them for upwards of a week.

Here are two old Forts in ruins, one on Castle Hill, the other on the Larboard hand, going into the Northeast Arm. The last cost Government a Deal of Money but it was never finished. Placentia was the spot where the French had footing for the last time by Treaty. They had a Settlement and carry'd on a large Traffic in Fish. They gave much uneasyness to the British Settlements in St Mary's Bay, Ferryland etc., from which places remonstrances were sent Home to England in the years 1709 and 1710, praying that whenever Peace was concluded with France the French might be excluded from having any Settlement in Newfoundland. The Government was attentive to this object, for when the Allys sent their Ambassadors to Gertrudeburg [*Gertruydenburg*] in 1710 to Treat the French for Peace, the English Plenipotentiary propos'd, among other matters, to the Marquis de Torcy, the French Ambassador, that the French should entirely abandon Newfoundland; but this Conference being broken off, the War continued untill the English were defeated at Denain, when a Peace was concluded at Utrecht, 30th March, 1793, in which it was stipulated that the French should evacuate Placentia and all their Settlements, but that they should retain a Right to come and fish here in the Season, and dry it ashore, but that they should not remain there during the winter.

When the *Boston* was sailing for Placentia Harbour and had shot some Leagues up the Bay it set in to be hazy. No Officer in the Ship had ever been at Placentia. From the Hazyness of the weather our view was very contract'd. Much care was necessary, for I believe no Gentleman on board knew with precision the Marks for entering the Harbour. Had they been known the weather was so thick that they could not a been made out. When we thought ourselves off the place and fired two Guns as the Signal for a Friend, a good Lookout was order'd to be kept to catch sight of the Fire from the Gun on the glacis* of the Fort, in answer to our Signal. It was observ'd, the *Boston* went in in great Stile, dropped her Anchor and was moor'd in safety.

I have been very minute in this particular, by way of preface to the following observation. When a Ship is under Sail in hazy weather, has Land in sight on both boards, is within Soundings, has Rocks and Sandbanks laid down on the Charts near where she supposes herself and is entering a Harbour or Bay, all hands are on Deck. Silence is order'd. The Sails full of Wind, the Sea dashing against her Bows, the Waves in contest against her sides, and she in motion, gliding on the Liquid Fluid with immense impetuosity. —All yet is Silence! The Captain speaks, he gives his Commands, they are executed in quiet Alertness. All, All are Mute but one— the man heaving the Lead. Fearfull the lurking Rock every ear attentive to his Voice hears him sing "By the Lead, Nine", attentive still, he says "By the Lead, seven". All is Calm, there is no uproar, nor no voice but his is heard. Every Soul thinks what a slender barrier there is between them and Eternity. They pause, the Ship still driving on, listening to the man at the Lead. How awefull is this moment and how important it is imprest on the mind capable of Reflection! The Sea roars, the Masts cracks, the winds whistle, the Elements in Tumult, but the man at the Lead, lashed to the Chains, sings "By the Lead, five". His voice is hollow, pompous, grand and serene. This is impressive, and the more harmonious and lofty his voice is the more the influence stampt on your mind in regard to the existence of Danger.

Whoever has sail'd in a Vessel so circumstanced with a cool, quiet, serene and undisturb'd mind, and a Heart mercifull, compassionate and open to sympathy and comiseration, will admit the force of this remark. But the difference between a good voice at the Lead, and a bad one, is as great as between an eloquent Orator or the man who only says Yes or No.

[*Early in the 1660s the French founded a settlement at Placentia which they fortified strongly and which flourished. In 1692 Commodore*

* Slope of cleared ground in front of the ramparts of a fortress.

Williams, with a squadron, attempted to seize Placentia but found it too strongly defended. French from Placentia assisted in the taking of St John's in 1696. The Treaty of Ryswick left them still in possession of Placentia and the English settlements were perpetually open to raids by the French. In 1708 the French from Placentia attacked and seized St John's once again. By the Treaty of Utrecht Newfoundland and the adjacent islands were declared to belong to Great Britain but liberty was given to the French to catch and dry fish only on that part of the coast lying to the north of Cape Bonavista, and stretching along the western shore as far as Point Riche; they were not to make any fortifications or remain in the island longer than the time necessary for curing their fish. The fortifications were repaired by the British in 1762 when the French were again in St John's.]

VIII

An Expedition to Torbay

St John's Harbour, July 18th, 1794. We are at anchor in this place again, having left Placentia on Monday, the 14th of July. As soon as we got out of the Bay we were completely closed in a Fog. After beating down the Bay before night set in, it was thought prudent to come to an Anchor. We hail'd a Fishing Boat; a person came on board out of her who said we were off Point Breme and distant not more then a League. This Point is about half way from Placentia down the Bay to Cape St Mary's. We remain'd at Anchor off this Point untill Wednesday the 16th July in a Fog so thick that you could see neither Heaven or Earth. On the evening of this day it clear'd up. We got under weigh and passed Cape St Mary's before night. The next day we sail'd along the shore, by the Bay of Bulls etc. and this night we came to anchor in this Harbour.

Between the Bay of Bulls and Petty Harbour is one of the most singular natural Curiositys in Newfoundland. This is a natural Fountain and is occasion'd by the following concuring circumstances. By the Sea, under a Chain of Rocks, is a large Cavern, which runs many yards underground. At the extremity of this Cave there is an aperture or Hole which runs up to the level or surface above. At the entrance to this Cavern the water is very deep. When the winds blow strong on shore a very heavy Swell is roll'd into the Cave with amazing velocity, it is hemmed in on both sides, and when the waves meet with the resisting Rocks at the further end it forceth the passage upwards with most extraordinary strength—so much so that the waters rise into a Column into the air and is to all intents a grand and magnificent Fountain. This Fountain, view'd from the Sea, has a fine effect. It appears to be inland about Half a mile. In the distance there is a rise of Land, and when ting'd with azure blue, which it generally is, makes a charming Background to show off this Column of water to the greatest advantage. [*Described by James Yonge in 1663.*]

Sunday 27th July. I set out upon a Pedestrian Tour from St John's, for Torbay, a place distant about nine miles, meaning to return the following day. I took an honest, good natur'd Welch Lad of the name of Bevan, who belonged to the Ship, with me. Our way to the place was through an Indian Path as perplexing and difficult as that before spoken of going to Portugal Cove. We enter'd the woods and proceeded vigorously and jovially on our Journey but we had not travelled long ere the Clouds grew Gloomy, the Sky obscur'd and all around portended a Heavy Storm. We kept advancing on our Route and the Pillars of Darkness which floated in the Atmosphere, by their appearance, foretold that they would be speedily in our presence and favour us with a part of its liquid fluid. Presently a burst of Thunder assail'd my ear, which told me that the wind being concentrated was more potent then the objurgated Cloud above me, and had forc'd a Passage by means of which channels were open'd, the air diluted, and the waters would dissipate itself immediately on the Objects beneath. I was not disappoint'd in my expectations for the Rain that fell directly after the Thunder Clap was one of the heavyest I was ever in. I have been in England often exposed in the open air to severe Falls of Rain but I never was wet through in so short a period as I was this day. The drops of Rain which fell would cover a Half Crown Piece. In about five minutes I was as wet as water could make me. When Rain falls in this Country it mostly is in the perpendicular direction, the wind dying away, not the gentlest Breeze is perceivable. This disastrous and unlucky event, it being the will of the Almighty, we bore with Resignation and Patience, trudging on—the Rain Pelting, the Thunder Roaring, the Bows and Sprays of the Trees slapping our faces; we never grumbl'd, save only observing now and then "I wish I had known of it". Through thick and thin, on we went.

Soon after the Rain had abat'd we came to a Morass, covering several Acres of Space—I cannot call it Land or Ground, or barren Rock—because the Space was cover'd with unusual long, bushy moss, amidst Slush and Mudd; it appear'd a perfect quagmire—a whole connected space of Quicksands which I suspected even the winds would agitate and throw into motion, like a gentle swell at Sea. "Well," thinks I, "if I venture on this Boggy fen I shall for certain be smother'd." But my Welch Companion Bevan gave me advice which at once put me out of all fear for myself, by saying "First in the wood, but always last in the Bog, Mr Thomas! Now I will lead the way if you will follow." I thought there was some advantage in warding off danger in having this Lad in the Bog before me, but on considering I was not without my *alarms* by reason that Bevan was but a Stripling, a mere feather of a Youth; his weight would be but a light impression on the quivering Bog surface, whereas my weight was at least Sixteen Stone, therefore the sward that bore him safe perhaps would not resist my pressure, but give way and admit me to the Gulph below. Wishing to preserve a life so valuable as mine, I was resolved not to go in untill I had, as far as my situation would permit me, equip'd myself against all fatallitys on that head, for which purpose I procur'd a Pole, its length longer then a Rope Dancer's. As soon as I enter'd the Morass I carry'd it before me, ready in case the Moss sward had given way and I had slipped in!—to have slung the Pole across the gap and prevented my going *down* further than my Shoulders. My care was needless, for we got over the worst part perfectly safe. The figure annexed will give you an Idea of carrying the Pole.

We came to a small elevated spot, here we rested. I looked back on the Swamp which we had just passed over. Bevan, who is a Native of Breckonshire, said that the Bogs in the Black Mountain, in that County, and all the Bogs in South Wales put togather, would not make a more horrible space then what this appear'd to be. I here examined my Shoes which I found to be nearly torn off. Being in no danger of meeting anything human I pulled off my Stockings, Coat and Waistcoate, Hatt etc. and gave them to Bevan to carry, they being as wet as if they had been steep'd in a Bucking Tubb.

I will say a word or two about this Waistcoate and Jacket. My Waistecoate was a Red one. Some few years ago, when I resided in London, in my boyish days, nothing would serve me but I must have a Red Waistcoate, trimmed with Gold. It was quite a natty thing. I remember my acquaintance laugh'd at me much for this proof of foppery and Nonsense. At the same period, which was the celebrat'd contested Westminster Election between Lord Hood and Lord John Townshend in 1789, in which Mr Chas Fox was so great a *principal*, the Supporters of Fox's Party always wore a uniform, in compliment to Charley. I *was* one of the foolish many. I bought a uniform and wore it! To be sure, at Elections all Scandal is licensed. But of the Coat, why this uniform Coat, which I had made five years ago, I had got alter'd into a neat Jacket, and had worn it on this day. When I was handing it to my Travelling Companion, all Slush, Wett and dirt, and my own person the picture of distress, it brought to my mind the pasquinades that were thrown out at the time, particularly that of—Time will show it! But the person to whom the authorship of most of these Libels were attributed to has, I am told, been exalted to the *Pillory* himself. This is Mr Frost of Spring Gardens who, at that time was Lord Hood's Solicitor.

Time did show it. On looking at my Jacket I found that time did show it . . . for the respectability, Gentility and Utility of this piece of originally blue Cloathe was strangely alter'd. Here it was now, by the side of a Swamp in the Barrens of Newfoundland, threadbare, wet, dirty and altogather of so ungentlemanlike look that had I met with it under any other circumstances it would have struck me as being a Deserter from the Gibbet. True it was there was some difference in the situation, there was a wide breadth between. The Atlantic Ocean is somewhat larger then Covent Garden. But my poor Coat, how showy thou was when first exhibited in the Hustings of that place of Cabbages and Potatoes! —and what an unhappy Remnant now remains of thy former Greatness and Splender, in this forlorn and solitary spot. I now perfectly fell in with the Idea of Mr Frost that Time had shown it. That the predestination of my Coat might be full and complete I resolv'd to perform, myself, what was wanting in the completion of its Miserable History, for which purpose I afterwards gave this Garment to a Fisherman who went out on a Banker to Fish on the Grand Banks. So much on the Supporter of the Blue and Buff Squad. [*Charles Fox of the Whig Party wore the colours, buff and blue, of the American Rebels.*]

As to the Red Waistcoate, no Gold was left on it, being oblig'd, from bitter Necessity, to sell the Gold Lace to an Embroiderer in the Strand in London, in order to raise money to assist in removing my *Baggage* from London to Portsmouth, to join my Ship there, on the War breaking out. For this Lace I receiv'd *Eighteen Pence*, which convey'd my *Lumber* to Westminster Bridge. This was a good lift on the Road, being only seventy-one miles short of the

The Harbour of Placentia. Watercolour from the log of H.M.S. Pegasus, *1786*

'A Representation of the Fish Flakes, and Manner of Drying Fish; in Newfoundland, 1794:
1. The Fish placed in Faggots
2. Laid on the Flakes to dry
3. Being Dried:—Are placed in Piles'

'A Method of carrying a Pole, recommended to those who cross the Morasses, in Newfoundland in Summer, 1794'

'A Pasado [posada], *near Xeres de la Frontera, in Spain'*

seventy-two! But then this *trifling* falling short of the place was nothing when put in competition with the *usefull* information I got in the Transaction!—For altho I only got Eighteen Pence for my Lace yet my Taylor, who was a very honest one and a *Friend of mine*, charged me only seventeen Shillings for the Lace alone, so for Ware and Tare it only cost me Fifteen Shillings.

This Red Waistcoate I had a remarkable respect for and I consider'd it the most favoured article of that kind in my Wardrobe and seldom wore it but on *State* occasions. On the Wars breaking out, and the Gold Trappings being dispos'd of for the National purpose before stated, I made it a common *hack* because I thought red was figurative of my trade, which was *War*, and yet I was not a little vexed by despoiling my Red Waistcoate in this day's vulgar march.

I shall now recall your mind to my situation on a Little Hillock, going from St John's to Torbay, dripping wet, with nothing on but a Shirt and a pair of Linnen Drawers, and just escap'd over a Morass more frightfull to the eye than deceptive to the feet. On my turning my front towards Torbay I found, on my right hand, a Rock; at its foot rose a small Rivulet which we had to cross. For that purpose there was an Old Stump, and a Pole laid on it; we then came to a Morass with Old dead Sticks laid longways for you to walk on, at the extremity of these Poles were two small Knolls or Hillocks between which the Path goes. My Companion first, started over the water with two long Poles in his hand.

Before night we arriv'd at a Hutt, in sight of Torbay. We met a Weoman at the door going for water. I thought I would have a little fun with the Weoman by telling her we had been Shipwreck'd. Our appearance was miserable in the extreme.

"Pray, my worthy Soul," says I, "What Country do you call this?"

"Why," she reply'd, "This Country is call'd Newfoundland." I then, with nothing on but my wet Shirt and Drawers (which stuck as close to my skin as Turpentine doth to the Bark of the Fur Tree) clasped my hands, made an ejaculation by saying "How unhappy is my lot, what a distress'd object I am, how unfriendly the Fates have been to me! Have not I cause for complaint that I should have travers'd the Ocean in so many directions and never met with so complicat'd a Disaster before this day?"

The Weoman stared, and cry'd "Where, Sir, Where?" I pointed to a Promontry which is the angle of Torbay.

"Aye," says she, "It is on Cape Blackhead. What! Is all *gone*?"

"Everything, except the Bundle of Biscuits which the Lad has in his hand." (Which was my Blue Jacket and Waistcoate ty'd up in a Handkerchiefe.)

"God Save me," says the Weoman, "I'll go in and tell the people." So she went running into the House.

As soon as her back was turn'd we made off for our own Quarters, which was a kind of Public House, leaving the Weoman and her family at large to *plunder* the Wreck and put what construction they pleased on our abrupt departure.

We enter'd the House of Entertainment in Torbay, concerning which I had made enquirys before hand. I shall relate no adventures which occur'd here further then speaking, according to my usual practize, on the heads of the House. The pair of Landlords certainly gave scope for my Pen. The Master's name was Timothy Fachairy, an odd name!—He was an Irishman, Six foot high, age about Thirty, athletic, bony, vigorous, the picture of good Health. Now what age do you suppose his Wife to be? Not more then Forty, to be sure. But she was forty, and thirty added to that. I make no doubt she was seventy years of age! What a blooming Bedfellow this Irish Hero had got.

A short History of this loving Couple (for I am sure I saw nothing to warrant a contrary observation) is simply this. The now *young* Mrs Fachairy's first Husband being dead it follows that she became a Widdow. Her present Spouse was then her Servant. He, knowing that she was well situat'd in point of circumstances, had a comfortable House and Furniture, upwards of £350 Sterling in Dollars, had more Fishing Flakes and more Fishing Boats then any other Five persons in Torbay, he very wisely thought it an eligible match.

Torbay is a small, wild Bay only used by small Boats. Here are some Noble Rocks and a small Waterfall. There is about Thirty Houses or Hutts scatter'd on each side of the Bay. I sketched a view in the environs of this Bay but have nothing further to add on its Scenery. [*This sketch is not in the Journal.*]

I have one remark to make on Torbay and that applys to all the Outharbours in Newfoundland. Here they have no Church nor no Clergyman, they have an unconsecrat'd Burial Ground where the dead are deposit'd. The Funeral Service is read by one of the Fishermen. It is no uncommon thing for the Inhabitants of one Bay to send for a *Learned man* who can *read*, from a neighbouring Harbour, to perform the Obsequies over a departed Christian. The Burial Place is not fenced in but open, so that Animals of all descriptions has free communication to perambulate the Sacred Spot.

In regard to Religion, the majority is Irish. In the Outharbours and Bays they have no Priest amongst them, therefore if there is a person amongst them that can *read* the other Inhabitants attend him when he performs the Catholic Service as well as circumstances will admit. If they have a Christianing or a Wedding they have to go to St John's, Placentia, Harbour Grace or some other place where a Canonical Gentleman is established, and will have to travel a great distance before they can have their Children initiated into Christianity, or the Lover have his Gorgon Knott made fast. If a Clergyman was to make his appearance in his Canonical Robes at one of these Outharbours I have little doubt but the Weomen and Children would be scarified out of part of their senses and avoid him with the same degree of alertness that they would a Black Bear or a Flock of Wolves. On the Ministry of Sacred Religion of the Protestant Church I shall speak hereafter.

On Torbay I have no further comments to make. We return'd on the next day by the same path we came, with the loss only of a pair of Shoes, and went on board the Boston, in St John's Harbour, the same evening.

[There seem to have been six or seven Roman Catholic priests in Newfoundland in 1794. The Rev Patrick Phelan was at Harbour Grace, Father Yore at Ferryland and Father Edmund Bourke was at Placentia. Dr O'Donel had been appointed the first Prefect Vicar Apostolic in 1784. Prior to this date Roman Catholics had been actively persecuted. Doubtless other Roman Catholic priests had been active in Newfoundland but few have been recorded.]

IX

Aquafort Harbour and Ferryland

Aquafort Harbour, August 7th, 1794. The *Boston* came to Anchor in this Harbour this day. We sailed from St John's on Monday the 4th, in Company with His Majesty's Ship *Amphion* of Thirty-two Guns. We are bound on a Cruize to the Southward. We put in here by the Request of Captain Sawyer of the *Amphion* to shift his Ballast and trim his Ship, she not being able in her present condition to attempt sailing with the *Boston.* I expect to stop here for a day or Two. On our Passage by the edge of the Grand Bank we spoke a Brigg which had been Fishing on the Banks for Twenty-one days, in which time she had catched the very enormous number of Twenty-two Thousand Fish! Here was a capital Haul. Could they have empty'd their Netts at Billingsgate the produce must have been very great. She was making the best of her way to St John's. If she makes another Trip and catches Ten Thousand Fish she is entitl'd to the Bounty given by the Parliament of England. But of this hereafter. [*The log says: "August 5th/25th moored in Aquaforte Harbour".*]

As we come to the Entrance of Aquafort Harbour the appearance is somewhat striking. On the Starboard hand there are Magnanimous Rocks, with two small ones just perceivable above the water, detached from the Mainland. On the Larboard hand, and right in the mouth of the Harbour, is a large rugged Rock, and a small one to the left, nearly in the mid way between the large Rock and the highlands on the Larboard hand. At the upper end of the Harbour is a small cultivatable spot, with a few Fishermen's Hutts scatter'd about. As you sail up the Harbour the Hills on both sides are nearly coated with Spruce Trees, the never failing embellishment for a Newfoundland Landscape. On the Larboard side you see, within about six miles, these remarkable Hills before spoken of and called the Butter-Potts. On the whole this is as pleasing a

Picture as any I have seen in this Country. I have sketched a view of it. The entrance into this Harbour is between the large detached Rock and the high craggy mountainous Rocks of the Main land. It is not of difficult access and the water is deep enough for a Ship of any burthen.

Aquafort Harbour is very properly named. Aquatic signifys abounding with water and Aquarius, the Waterman of old, was also one of the Twelve Signs. The name of the place at once bespeaks its qualitys. Here is good anchoring Ground and plenty of room for a large Fleet to moor, and ride in safety. Several Rivulets and small Springs of fresh water discharge themselves into this Harbour. There is also a very considerable Cascade in this Harbour, which emits down upwards of Five Tons of Water every minute. It is the most considerablest of any I have yet seen in this Country. This Harbour of Aquafort is not more then three miles from Ferryland, and four from Capelin Bay, a place which I have spoken of at large in some distant pages.

In regard to the Settlements in this Harbour there is now only Two Familys left. At the head of the Harbour there is eight or nine Houses, but they are all desert'd except two. The persons who lived in them return'd, I believe, not as rich as they came, after labouring hard after the Fish for several summers. The low price they got for them, the dearness of Pork and the severity of the winters proved how abortive the *design* was of making a Fortune in Newfoundland; so they went for Europe without *first* settling with the Merchants before they sail'd.

While our Frigate lay at Anchor in the Harbour I avail'd myself of going through the woods to Ferryland. I had occasion to call on business on Mrs Keene who lived in a place called the Grove. She is now a Widdow, is left in good circumstances having fourteen Cows, which in Newfoundland puts the proprietor on a par with Job in point of Riches. Her Husband came over from England about Fifty-Five years ago as an Adventurer—what is called here a green man, which means a man that has never been in a Fishing Boat on this Coast before. By dint of Industry and Perservance he became the most affluent Fisherman in Ferryland; but four years ago he quit'd Ferryland and took a Voyage for the Elyssian Fields. Others say he was ferry'd across the River Styx, but without truth as there is no man free from error. But be that circumstance as it may be, true it is that Mrs Keene did not waste *much* after his death by pining for I fully believe she weigh'd at least *Seventeen* Stone. Her corpulency was larger in proportion to the height so you may judge of the taperness of her Body. The reason of my being thus particular on Mrs Keene (concerning whom I have nothing ill to say) is to introduce a remark which occur'd at her House.

After I had been within her Dwelling some time and was going away—"Sir," says she, "I am sorry I have got nothing, I never was so *empty* before." By which she meant that she had got no Gin or Rum to give to me. Well, thinks I, if you are empty *now*!—looking at her Bulky Frame—what must you be when *full*! "My Dear Old Soul," says I, "Pray put no apologys, for if you had a *Butt of Gin*, with a Spiggot and Posset in it, not a Thimblefull of the Spirits for me!" I bid her Adieu, and with my good wishes and acknowledgements left, assuring her that I would *speak* and *think* of she when my eyes could not have the Pleasure of beholding her. I now leave Mrs Keene; God Bless her, says I, for as the Almighty has given her plenty in this life, so I hope he will be mercifull to her in the next. From the little I saw of her I am confident her hopes are great and her pretensions well founded.

In Ferryland is a kind of House of Entertainment called the London Inn. It is now kept by the Widdow of Captain Tree, an American Loyalist, who lost a considerable Property when the British Troops abandoned Boston. They came and settled here. Mrs Tree is in a very comfortable situation, has a large and roomy House and Genteel Furniture. A Gentleman may have as good a Dinner and Rest at this House as any in Newfoundland. I Din'd here the day I made the Tour on Four Covers, Viz. a Boiled Leg of Pork, Fowls, Lamb, Ducks, Pudings, Green Pease and other Vegitables, served up with Sauces and Gravys. Had an Epicure been one of the Guests he could not a found fault with a single Dish.

Mrs Tree is about fifty, rather corpulent, but in possession of one of those faces which is the Frontispiece to Good Nature and the Emblem to Sociability and calm serenity. She related to me the History of the American War and the *fatal* consequence of its effects to her Family, the Terror of her mind when she heard the Cannon roar at the Battle of Bunker Hill, which produced on her understanding a continuous torpescenty that she could not get rid of untill she had made her escape from the Country which was then the Seat of War. She told me that she had, at this time, a Son on board the British Ship the *Royal George* of 100 Guns, who was born in America, serv'd under General Washington in the American Army, and was at this time a Citizen of the States of America; that he belonged to an American Ship from New York to London, that when the Ship arriv'd in London he being ashore one evening was *press'd* and *Forc'd* on board an English Ship of War. She said that if the American Minister was to apply to the Court of St James for the Enfranchisement of an American Citizen detain'd on board a British Ship, the English Government *dar'd* not refuse his enlargement. I told her that England was a Country of Resources and Riches that gave her such weight in the Political World as to make her displeasure *dread'd*, therefore no Power on earth would be permitt'd to deliver their Credentials if the word *Dare* was part of the prologue to the preliminary. To say more on this controversy between Mrs Tree and myself—I cannot but admit but what it wrote a consideration on the subject in my mind, and the following is the fruit of my Reflection:

It is held unlawfull for our Offspring to resist the *will* of the Parent. It is likewise deem'd un-natural in a Native to fight against his Country, which has foster'd him, whose Laws have protected him in the enjoyment of his Property and in the Freedom of his person. So fully doth the Constitution of England set up this principle that on our engaging in War we *instantly* issue a Proclamation telling all our Subjects to quit the Service of that Power against whom our Arms are directed, on pain of death, which punishment can be inflicted by the antient Law of the Land. Now if one Kingdom or State says that this Law has Equity and Justice for its basis it surely must be confess'd that the other Countrys have a right to enact the same Laws in regard to their own Subjects. America is acknowledged by all the Powers of Europe a *Free* and Independent Republic, and the instant that instrument was signed, that very moment, *all* her Citizens or the persons born in the Land became free, and were absolv'd from their Allegiance to any other Power.

To illustrate the Business it is only necessary to suppose an American is a Castaway on the Island of Sardinia. America shortly after goes to War with the King of Sardinia. She first passeth a Law making Death for any of her Citizens to be found in the Service of any Foreign Prince. The American left on the Island is *forc'd* into the Service of the King of Sardinia, in which Service he is actually *taken* by the success of the American Arms. This man, by being taken in Arms against his Country has fell (altho not intentionally) under the Rod of the Law; nothing but death can expiate his Crime.

So explored and admitted are the foregoing Hypothesis in regard to England that in the late War if a Naval Officer wanted to take a Spanish Boy on his Ship as his Servant and for the benefitt of learning the Language from him, he could not be receiv'd on board untill leave had first been obtained from the *Admiralty*. The same objection was also against Holland and France; and in the present War two instances have come to my knowledge, where two Gentlemen of the *Suffolk* of 74 Guns each wanted a French Servant from amongst the Prisoners in Forton Prison, but no Liberation could be admitted untill leave had been obtain'd from the Admiralty.

In the American States some anxiety has been given in regard to American Sailors being detain'd on board British Ships of War. Very much difficulty has arose in the English Service on this head between the American and the English Sailor. There is no external marks for discrimination, and it is easy for a man who wishes to evade the English Naval Service to say that he is an American. The most serious circumstance of the kind which has fallen in my knowledge has occur'd at Newport in Rhode Island, where acts of violence were committed on the Captain of His Majesty's Ship *Nautilus* and his First Lieutenant as the people said that there were American Sailors detain'd on board the *Nautilus*.

Mrs Tree having led me into a digression which I never intended to volunteer in I must be pardon'd for discanting on the Rights of Nations. I shall return to my domestic seat on an old, broken Chair in Mrs Tree's Parlour. Opposite to my Chair hung two stuffed Newfoundland Wild Ducks of beautifull Plumage. I had a design of begging or buying one of them. I made some remarks to Mrs Tree on their size and the colour of their feathers. Learning that there were numbers of them killed on the Ice in Winter I presum'd to ask if she would sell me one of them to take to England as a curiosity.

"Most readily," says she, "I will not let you have one, but I will *give* you *both* of them," at the same time rising from her Chair she unhooked both Birds and laid them on the Table by my side. "There," says she, "such Birds as them are not to be met with in

England or Wales, many a good Dish do I make with them in the Winter."

I return'd her at least a Boatfull of Thanks. But on my eye ranging round the Room I saw as many Punch Bowls as would rise a Chinese Temple as high as that in the Royal Garden at Kew.

"Now my Dear Soul, Mrs Tree," says I—at the same time gently playing with the flap of her Handkerchiefe which was hanging loose—"cannot you oblige me further by selling me one of those Punch Bowls?"

She told me to select one out, which I did. She put a very moderate price on it and I paid her for it. I told her that on my arrival in England that Bowl would be filled with good Punch, when me and my Friends would drink to the Health of Mrs Tree of the London Inn in Ferryland, Newfoundland.

"So, Sir," says she, "You have *Friends*, have you?"

"Most undoubted Madame, a number in England."

"I should like to go to Britain with you for the sight of a *Friend* would be very entertaining to me, having never *yet seen one*." Then she asked me if I would like to drink a Glass of Punch with a Party of her *Friends*, and of course her Friends would be my Friends. I reply'd I had no objections.

"But," says she, "my Friends are my Irish Fishing Servants now in the Kitchen who, I am confident, will be as noisy and as merry and as *friendly* with you as your best *Friends* in England, providing you pay for the *Liquor*."

This, certainly, was no bad sally of Wit of the good Lady's, and was a home stroke, for I confess on searching the Catalogue to see the names of *all* which I have been acquaint'd with, I cannot put a mark against the name of a single individual, at this moment, to say for certain—That is my Friend. And yet I have had as many persons as most that would walke and talke and Drink with me, and shall again if ever I return to England.

In addition to the Ducks which she gave me, and the Bowl which I bought, I also purchas'd of her some Fowls and a whole Lamb, which a man killed and Dress'd, and I sent the carcase on board in a Boat. Before my departure Mrs Tree told me, in a good humour, that I was an acquisititive Viseter. She wished me well, as she hop'd I was a good man. I told her I was like a Magpye, given to chatter.

"Magpye" says she, "What's that?"

"Why, an English Magpye, to be sure. Did you never hear of one?"

"No" says she. Then I gave her an account of an English Magpye, the description of which pleas'd her much. She said she would like to have a Stuffed one brought over. I promized to do all in my power towards satisfying her curiosity, and if the *Boston* sails again for the Newfoundland Station I will, most assur'dly endeavour to bring or send her some.

Mrs Tree not having it in her power to supply me with the number of Fowls I wanted I was obliged to perambulate the Settlement in search of them. Amidst the rugged Barren and Houses I met a Boy of the name of Thomas Gosecoat, a Devonshire Lad, and Servant to the Revd Mr Cole, who is Pastor to the Flock at Ferryland. This Lad I knew before, when the *Boston* laid in Capelin Bay. Of his Master I will have something to say later. [*There seems to have been no clergyman in Ferryland in 1791 or earlier, but in S.P.G. Reports of 1792–93 it was noted that two letters had been received in the course of the year from the Revd Samuel Cole, lately appointed missionary to Ferryland and Bay Bulls. In the Report of 1794–95 it was noted that Mr Cole had been in England that winter and that though he had intended to return to Newfoundland in the spring he had resigned his appointment having the prospect of some ecclesiastical promotion in England. His mission included harbours between Ferryland and Bay Bulls.*]

This Lad pilot'd me to a House where his Master, the day before, had bought some Fowls at 2/6 the Couple. There was some of the same Brood left. There was no person at home except a Weoman, the Mother of the Family, and she was ill in Bed. After thumping for some time at the door I heard a voice in the adjacent place (I cannot call it a Chamber). I went into it and beheld the Weoman in Bed, apparently very ill. I told her my business. She said she had some Fowls and the price was 2/6 per Couple. Having seen them, I told her I should not give more then 2/- the Couple. I now began to ask her concerning the state of her disorder, the Symptoms etc. . . She related, at large, how many weeks she had been in Bed, how old she was, how many Children she had got, the age of her Husband, the part of Ireland she came from, how hard the times was, how slow the Fish bite at present and that there was nothing to be got but Flint Biscuits in Newfoundland. I thought this was a singular relation of her diseazes.

"But the Fowl, Madame, will you not sell me the Fowls for less then 2/6 the Couple?"

"No, by St Patrick, I will not, no, not a single Farthen."

I thought I must work on the sympathetic!—so approaching her Bedside with diffidence, and a look which symbolis'd Faith and Compassion—"My dear Weoman, I do not wonder at your illness, for the very name of your complaints is enough to give you the Hydrocephalus, without being in possession of them. But Hope—Hope—my dear Creature, is the chain by which our life is linked. You certainly are, at this moment, in Trouble and great Tribulation. But you and I, and all sufferers, have this certain and positive Fact—that there is, in this life, an end to *Pain* as well as to Pleasure. But my good Female, the Fowls. Come let me have them for 2/- per Couple."

"No," says she, "not if I was sure I should be forc'd to eat them myself."

"Well," says I, "You are very uncharitable to a Sojourner like myself."

I happen'd this day to be dressed all in Black, my hair curl'd close to my head, as I generally wear it. With this dress and grave demeanour I have more then once been taken for a Clergyman. When I was at St Pierres the French called me "the *Boston*'s Priest".

I now reassume my position at the Bedside.

"My Fair Creature, we have talked so much about the Sorrow of this life, *dear* and *cheap* Fowls, Plagues and Distempers, Ireland and Whale Oil!—But not a word has yet transpir'd about the Faith! Not a sentence on Religion. What Religion are you of?"

"A Catholic, Sir,"—to which I subjoin'd "And so am I too!" She hastyly added "I am glad of it."

I offer'd my desires to say Vespers, which she seemed glad in her Heart to accept and join in. It is a most extraordinary circumstance, but I had in my Pocket, at that time, a Pyx containing the Host which I had been given by the Wife of an old French Baker at St Pierres. At the sight of this Pyx, having such a Relick about my person, she could have no doubt but that I was a Roman Catholic!

I kneeled down by her Bedside, repeated the Paternoster and other Ritual solemnitys, according to the Church of Rome, with due decorum, fitness, order, and as she said, dignify'd Grace. This much I will say of myself—that during the ceremony my mind was fervent in the cause of God and my heart glowed in the opportunity of rendering my thanks to the Almighty for the daily Blessings and nourishment which I receiv'd from His Divine hands.

This Religious Scene being over I press'd the Weoman to rise and to take the air, the day being fine. She promiz'd me she would and begged me to retire. I retreated, and soon after she made her appearance, Pale and Dejected. I now began on the old Lyne—the Fowls, and hoped I should have them for 2/- the Couple.

"Yes," says she, "You shall have them for Two Shillings a pair, for your Religion's sake."

I thanked her and was sorry we could not live in the same Village together. She went to the Door and called the Fowls in, tyed their Legs, and sent them, by a little Girl which she beckon'd from a Neighbours door, to my General Depot at the London Inn. Parson Cole's Boy made his appearance before I gave her the money for the Poultry. His Master having paid 2/6 for the same Brood, she was fearfull it would come to his ears of her selling them to me for less money. She spoke to the Boy on the Subject, to keep it from his Master's knowledge. We had some conversation as to the Sin of this matter in selling her Fowls cheaper to one *Clergyman* then another. She said that she had committed a crime because she ought to treat her Neighbour best, besides Mr Cole was always ready to lend her any spiritual aid she needed. I told her that the argument she used ponderated in my favour by reason I used the Sea and had few opportunitys of pertaking of the good things on Shore, therefore it was a Charity to relieve the wants of the Buffited Mariner. I now take my Farewell of Ferryland for, with my live and dead Stock, I got on board the *Boston* the same night.

I have been ashore more then once at a pretty little spot in this Bay. We call it Jerseyman's Plantation because a Jerseyman was the last person who Resid'd here; but it is now deserted, the man, having failed, became a Wreck in point of property, with the rest of the Settlers in this Bay. This little Plantation forms one of the charmingest scenes I have yet beheld in Newfoundland. The unfortunate possessor has left behind his House, his Fish Flake, his Store Room, his Garden and his burying ground. The spot is formed of a shelving Rock which serves as a Landing place and a

Fish Flake on which he used to dry his Fish; near the Flake is a spot where one of his family has been bury'd, which is enclosed with Spruce Sticks and Poles. Above the Flakes and the Mausoleum is a low Rock running several yards which separates the Upper Garden from the Lower Garden. On this spot is an Old, Dead Tree. At the upper part we suspended a Handkerchiefe as a signal to the *Boston* to send a Boat. On the left hand is a third cultivated spot, higher then all the rest, and also separat'd by a long, low Rock. The whole is bounded on the land side by Spruce Trees, and next the Sea by some formidable Rocks, except where the Fish Flake and the shelving Landing place intervene. The whole of this arable spot contains about two acres. I shall be very minute in my remarks on this pleasing Residence. Before I landed at it I knew the History and the Fate of the last Resident.

When I first landed at the Plantation I was struck with the accessible and natural formation of the shelving Landing place; I could not but admire its propriety and fitness for the free communication with the water. Looking on the left I saw a high Rock, advancing I came to the Store Room—I went in. Here I saw part of two Casks of dry'd Capelin, some broken Hoops and staved Kegs. I then went into the Dwelling House, the doors was taken down and the wind blew in in all directions, through the crevices. A rotten Rope end, an old shoe, a rusty Nail driven here and there, the old lanyards on which a Bed had been suspend'd, a broken Porringer, an old Tea Kettle and a pair of ragg'd woollen stockings—all these emblems, the tokens of wretchedness and Misery, told the fate of the last Inhabitant. I retreat'd from the House to perambulate the little Domaine. Here I found Grass in great plenty, Raspberrys in such numbers that a Peck of them might be gather'd in a few minutes had they been ripe. Roses grew here spontaneously and so numerous, they being then in Blossom, that the fragrant flavour was diffus'd all around. Here are also Wild Pear Trees and plenty of Currants, with Partridge Berrys, Stone Hurts and Maidenhair Berrys in vast quantitys.

A few yards from the House was a fine Spring of Fresh Water which supply'd the domestic wants of that article, and tons of Wood was within two minutes walke of the House. Here was his Fish Flake for drying his Fish, and in this little spot was compress'd all the necessarys of life, so that here there could be no want.

On an Eminence in the Upper Garden or Plantation grew an

old Tree, but by length of days and piercing winds he was *now* dead. On this dead Tree the inhabiter of this Plantation used to hoist a Signal to the people at the head of the Harbour in case of Distress such as Fire, being out of Provisions or when he was viset'd by any dreadfull Malady. Immediately below this Tree, in the Lower Garden, was the Cemetry or Family Mausoleum, if I may call it so. There had been only one person enter'd there. It was fenced in with Sticks and Poles of the Spruce Tree, which was sufficient entablature to point out the Sacred spot, for in that Grave perhaps lay the Ashes of one who once gave Pleasure to the eye, Satisfaction to the Heart, Gratitude to the Senses, Information to the Ignorant, Cheerfulness to the mind and Mirth to the circle. But now, clad in the Robes of Death, his body enter'd in the very spot where Herbs grew which fed his Hunger when living—but now how revers'd. His Body has become food and Nourishment to the same specie of plants which, when living, had been his daily Provender. I have called his burial place a Family Mausoleum. Why not call this humble Fence of Sticks a Mausoleum? Would not all the Family, had they dyed in Aquafort, a been deposit'd by his side? Is not this Mausoleum as magnificent and splendid and as noble in the Eye of God as the Grand Edifice, the family Mausoleum of the Darnleys, in Cobham Park in Kent.

In some lines back I have spoken at large on the Fruits, the Fish, the Flowering Shrubs and the beautys of this charming little place. I wondered, indeed I could not believe, while I looked on one side of the Picture, how it was that an industrious man could not live in this Paradise, as it appear'd to me to be. I thought had I a Partner whom I loved and have seen her here, it must be the Garden of Eden in perfection.

But shall I tell you the Season of the year in which I was here? It was the month of August—the *May* of Newfoundland, the finest Season of the year, when the Gates of Nature are unlocked and the Vegitable Kingdom gusheth out like a torrent from its bed; whatever it toucheth it is conducive to quick maturity. I have as yet but given you one side of the picture. Shall I turn the Landscape and exhibit the other side of the picture? I certainly must, and the difference of colouring will be immediately obvious.

Let your Ideas be carry'd to the spot just describ'd. Figure to yourself the earth cover'd with several feet of *Snow*, not an Herb to be seen. Then, if you venture out your life is in danger.

The Sea, from being coated over, refuseth the usual assistance, no food to be got from she. As to the earth, on *that* God has put a strong and mighty *lock.* On the face of the earth there is an immense Barrier which separates it from man; it is cover'd with an impenetrable Mass of Snow. But avast! How do you like this side of the picture? Are my shades deep enough? Are you a man for a Frost Piece? Are your fingers pliable and warm enough to handle your Pencil to throw a group of Skaters into a Sketch taken in a Frosty Season on the Serpentine in Hyde Park? Have I not said enough on the Jerseyman, poor fellow?

The day on which I was last at this Plantation a number of persons from the Ship went ashore there, amongst which was Mr Irwin, a Master's Mate and Mr Rawlings, the Captain's Clerk. I have said much of the Old, dead Tree which serv'd the purpose of an Ensign Staff and which is so conspicious an Ornament in the Landscape. The two Gentlemen before mentioned (one of which rivals, in point of size, the famous Colossean Statue at Rhodes) must needs try their strength against this hoary Tree and at once destroy the Signal Staff, and level his antient head with the vilest Reptile that crawl amongst the Grass. They set their shoulders in contest against his rotten sides, some of his wither'd Limbs parted from the Body at the first shake and he was not long able to resist by reason of his Stump was porous, and his whole frame perished. Down he came, poor Old Gentleman! This Transaction occur'd in my absence. When I arriv'd at the place I upbraid'd these two Young Gentlemen for attacking an Inhabitant so venerable in years, so antient in look, particularly as by his erasure they had despoil'd a principal figure in the Landscape.

At this place we stocked ourselves with good Hay. The Butcher and his Mowers and Haymakers going on Shore daily for that purpose.

There is another pretty spot which forms a pleasing Landscape. We call it the Watering Place because we got Fresh Water here. Our people were ashore at this place brewing Spruce Beer, Cutting Wood, washing their Linnens etc. The Launch was always employ'd on this duty carrying the empty Casks and numbers of our people were always ashore picking Berrys and recreating themselves. There is about Two Acres of space which might be cultivated; in the middle riseth a Spring of Water, at the extremity is an opening into the Woods. All the other parts are bounded by impenetrable Thickets of Spruce Trees. When view'd from the Bay and having a number of figures on the Beach it has a striking effect.

[The log of the Boston *for Monday 11 August 1794 records "16 Puncheons of Spruce Beer completed and got all the brewing utensils and wood out and prepared for Sea".]*

X

On the Banks of Newfoundland

14th August, 1794. Our Frigate and the *Amphion* quited the Harbour of Aquafort on Monday morning last, the 11th instant, and here we are on the outer edge of the Grand Bank, cruizing backwards and forwards in the Latitudes of falling in with American Ships bound from the States to Europe. We have spoken with several Vessels. I understand we will Cruize in these Latitudes a fortnight or three weeks. When we return into Port I will give you some observations on the American Shipping Trade, for the present I shall employ my leisure hours in giving you a description of the Island of Newfoundland, its Lakes, Soil and Original Inhabitants. I shall endeavour to be minute and particular in that part which relates to the first settling of the Colony here, for which purpose I have consulted the best Authoritys extant. If an error should be detected in my Anachronism you will take it from its right source—The head and not the heart!

Newfoundland is a large and extensive Island in the Gulph of St Lawrence. It contains some Thirty Thousand Square Miles, which is a circumference little short of the extent of Great Britain. This Island covers so considerable a space of the Globe that its dimensions are inferior to only Fifteen Islands yet discover'd in the habitable world. Its shape is Triagonal and it measures Three Hundred and Fifty Miles in length and Two Hundred miles in breadth. It is situated between Forty Six Degrees, Forty Minutes and Forty Two Degrees, Seven Minutes North Latitude, and between Forty One Degrees, Fifty Two Minutes and Fifty Seven Degrees, Forty Minutes West Longitude. It is bounded on the East and South by the Atlantic Ocean, on the West by the Gulph of St Lawrence and on the North by the Straights of Bellisle, which separate it from the frozen Regions of Labrador.

[*A.T. was not far out. The island of Newfoundland is situated between 46 37—51 37 N latitude and 52 44—59 30 W Longitude. It is 317 miles long and 316 broad, triangular in shape and 42,000 square miles in area.]*

The Climate of Newfoundland in Winter is exceedingly severe and keene. The Sky is generally overcast and a thick Fog fills the Atmosphere with a dismal, Cloudy and heavy mist which gives all living Creatures that move in it the appearance of heavyness of mind and the gait of sour sulleness. Because of its Northern position, and the still more Northern situation of the neighbouring Continent of Labrador (or the Esquimaux Country) in which are monstrous Mountains of Ice and trackless deserts of Snow, the winds blow from one point for Eight months of the year. This gives such a degree of cold that it is beyond the beliefe of any but those who have felt its piercing blasts in Hudson's and Baffin's Bay and Greenland.

Thus from the affinity of Newfoundland to the Continent of Labrador the cold, in some particulars, receives additional strength so that here Winter reigns in great and mighty force for Seven months of the year. During this time the earth is hid from the Eye of man, being cover'd with Snow and bound down by a strong cement. When the Sun shows its genial rays its warmth has little effect towards solving so thick a Mass of Ice and Snow. But when, by motion of the Globe, this Island is brought to a more temperate heat the Sun darts forth its rays, the Ramparts of Snow are turn'd into a Solution of Water, the earth is uncover'd, Vegitation begins, Fruits and Plants of every kind Flower and arrive at *maturity*, then begin to wither, decay, drop their heads and sink into the earth again. And all this change from infancy to Maturity, and from Maturity to death, is perform'd in the short space of June, July and August. The seasons here are divided into two parts—Summer and Winter. The names Spring and Autumn will never occur to your Ear here for the Summer bursts upon you all at once. The Sun, who is the source of light, the father of the Seasons, and the fostering hand of the world, instills his beneficial heat into all his Plants and Herbs and brings them into perfection in a very short time.

The Summer here is in the extreme of heat. You will sometimes find it is so hot as to burn the Fish as they lye to dry on the Flakes. *[It is true that fish will become sunburnt if spread on a hot day when there is no wind.]* But the weather here is very subject to change in the summer time. When we laid in St John's Harbour in June last the mornings were frequently frosty, about Ten O'Clk it would be quite hot and by Noon perfectly sultry. It often happens that one hour is hot, the next hour cold, then a Fogg, afterwards clear, then Rain—so that it commonly falls out that you get Four or Five kinds of weather in one day.

The Lakes in Newfoundland are very numerous. Many of them are of great extent. From the summit of Signal Hill, near St John's, I had Seven in sight at one view. These Lakes are all good, fresh Water and in them are abundance of all kinds of Fish, with Otters, Beavers and a variety of wild Fowls. It is very seldom that you can go more then Three miles but what you fall in with a Pond or Lake. This sheet of water is generally the head of a Rivulet which meanders amongst the stumps of Spruce Trees and stones untill it emptys itself into some Harbour or Creek. These Lakes are, in point of numbers so many, and the spaces which they occupy so extensive, that it is admited as a fair Hypothesis that for every square of four yards of Land there is one square yard of water—but the Rivulets are included in this calculation.

Every Harbour, every Bay and every Inlet you enter it is surprizing to see the many fresh water streams that rush down with heedless violence to be swallowed up in the boundless Ocean. Some travel roughly along a hollow malancholy Channel abutted with Rocks, and eternally shaded from the Sun, viset'd only by herds of Wolves and the Croaking Eagle, others creep amidst a heap of loose stones, old Trees, small swamps and impenetrable Thickets untill it appears on the Beach as a gentle Rill, where it softly insinuates its slow approach, its humble wish to be united with the waters of the deep. Again I see a Mountain whose acclivitys descends suddenly to the edge of a frightfull precipice, from its summit bursts forth a Column of hoary liquid. Its agitated motion, its extended particles, its dashing limbs, its foaming head, and lastly its solemn, Grand, Awefull and Tremendous Noise declare aloud to the listening elements its Anger and displeasure at being thus hurled down the monstrous rock to mingle its transparent and gratefull fluid with the briny waters of the unfathomable Ocean. This picture of the Cascades in Newfoundland is not too highly varnished. Every Harbour has its Cooto (as they are called) or Waterfall. In Cape Broyle there is a fine Cataract.

It is a fact admited by all Travellers and Navigators that the North is better water'd then the other quarters of the Globe and the reasons they give are perfectly obvious to the uninformed. This Country is full proof of the assertion, for in traversing the Shores of this Island you will find in every four yards a Spring of Fresh Water oozing out.

The Bays, Harbours, Creeks and Coves in this Island are superior to any others in the world in point of numbers and safety. Secure retreats for Ships are met with at every three or four Leagues distance. No Country of its size affords such a good number of Bays and safe Harbours which are of easy access and good Holding Ground. Within the distance of three Leagues I shall notice no less then five harbours, viz.—Cape Broyle Harbour, Capelin Bay Harbour, Ferryland Harbour, Aquafort, and Fermose. If I was to carry my eye further on the Mapp I could instance parts of the Coasts where Shelters as numerous as those just noticed. But yet, with all these precious Havens and Places of Refuge, which would be so great a Blessing to some Countrys, Shipwrecks are very common on these shores. These dreadfull scenes are occasion'd by those teazing Fogs which are eternally hovering about the Coast and prevent the poor Mariner from seeing his danger.

A Shipwreck on this Island presents to the unhappy objects nothing but dismay and certain death if it happens in winter, and when the poor sufferers get on shore, even then death is inevitable. There is no House near, his Cloathes are completely immers'd in water, rigid winter in all its bitter force is Sovereign Master of the earth. The Shipwreck'd Sailor, poor fellow, is soon frost bitten, he is benumb'd, he lyes down and perisheth in the cold—he is frozen to death!

I shall here break the chain of my relation and observations of the waters of Newfoundland to introduce a Narrative or two which will illustrate the fatal effects of the cold. The first is this:

The *Boston* Frigate was on this Station last year. In the month of October when she laid in St John's Harbour three of her Seamen deserted. The Frigate sail'd for England in December, heard nothing of her men untill her return to this place in May last, when we learned that these unfortunate men had attempt'd to cross a slip of land no more then Twenty Miles athwart St John's, to the Bay of Bulls, but they missed their path and were found frozen to death in the woods. From their dress and other concurring circumstances no doubt was left but that they were the *Boston*'s people. They had got within three miles of the Bay of Bulls when the poor deluded fellows wandered into a path which led to the wreck of a deserted Iron Foundry which the French had made some progress in establishing when they were in possession of Newfoundland. Their bodys were found lying close togather, and in a perfect state, the frost having kept them from putrefaction.

We have, at this time in the *Boston* a man who in April last was wreckt in a Brigg, in foggy weather on Cape St Mary's. He and three others got on shore after their Vessel went to pieces. They found means to convey on shore a few articles of provision. The Cape was desolate and uninhabited. They lighted a fire and continued rambling along the shore for three days in a deplorable condition, all of their fingers being burnt (as it is called) with the Frost. On the fourth day they separat'd, the other three being unable to proceed. Our man, who is a Gunner's Mate, kept advancing along the shore in the hope of coming to some Settlement. Luckily he saw a Boat close to the shore. He made a Signal. She came and took him in. He was a perfect spectacle having eat nothing for two days, his hands and feet were Frost Bitten; altogather *[he was]* in a shocking situation. The Fisherman gave him every comfort in his power. They then went in search of the other people and found the place where they came on shore. The little Punt, in which they saved their lives, and which was haul'd on the Beach, was gone; from that they conjectur'd some assistance had arriv'd and it is to be hoped their lives was saved. We met with our man at St John's. When he came on board it was expected he must lose one of his Feet, but he recover'd and is now perfectly well. We have three other men on board as Sailors who enter'd under similar circumstances. All were *frost burnt* in March and April, but with good Treatment none of them have lost as much as a Finger.

In the month of December last a poor Irishman was sent on business to the Bay of Bulls. Before he got half way he was nipped by the Frost and fell down under the severity of the weather. Fortunately some people coming from Bay of Bulls met with him and carry'd him back, and by putting his Body into a succession of warm Blankets he was restor'd to life. The great variety of instances which occur every Season of persons being Frost bitten are numerous but I shall content myself with the fore-going Recitals.

The Navigators who first viset'd these shores were Ironical

Souls. The names they have given the places are not a little laughable. I shall present you with a short List of them. I shall begin with the Islands which are:

Funk Island	Fox Island
Fogo Island	Shagg Island
Stinking Island	Eye of Ireland's Isle
Gull Island	Scurvey Island
Goose Island	Dead Island
	Plum Island

The Whimsical Bays, Harbours and Capes are:

Point Lance	Come by Chance Harbour
Cape Spear	Maggoty Cove
Cape Race	Cape Ballard
Black Head	Piper's Hole Harbour
Petty Harbour	Paradize Sound
Glam Cove	Fortune Bay
Mutton Cove	Point Enrage
Bay Dispair	Bay of Exploits
Rencounter Bay	Loggerhead Bay
Ragged Harbour	Tickle Harbour
Bloody Point	Hearts Content
Horses Chops	River of Exploits
Old Man's Bay	Hearts Delight Point
Taylor's Bay	Random River
Harbour Grace	White Bear's Bay
Bay of Wolves	Bay of Islands
Cod Roy River	Witless Bay
Hares Bay	

This catalogue might be considerable lengthened. [*Many of the names of places in Newfoundland are English corruptions of French, Spanish and Portuguese words.*]

There are a vast number of Islands scatter'd about the Shores of Newfoundland but few of these are inhabited. In Conception Bay is Big Bell Isle which is the most fertilest Island in all the Country.

At some Leagues distant from the Northern Shore are the Islands of Fogo, Stinking Island and Funk Island. They are generally called the Funks from the stinking Smell which salutes your

Nose on landing on them. I have mention'd these Islands as a Preface to the following remarks. I shall be particular on Funk Island. My observations on that place will apply to the other Islands.

Funk Island is a barren spot inhabited only by Penguins and other Birds. The astonishing quantitys of Birds which resort to this Island is beyond the beliefe of any person, except those who have witnessed something similar in other parts. As soon as you put your foot on shore you meet with such Thousands of them that you cannot find a place for your feet and they are so lazy that they will not attempt to move out of your way. If you come for their Feathers you do not give yourself the trouble of killing them, but lay hold of one and pluck off the best of the Feathers. You then turn the poor Penguin adrift, with his Skin half naked and torn off, to perish at his *leasure*. This is not a very humane method, but it is the common Practize.

If you go to the Funks for Eggs to be certain of getting them fresh you pursue the following Rule:—You drive, knock and Shove the poor Penguins in Heaps! You then scrape all the Eggs in Tumps, in the same manner you would a Heap of Apples in an Orchard in Herefordshire. Numbers of these Eggs, from being dropped some time, are stale and useless, but you having cleared a space of ground the circumferences of which is equal to the quantity of Eggs you want, you retire for a day or two behind some Rock at the end of which time you will find plenty of Eggs—fresh for certain!—on the place where you had before cleared. While you abide on this Island you are in the constant practize of horrid crueltys for you not only Skin them Alive, but you *burn* them *Alive* also, to cook their Bodys with. You take a Kettle with you into which you put a Penguin or two, you kindle a fire under it, and this fire is absolutely made of the unfortunate Penguins themselves. Their Bodys being oily soon produce a Flame; there is no wood on the island.

I had the following information from a person in St John's whose veracity I can depend upon. "About Twenty years ago, when this kind of Traffick was Lawfull, I made two Trips to the Funks. In these Trips I gather'd, with one person with me, half a Ton of Feathers and as many Eggs as sold at St John's for Thirty Pounds! While I lay at the Funks a small Island of Ice drifted into the Cove where my Shallop lay. Having occasion to go to the Shallop one morning on the Ice was a large Greenland Bear and one White

Fox. I killed them both. The Bear was of that enormous Magnitude and Bulke as to weigh seven Hundredweight, which was a valuable Prize." These animals were on the Ice when it parted from that frozen Continent of Frost and Snow about Greenland, and had drifted this far living on Seals etc., which at times get on the Ice.

This skinning and taking the Eggs from the Funks is now prohibit'd and they are allow'd to take the Birds only for Bait to catch Fish with. The Funks being a distance from the Land, are so uninviting and desolate that they are seldom viseted, unless by Pirates and Robbers to steal the Feathers and Eggs. About three years ago some fellows were detected in this kind of Plunder. They were brought to St John's and flogged at a Cart's Tail. But I am told there is quantitys of Feathers purloin'd from these Islands every year. The Islands are called the Funks or Stinking Islands from the quantity of Dung which the Birds occasion which in warm weather sends forth a horrible stench.

[Jacques Cartier visited the "Isle of Aves", off the northeast coast of Newfoundland in 1534 and wrote of the numbers of these birds: "in less than half an hour we filled two boats full of them". The island was later known as Penguin Island and then as Funk Island. These birds were Great Auks (Pinguinus impennis), a now extinct species of the family Alcidae. They were the largest of the North American divers. Many of the early settlers visited these islands to take the birds for fresh meat and for bait. The slaughter of them on a large scale resulted in their being wiped out for ever. The use of the word Penguin for Great Auk was very common. By 1794 their numbers were already on the decrease. The last recorded was in 1845 or 1855. In the Letter Books of the Colonial Secretary's Office there is a letter under the date of 4 September 1794, stating that the destruction of these birds for the feathers was forbidden. It notes that "they afford a supply of food and bait and are useful in warning vessels that they are nearing the land".]

I shall now recall your attention to the Mainland of Newfoundland. Of its Soil I promiz'd to say something but this I have so blended with other matters that little can now be said of it under one general head. This I must observe—that it is one continued Rocky surface, and where Spruce Trees do not grow it is sometimes cover'd with Moss, in other places it is perfectly bare. Everywhere cultivation is deny'd by its Rocky Crusts and Swampy Ravines. To use the Plow is impossible, and yet on the borders of a Harbour or a Cove you will see Green Platts and apparent cultivatable places; but on examination you find it little better then the Moss whose Roots are immers'd in water.

There is a Noble Animal to be found in the Woods in this Country which far surpasses anything of its specie in Europe. This is a remarkable large Deer. They are very numerous, go in Herds, are of a cream Colour, and some of them so large as to vie with an English Ox. I saw a man at Placentia who assur'd me that last Fall, near Long Harbour, he killed a Deer the Forequarters of which weighed 159 pounds, which is an amazing size. They are, I am told, formed like those in Europe. With perfect Beauty they walke in great State and when a Herd of these noble Creatures are moving along in Majestic Order what a Grand Scene they exhibit. [*These are the Caribou* (*Rangerifer tarandus terraenovae*) *of which there were great herds in Newfoundland. They were hunted and killed in great numbers, particularly after the opening of the railroad, until they were in danger of extinction. They are now protected by strictly enforced Game Laws.*]

Secure in the Barrens and Woods of Newfoundland you would suppose that they were more safer from the Hunter then if they were in England, where the Staghorn forms so considerable a part of the Sportsman's establishment, but the reverse is the case. Every usefull Creature on the face of the earth has its Enemys. In Newfoundland the wild Deer has a set of foes more implacable then the Buckhound or the Huntsman, and these are the Wolves. These fierce animals hunt and destroy a great number of Deer. As soon as the Deer finds he is pursued by Wolves he immediately makes for the Lakes, in which is a safe Asylum, provided he is too nimble for the Wolves that are in the chase. As soon as he arrives at the edge of the Lake he dashes into the water and swims to some distance from the Shore. The Wolves, who are close at his heels when he takes to the Lake, durst not follow, as they never go in the water. When they see the chas'd Deer in this safe Retreat from them they set up a horrible Howl, declaring their anger and disappointment.

I have not yet told you of another potent enemy which the Deer has, who acts in *concert* with the Wolves to encompass their deaths —and this is *Man*, for on the Wolves being unable to continue the chase, here man immediately takes it up, and in this manner. The people of Newfoundland have their witts about them as well as the Inhabitants of other Lands and this instinct of the Deer's making for the water when in danger is a circumstance they are well acquainted with. They have so profited with this knowledge that the Hunters have Punts or very small Boats on the Lakes in the Interior and desert parts of the Country where the Deer are suspected to frequent. In these Punts they set for days togather, arm'd with Guns and Tomahawks, watching for the Deer which the Wolves hunt into the water. The moment the Deer makes his appearance in the water the Hunters row after him. If they perceive that he is vigorous and swimming off they discharge their Pieces at him, but if they observe that he is faint with fatigue and weary with Toil and Labour he has sustain'd by the length of the chase they row up to him and kill the poor Deluded Creature by repeated Strokes of the Tomahawk on his back. After it is killed it swims on the Surface. *[Caribou cross large lakes in migration without being chased by wolves.]*

It sometimes so happens that a Flock of Wolves will chase a Hundred Head of Deer into the water at a time. This is a fine Harvest for the Hunter, for he rows his little boat amongst them, cuts away with his Tomahawk and deals death around with all the dispatch possible. He first stabs one in the vital part, then cuts another's Backbone asunder, shoots a third in the head, but always endeavours to get a stroke in the back with his Tomahawk, for if that bone is injur'd he is so maimed that he cannot escape and they kill him afterwards at leisure when the Herd is dispers'd.

I must ask you to figure to yourself the supposed sight of seventy or eighty of these large animals swimming in a Drove and a little Boat, not larger then a Bucking Tubb, in the midst of them, killing and wounding as many as he can with his Hatchet and Gun. The man in the Boat, you must think I am sure, is in a perilous employ and your wonder must be excited that his Boat is not upset. This paves the way to my telling you that the native Indians of Newfoundland are as expert and as dexterious as any people in the world in the Management of Boats. I shall describe one of their own for your information. The Frame is made of light wood which is entirely coat'd with Skins of Seals or other Sea animals. The Boat is sometimes ten, twelve or perhaps only eight feet long. There is a complete Deck to it, except a small round opening in the middle, of width sufficient to admit the Body of one man. Into this hole the Person who is to manage the Boat gets. He then covers his Arms with the Guts of Whales, and his Body etc. with the skins of Seals; that part of his dress which is on his Body is made fast to the Skins which form the Deck and that part of his covering which is attach'd to his Neck is made fast so that with these precautions (the Skins being waterproof) no water can enter the Boat. The Indian thus equip'd, with his Paddles in his hands, his Tomahawks and his Darts made fast to the Decks, he proceeds to Sea or to range the coast in search of Game. He is not afraid of a Gale of Wind nor of a heavy Sea breaking over him for if his Boat is overset he soon rights her again and brings her into a proper position. If the Tempest is so violent as to roll his Boat over two or three times he care not a Barley corn for it for he is well initiated to the water and is so masterly in the management of his Prow that it must be a terrible contest of the Elements indeed that can discomfort him.

I could be much more diffuse on this head in regard to Canoes had I not some remembrance that you have a connection with a Gentleman who belongs to the Royal Society who has it in his power to show you one of these Boats, which is in the Repository of the Society, under the Adelphi in London. It is placed under the head of a Greenland Canoe and is exactly the same as the Canoes used by the Indians of Labrador and the Natives of the Northern Shore of Newfoundland. They all belong to the same origin.

[This description of Northern Newfoundland Indians almost certainly refers to Esquimos and not to the Beothuck Indians and this must be a description of their kayaks and harpoons.]

I have led myself considerable astray by the Subject of these Indian Canoes. Your attention must be fixed to the Scene of Action —I mean the Deer in the Lake and one of these Canoes just described, with an Indian in it. What Havock must one of these fellows make! It signifys but little getting a Cuff and being capsiz'd for he riseth without any Injury and attacks again the flying assailant; and this he will repeat with such vigour and success that a number fall by the Art and force of his Weapons.

From the circumstance of the Deer flying, as it were, to the lakes and the Wolves following them, opens a Harvest of a different kind for the Hunter. On the Wolves coming to the edge of the water they stand gazing on the Deer, who is out of their reach, and they scatter about the Banks in the hopes of their coming out. After the Hunter has dispers'd the Herd of Deer he approaches the Shore where the Wolves are, in his Boat. He fires at them as often as he sees one and generally kills some, but this is very dangerous as the Wolf is a revengefull Animal and much circumspection must be used when you quit your Boat, that you are not waylaid by them.

There are a great number of Deer killed in Newfoundland by the Gun on the Barrens. They are uncommonly shy and are endow'd with the faculty of smelling Man at some distance should he be so unfortunate as to fall on the weatherside of them when he is in search of them. It is a chance if you get a sight of them for the moment they smell you they will run at full Speed. When you get a Shot and kill one you take his Bowels out and cut his head off, his Body is cut into four Quarters, leaving the Skin on. As there is generally three or Four Hunters togather on these excursions they find means to carry the Body to the Harbour or Bay from which they came, leaving the head and his noble pair of Antling Horns behind.

The scenes of these transactions always happen a long way in the Tractless and Interior part of the Country, for the Deer will never come within several miles of the Residence of any human being. When the Hunter starts from his House, in addition to his Gun Ammunition he provides himself with a Pocket Compass without which it would be dangerous to stir two miles, a Flint and Steel to kindle a Fire with, and to these you must add Pork and Biscuits. When in the Woods the Hunter often gets a fresh Meal if he kills a Bear. The Skin is only usefull if he is a long way from Home. He eats a part of the Flesh and preserves only the Fur.

A Gentleman of St John's has made me a present of a pair of uncommon large Deer Horn. They are so long, and extend so wide, that he found it impossible to give them House room, but he had given them *Field room*, as they now lye expos'd to the open air in an enclosed Barren behind his House. How I am to get them to England I know not. I fancy I must agree with some Merchant, whose Ship is bound to London, to lash them to the Masts of his Ship, as they will not incommode him or throw any impediments in his way as to Navigation, unless it be from their extreme length which will endanger their escaping to the Sky. But if they arrive safe over Margate Flatts I shall begin to have some fears for them after they pass the Nore. When they make their appearance off the Grass Batterys at Gravesend my apprehensions will be considerable increas'd for fear my *Horns* should carry away the Ensign Staff at Tilbury Fort and the Spire of Gravesend *Church* at one and the same time. But if, by dint of Seamanship, the Captain should manage the Helm, and Tack in so scientific a manner as to steer clear of these *dangerous* obstacles to the free navigation of the Thames what must be our feelings on beholding Woolwich and the Church of Barking, beyond the Marshes, on the opposite side of the River? My Horns will never pass these objects, they are so near each other. We must therefore take my pair of Spreaders down, convey them up Barking Creek, prepare a Company of Pioneers to march them to clear the Country through Middlesex, Buckinghamshire, Oxfordshire, Worcestershire, untill they arrive at Wigmore, the place of my Nativity, where I mean to deposit this my famous Pair of Horns.

I shall resume the habit of Gravity and speak seriously on the subject of Newfoundland. On the Wild Deer and Wolves I have no further comment to make. I shall just recite the names of other Animals natural to this Country and then dismiss the Subject. Here are Bears, Beavers and Otters, Hares, Wild Catts, Musk Ratts and Foxes in great plenty. The Fur of the Bears and the Silver Fox are very valuable. When I was at Placentia I bought the Skin of a Wolf of a Hunter. It measures more then six feet in length, for it I paid fourteen Shillings.

The Inhabitants employ much of their time in winter hunting after Game. Most Familys have one of their people out. The Merchants and better sorts of Housekeepers have one Hunter out on the following conditions: Of all the Game they kill the Hunter has the Furrs to his own use and Benefit, but his Employer has the Bodys of the Animals after they are stripp'd of their Skins. For this advantage the Merchant finds the Hunter with Provisions during the Winter, but the Hunter must give the Merchant the first offer of the Furrs, and these poor fellows, being always under Obligations to them, they get for the Skin half its value. But once the Furr is in the hands of the Merchants they sell it at an enormous price or send it to Europe.

On my arrival in Newfoundland in May last I made enquirys concerning Furrs, wishing to buy as many as would make half a Dozen Muffs to give my Sisters and some Ladys I knew in England but after all Researches in St John's I could only find two Furrs of Foxes, which were valued as high as if they had been hung up for Sale in Ludgate Hill. The dearness of Furrs here is thus to be accounted for—the men who employ themselves in Hunting in Winter are generally poor fellows who have sold themselves in the Fall. After the Fishing Season is over, by a months Riotous living, they spend all the money they gained by the Summer Fishing, and after that is gone they pawn their Bodys or run into Debt, under the promize that next Season all shall be paid off—and to do them Justice I hear but few complaints on this head. One of these Poor Fellows is so situated that when he gets a Furr he cannot keep it untill the Shipping arrives from Europe, when he would get the same price which the Merchant does. Pressing necessitys and bitter want forceth him to turn it into money immediately. The Hunter, wishing to get an extra Gallon of Rum or to ingratiate himself to have some favour lets the Merchant have it at his own price. Thus when the conflux of people arrive in Newfoundland in the Spring from Europe they find all Furrs in the hands of the Merchants, who dispose of them at what terms they please.

The Indians who prowl about the Northern Shores cloathe themselves with Furrs which they get in Hunting. I have convers'd with a Hunter in Broad Cove, Conception Bay, who once fell in with a Party of Indians to the northward of Random River. His name is Smith, his Grandfather was an Adventurer to this Country. Smith and four others were upon an Expedition after Game and had penetrat'd considerable to the Northward. One morning they had descended a Barren Bluff; at its foot was a knoll or large Rock. One of them got upon this to look out, when casting his eye beneath, he saw four Indians who had not observ'd them. It was also seen that they had Offensive Weapons and had a Quantity of Furrs. Smith and his companions wished to be in possession of the Furrs, and yet they were afraid that the Indians would be a match for them; but however Right or Wrong the *Robbery* was determin'd on as the Plunder seemed considerable. They had strong hopes that by discharging a Gun and showing themselves in Battle Array with their Forelocks in their hands, on top of the Rock, that the Indians would be so affright'd as to run away. They formed the line on the edge of the Precipice and fired a Gun, immediately on which the Indians run away and left their Furrs and Cooking Vessels behind them. On this booty, Smith said, they made upwards of Twenty Pounds. At another time he fell in with a Place of Rendezvous of the Indians in the woods, but they were all absent. In the Tilt he found one Bear Skin, some Partridges and Fish. The Partridge and the skin he carry'd away, leaving the corner in which they found them empty and bare, as a Momento to the Indian to curse the faith of some perfidious white hand.

[This story probably refers to the Beothuck Indians of Newfoundland who were a distinct type of aborigine who peopled Newfoundland at the time of the arrival of John Cabot. During the first three centuries after the Cabots arrival Europeans treated them as pilferers and with injustice and cruelty. Governor Captain Hugh Palliser first made an effort to establish friendly intercourse with them and to protect them. In 1768 he sent an expedition up the Exploits River to make contact with them but none were met with. He also issued a proclamation to the effect that they should be treated with justice and brotherly kindness. There were then reckoned to be only 500 left. For the next sixty years succeeding governors tried to establish friendly relations between the settlers and the Beothucks. Proclamations were issued offering rewards to those who had friendly intercourse with them and threatening punishment to those who ill treated them; there were several expeditions made to befriend them. In 1829 a Beothuck woman named Shanawdithit died in St John's. She is believed to have been the last of the Beothucks.]

When I consider these Transactions, and reflect with what degree of impudence these storys are related in Newfoundland, I think us Britons need not express our surprize at the Arabian Bandettas which infest that tract of Land between the Persian Gulph and the Caspian Sea.

This Smith assur'd me that on a Lake near the Straits of Belle Isle, as he and a large party were reconnoitring, they met a deserted Canoe of the same kind which I have been so particular in speaking of before, that having shot some Lews which fell in the Lake, they thought of making use of the Canoe to fetch them on Shore. For this purpose he selected out the most active and expert fellow amongst them. They drew the boat into shallow water and four of them kept the Canoe erect while the man fixed himself in the Hole in the Deck. As soon as they let go the Canoe for the man to poize himself it immediately capsiz'd and turned over. The Bystanders soon righted the Boat again. The young man in the boat fixed himself in exact equilibrium, so that both sides did equally equiponderate, but the first motion he made with his Paddle the Canoe overset. Two more of the Party try'd to balance themselves in it but with no better success. Yet in this very same Canoe an Indian will pursue a Grampus and kill it at Sea, pursue his Game in it along the Coast and on the Lakes. As soon as he perceives an object he drops his Paddle, takes up his Bow and lets fly the Arrow, which he sends with such wonderful precision as very seldom to miss the mark.

There is another particular of great admiration and importance in regard to their manner of sending the Arrow. The Arrow is made fast to the Bow by very fine fibres, made of the Guts of Fish which the Indians soften in their mouths and make into threads by drawing thro their Teeth. The Arrow has plenty of play as all the fastening is veer'd out in a moment. The instant the Arrow has struck the object it sticks fast to the Game and with this thread or Line whatever they have shot is haul'd into their Canoe by it. By this sagacious dexterity whatever Game they kill they are sure of not losing. But these poor Creatures who show such a Natural Genius, such scientific minds, such a capacity for skill and knowledge and who exhibit such traits of Heroism, Science, Learning and Mechanical Art—that astonish us *overwise* Europeans, yet we deal with their Blood, buying and selling them in the same manner as we do Hoggs and Horses in Smithfield Market.

The Indians of Newfoundland are only to be found on the Northern Shore opposite to Labrador, from which Continent it is separated by the Straits of Belle Isle, which is about fourteen Leagues *[miles]* across, so that the wandering Tribes of the Esquimaux frequently viset this Coast. To no part of the shore seated on the Straits of Belle Isle do any of His Majesty's Ships viset, for here are no Settlements. The Straits are but imperfectly known. The shores on each side are barren and desolate and everything forbidding.

As I have mention'd Labrador before I will say that it is also called Esquimaux and New Britain. It is a Country twice as large as old England and joined to the mighty Continent of America in the New World. When first discover'd by Columbus, like all North America, it fell under the general denomination of Newfoundland, by which all America was known for many years after Columbus viset'd them. This name of Newfoundland is now apply'd to the Island which is the original cause of these pages. Labrador was confirmed to England by the Treaty of Utrecht, but it is of no value, unless Mountains of Ice and Provinces of Stone and Flint should become articles of Commerce to carry across the Atlantic Ocean. Then indeed there will be articles enough to employ all the Shipping of Europe, Africa and Asia. The British nor no other

Power have a single Cannon or soldier in all the Country.

[*One cannot help wondering what A. T. would say were he alive today and heard of the vast iron ore mines in Labrador and the Churchill Falls development.*

He is in error about the lack of cannon for that year. After returning from cruising the Labrador coast Captain C. Wemyss of H.M.S. Bonetta *reported on the armaments of four forts in Temple Bay and added that there were no fortifications on the coast of Labrador but at Temple Bay. His report is in the Provincial Archives. Some West Country firms were already doing business on that coast.*]

As this Island has been inhabit'd for such a number of years and was peopled by British and Irish, you frequently meet with Familys whose Grandfathers were born in Newfoundland. These are what I call the Natives. They speak English but they have a manner perculiar to themselves—the common people Lisp. When I came among them I thought some of the old Dimerips of Fashion [*Demireps*]—from the perilus [*purlieus*] of Rathbone Place and Portman Square had been transported as Convicts here, for every Out-harbour I viseted on conversing with the people, they would on answering my enquirys say— "Yes, *dat* is the way" or "O No, we *tant* do it so; but *den* we do it the other way, *tafter* we bring it home because it is *taffer*".

I believe that about ten years ago, amongst the Bon Ton, it was a fashionable qualification to Lisp. I have heard some Weomen of Rank say—"O T*hear*, p*ay* do not *thrubble yourthelf*" for "O Dear, pray do not trouble yourself". But how the common people of Newfoundland got this *accomplish'd* malady I have not yet been able to learn.

A person who has viseted the different Settlements and Out-harbours cannot but observe what numbers of Irish there are in this Country. I am bold in saying that there are four Irish to every one of any other Nation. At Placentia the people are all Irish or of Irish origin. This leads me to observe that had the Government of England been as partial to Ireland at all times as it was to itself we should long ago have seen this Island under the title of Newfoundland or *New Ireland*, for in my opinion it merits the appellation better than Labrador does that of New Britain, but it is a Limb of that pitifull system which so many Ministrys have shown towards Ireland.

In the Northern World, where Winter Reigns in all the majesty of unrelenting severity all animals change their Colour. They are generally *white* in Winter, assuming a dress similar to the then colour of the Earth, which is cover'd with Snow. In Newfoundland in Winter if you kill a Hare it is perfectly white, if you kill a Partridge *[ptarmigan]* it is perfectly white, and so of the principal part of the Animal creation in this part of the World. In this I perceive the work of something Devine.

Towards the North Pole, where are those mighty Oceans of Ice and great Continents of Frozen Snow, on these immeasurable bodys the great luminous lights shine which reflects rays that are called Aurora Borealis. The wonderfull brightness occasion'd by the rebounding of these lights from the glassy, snowy surface throws a transparency over all the surrounding Continents, which enables man to follow his occupation by night. Thus in Greenland and all the places adjacent, the Natives follow their business by night. They hunt by the Aurora Borealis when all living creatures are supposed to be asleep or at rest. The Animals, being white, are the colour of the Snow and thus those in search of them find it a difficult business to see them.

In Newfoundland I have met several sorts of Bees. There is a Black Bee which has its Nest in the Moss. There is also a Bee strongly resembling the English Bee which has its Nest in decay'd Trees in the Woods. A man, who is a Native of Annapolis, in America, tells me he follows this method to find out their retreat. In the Summertime he goes into the woods, and when he observes a Bee he lights a fire, this fire he sprinkles with Molasses and Sugar. The flames which ascend give a fragrant smell, and if there is any Bees in the environs the sweet scent is sure to attract them. If he observes any more gathering about he puts Honey on a piece of Paper and around it he scatters some Powder Blue or Fine Red Lead. The Bee, before he loads himself with Honey, is sure to smear himself with the Powder. When he flys away he looks at his Compass to observe the route which it takes, he also looks at his Watch and notes the minute it flys away. When he sees one on the Paper again with marks on him he then looks at his Watch, and from the time he has been absent he judges of the distance of the Nest. He then goes with his Compass in quest of the Nest. If he errs he repeats the fire and his observations again, but this is seldom necessary. He tells me the Honey he gets but slenderly rewards him for his trouble, and for the last four Summers he has never gone after them as he is oblig'd to go a long way in the Woods.

[There are eight species of bees native to Newfoundland. All are bumble bees. As only the queen survives the winter the store of honey is meagre.]

It is a received opinion that no poisonous animal or vegitable is to be met with in Newfoundland. The Woods are not pestered with any obnóxious Reptiles. Frogs and Toads are totally unknown. *[The green frog (Rana clamitans) has since been introduced.]*

Last Summer a Vessel which came from Dartmouth in England, in this Country found in her Hold, amongst the Coals, a Toad. The person who found it was a Fisherman who had never seen or heard of such a pleasing Reptile before. After viewing it minutely, and watching its motions with caution on its jumping the man's fears got agog and he thought it might be something incarnate, whose presence would communicate Death or some Fatallity little short. On Deck he went, where two men were, whose knowledge of a Toad was not superior to his own. They all went into the Hold togather and beheld the little creature with the same degree of surprize as a European does an Elephant. They had heard of Rattlesnakes and Reptiles which possess'd the terrible power of insinuating *death* by a poisonous quality, and in the eyes of this Animal they thought they saw Arrows of Destruction dart from them. Presently another person arriv'd who reliev'd their anxiety by explaining the propertys and nature of the Reptile. Afterwards it was taken ashore, where its presence was noised about with all the eclat and consequence that would attend the ushering in of a Tyger in a country Village in England.

I doubt not but you have heard of the Muscatoos which are so troublesome in Hott Climates. We have them in Summer here. They are very teasing. It is astonishing that an Insect so small as not to be discern'd by the eye a yard distant should have the power of *Bleeding* in so copious a manner. This little Insect will light on your hand and draw Blood in a moment, and the singularity of it is that it is a double chance if you *feel* him untill you *see* the Blood. His perforating little fang he so slightly insinuates, and so artfully wreathes through the skin, that you do not feel the incision untill he has introduc'd his poisonous Liquid and tasted your Blood. As soon as you feel him you kill him (for he is a true Blood Sucker, not quiting you in a hurry). If you rub the wound (which is natural from its tendency to Itching) you put the Poison he has instilled in a state of Fermentation and it riseth in a Blotch as big as a Hazel Nutt, and continues for a few days, when it subsides and makes a final exit. There has been many instances of people being so stung about the Eyes by them in the Woods as to have their Eyes closed up. People who go into the Woods in hott weather smear their faces over with Fatt Pork or some severe acid which the Muscatoos dislike and then they do not follow.

I have had occasion before, in more then one place, to mention how plentifull this Country is stored with Berrys. Nature has been abundantly gracious to this Country in that particular. All Countrys has something to recommend them, China has its Teas, Lapland has its Reindeer, Ireland has its Linnens and Italy its delicious Fruits. Newfoundland has its Fish, and to that I may add it has its Berrys, which are gratefull to the taste and so abounding that Horses and Cows and Goats live upon them when they are ripe. The Berry which is to be found in the greatest quantitys is Hurts, they are called Whimberrys in England. They grow in surprizing plenty under the Spruce Trees and Brambles. Partridge Berrys are form'd like a large Pea and coloured like the finest Vermillion when ripe. They make good Tarts. These are in great abundance. Here also are Stone Berrys, Gooseberrys, Raspberrys, Currants and Cranberrys, with a great number of other Berrys which produce excellent food. The whole Country abounds with them in the month of August and quantitys of Cranberrys are sent to England.*

The Berry of the Maidenhair Tea is one of the richest to be met with in this Country. Their form is that of an Ant's Egg, the colour is positively whiter than Milke and the flavour the most delicious and rich that can be conceiv'd, very strongly tasteing like the

---

* The common blueberry is *Vaccinium angustifolium Ait*, another blueberry is *V. myrtilloides* and there is also a ground whort. Partridge berries are also called lingonberries in trade; the plant is *V. Vitis-Idaea L variety minus Lodd*, and in Europe it is known as cowberry or red whortleberry. It is not clear if by stone berries A.T. means stone-containing fruits. There are several but a stone berry as such is not known. The gooseberry is *Ribes hirtellum*. The wild black currant is *R. lacustre* (*Pers.*) *Poir*, the bristly black currant is *R. glandulosum Grauer* and the skunk currant, which bears red fruit, is *R. triste Pallas*. Two species of cranberry occur—the small cranberry, commonly called marshberry (*Vaccinium Oxycoccus L.*) is plentiful; the large cranberry (*V. macrocarpon Ait*) is more localized.

Essence of Cinnamon. The flavour is more like Wintergreen. There are plenty of them in the Woods but it is very tedious to gather them as only one grows on a Spray which is often in Moss. When we laid in Aquafort I took three Boys with me into the Woods where there was great numbers of these Berrys. Altho they were in such great abundance and we had not to move more then a hundred yards, yet after two hours Labour our whole stock of Maidenhair Berrys did not amount to three half Pints.

The Maidenhair Plant is a humble but insinuating production, creeping through the Moss and just showing its head, as is afraid of the weather or some Foe. The poor people constantly make use of it. I myself have made use of it and by no means am dispos'd but to speak favourable of its pleasing flavour.

The importation of this Tea into England is prohibited and the reasons given by the common people are curious. They say that the Maidenhair Tea or the Leaves, bruis'd and eaten by the Fair Sex when pregnant occasions abortion. How far this is true I know not, but this much I am certain of, that did it grow in England my fair Country Weomen would contemplate on its virtues, and some, I am afraid would be tempted to try its prognosticated qualitys.

[The Maidenhair or Capillaire has tiny greenish flowers which appear early in Spring. Its trailing vines cover fallen trees and mossy places. It is a heath (Gaultheria hispidula (L.) Bigel). Anyone who has set out to pick the tiny white berries will appreciate A. T.'s experience and yet I remember when they were bought by the gallon for jams.]

Here is another Tea, which riseth to the size of a Shrub, and is called Indian Tea. It is used in the same manner as Maidenhair. It grows in great plenty and you may gather a hattfull in five minutes. The *Boston*'s people go ashore occasionally and stock themselves with these Teas which they use on board, as they have Sugar serv'd out to them. The Indian Tea grows on a Bush which riseth to the size of a Gooseberry Bush. Its Sprays shoot out trifoliated, pointed Leaves—the upper part green, the under part a beautifull Orange Colour. I have shaded some of the Leaves with Indian Ink, but it is an imperfect representation. *[Unfortunately this drawing is missing. Ledum or Indian Tea is found on all the Newfoundland barrens. Its use as a tea was common.]*

In Newfoundland is much business for the Botanist. The Barrens and Woods are well stocked with Flowering Shrubs and Plants which are strangers to Europe. Here are Wild Pears, Cherrys and Plumbs and a Shrub is found the Leaves of which on being infused in a small quantity of water and drank, will produce inebriation.* A variety of Tricks are played by wanton people with the infusions of this Shrub, the effects of which are as striking, although not as lasting, as the Liquid of Turkish Poppys.

I am but a sorry Botanist. I was one day ambulating the bank of a Ravine where I met with a very curious Plant. It was bulbous and had a Stalke about fifteen inches high, at the top of which was a Fruit about the size of a Walnutt, which was defended in a most extraordinary manner, for the side to which the Fruit adhered formed a Canopy over it exactly resembling an Indian umbrella. No mortal existence, I am confident, could execute a piece of Art so curious and masterly but a principal part of its singularitys are yet to come, for the Leaves, four or five of which ascend from the Root and which are formed alike the fingers of a human body, is open at the top and perfectly hollow. It grows erect and it is green. The Stamens of the plant are very numerous and fine. When I stoop'd down to look at them I found each of the fingers full of water, some contain'd a Gill at least, which appear'd to have been there for a long time. The more I survey'd this Plant the more it struck me with surprize. I was confident that those fingers were tubes given by Providence to supply its Roots with regular moisture when the heavens had ceased from raining on earth for some weeks, but I was surpriz'd to find it on the border of a Ravine, or indeed in Newfoundland, where the air is commonly moist. I was sure it was a native of a dry Soil and a Hott Climate. I broke off one of the Stalkes (which are very slender) and, on minutely looking at it, I saw that its Canopy formed a perfect and complete umbrella—its fibres as fine as the finest Silk. Holding it in my hand I utter'd a Solilquy—Surely Thou art a Native of a more gratefull Clime then this. Asia, or the sultry Plains of China claim Thy birth; Thy position and figure declare Thou art a Sojourner here and hast basely suffer'd for Thy temporary emigration.

---

* Juneberries in several species (*Amelanchier spp.*) are commonly called wild pears or chuckley pears. Sometimes chokeberries (*Pyrus arbutifolia* (*L.*) *L.f.*, *P. floribunda Lindl.* and *P. melanocarpa* (*Michx*) *Willd*) are also referred to as pears. The cherry is the red wild cherry (*Prunus pensylvanica L.f.*) The plums are probably choke cherries (*P. virginiana L.*) which are dark in colour, almost purple when ripe. The shrub with the intoxicating properties may be a myth; I have found no record of it.

When I had finish'd I fancyed to myself that the Plant answered me thus:—It is a fact that I am a native of China, where I rare my head to several feet in height. From my slender frame, my delicate Texture, my fine fibrous Canopy, its Silky surface, its spiracle Dome, its zig-zag edge, and what is of greater importance then all the shelter which I afford that valuable (although unknown) Fruit from injury untill I bring it to maturity, and from my thin, slender stalke—from the union of these plain and external propertys I can *boast* that it is *from me* that the Chinese took the hint of making umbrellas. As to your finding me here, to that I say nothing except that my specie is not confined to Asia alone. Here I remain un-noticed and unmolested, untill casual accident bent your course to this untrodden spot.

Having painted to myself this suppos'd answer I was resolv'd to make the most of the hints, and walking further I met two or three more of the same Roots, which I gather'd and carefully brought out of the Woods. I have availed myself of showing these Plants to those who I suspect likely judges, but have gained no information, so that at present I shall class them as nondescripts untill an opportunity offers to gain better information.

[*This description undoubtedly refers to the Pitcher Plant or Indian Dipper* (*Sarracenia purpurea*) *which is the floral emblem of Newfoundland. It was chosen as such by Queen Victoria and has appeared on some Newfoundland coinage. The curiously shaped leaves, which are lined with hairs, hold water and act as traps for insects. These decompose and supply the plant with nutrients not otherwise available in the bogs where the plants grow.*]

Newfoundland has a variety of Water and Land Fowl, many of which are beautifully feather'd, and were a collection in one spot the sight would be new and pleasing to the Eye of the European. Partridge is as large as the English Hen, are white in Winter, except their Red Gills. They are a desirable Bird for eating. Here are Wild Ducks and Geese of various kinds which frequent the Lakes, Eagles which frequent the inaccessible Rocks, Hawks much larger than those in England, Curlews of a delicious taste, Birds of their motions answering the British Blackbird, but their colour widely different, Thrushes which are Red, Lewes that are beautifull and larger then a Goose, with a vast variety of other Birds of different sizes. The Coast abounds with Sea Birds. Here are Sea Gulls so large that from the extremity of each wing, when extended, measures Four feet, Penguins, Hegdowns, Muirs and Tuirs, Ice Birds, Mother Carey's Chickens, Loons, Noddys, Sea Parrots, Sea Pigeons and a number of other Sea Fowl.*

St John's Harbour, 25th August, 1794. Our Frigate and the *Amphion* arriv'd in this Harbour this day, being return'd sooner then was expected, having learned at Sea that Sir James Wallace, Governor of Newfoundland, had arriv'd here from England. We found the Admiral, Sir James, who had been here a fortnight, with his Flag on board the *Monarch*. The *Andromache* Frigate and also the *Bonetta* Sloop of War are here having assisted the Admiral in convoying the Trade to this Country. They bring a complete confirmation of Lord Howe's Victory over the French Fleet *[1 June, off Brest]*, but I am sorry to find that the Duke of York and the Allies are fast losing ground in Flanders.

From the shortness of this Cruize I was unable to fulfill my promize of giving you an account of the first peopling of Newfoundland. That subject I must defer till another opportunity.

[The log records "August 26/29th—Moored in St John's Harbour.

Sir James Wallace was on the Newfoundland Station in command of the sloop Trial *in 1763, and of the* Rose (20) *in 1774. He distinguished himself in engagements off Rhode Island and New York during the American War of Independence and was knighted in 1771. In 1779 he repulsed a French attack on the Channel Islands. He was appointed in command of H.M.S.* Warrior (74) *in 1790, Colonel of the Royal Marines in 1793, and later the same year Rear Admiral of the White and Governor of Newfoundland. In 1795 he was Vice Admiral of the White. He died in 1803.]*

---

* A.T.'s hawks are probably rough-legged hawks (*Buteo lagopus s. johannis*); his curlews probably the extremely abundant Esquimo curlews (*Numenius borealis*) of that period, but the Hudsonian curlew (*N. phaeopus hudsonicus*) also occurred. The British blackbird could have been a robin (*Turdus migratorius*). The red thrushes are probably red crossbills. The sea gulls are great black-backs. Lewes may have been loons, but this makes it doubtful as to what A.T. meant by loons. Sea parrot was then the local vernacular for the puffin.

XI

There is a place call'd Titti Whitti...

[It is doubtful if any place has been so variously spelled as this. The village and cove are known today as Quidi Vidi (pronounced "kwida vida" or more commonly "kitty vitty"). By one theory the name comes from the "gut" or narrow harbour which divides the great wall of rock extending northward from St John's and was called Qui Divida. The village there is historic and efforts are being made to preserve it, the lake is the place where the Regatta is held and it has a city park beside it. Fishing is still carried on from the village. In 1794 the Chief Justice D'Ewes Coke was said to conduct a fishing business there.]

You must know that there is a singular place about Two miles from St John's call'd Titti Whitti. I have been to this place several times but on this day I made a kind of solemn viset—a sort of Pilgrimage. Had I been on the road to Mecca I am sure my thoughts could not a been better stored with Religious Sentiments, or my face cloathed with stronger marks of Gravity and Seriousness. Every Horse I saw I consider'd him as a Pensioner on the Grand Signior for having been so fortunate as to carry a Pilgrim to the Kaba, or the House of God at Mecca, and every Fisherman I saw moving I thought was a Musselman who had design to viset the Tomb of Mahomet.

There is a road to Titti Whitti through the Woods. On the left hand is the large lake of Titti Whitti, and from it runs a Stream of Water of some magnitude. Before it falls into the Sea it forms a Cascade, it then meanders through and under some Fish Flakes and falls into the Ocean in a little Cove called Titti Whitti Cove. There are Seven or Eight Houses and Fish Flakes down in a hole which forms a kind of Amphitheatre; the Rocks round it rise to a great height. There are three pieces of Cannon placed about to defend the Cove. Near me were several grassy spots where the bodys of Frenchmen were bury'd. They were slain in Battle when the Troops of that Nation got possession of this Island the War before last. The Sun was transcendently bright and the air serene and calm. I found myself weary. I sat down. The Ocean, the Lake, the Cascade, the Rivulet, the Graves, the Rocks, the Cannon, the Houses, a Gibbet (on which was suspended an unhappy object as a monitor to the living to refrain from the dreadfull act of spilling human Blood)—all these objects were press'd within view of my Eye. Around my person, and in reach of my hand, were Berrys, more then would suffice hunger. . . . As I sat thought crowd'd on thought . . . That Rivulet—I wonder how many years it has meander'd in that course, and how many Thousands of Tons of Water has it discharg'd into the Ocean? But I must not enquire. I saw it meander prettyly along, and as I thought on the word *meander* I began to ask myself how it is that our English Poets, in speaking of Purling Streams, Serpentine Waters, gentle Rivulets and little Brooks always throw in the word *Meander*. No Poet can possibly exist on the Banks of a River, or carry his Ideas with him into his Closet, and reject out of his Wallet the word *Meander*.

I have heard of a Waterfall (Niagara, in America) the noise of which is so violent that it may be heard at a distance of Fifteen miles off. The seat which I now occupy is distant about a mile from the Cascade of Titti Whitti. I have not the propertys of Dionysius at Syracuse,* yet my Ear distinctly receives the turbulent clamour of the dashing waters amongst the ponderous stones and bulky Rocks which forms the Waterfall at Titti Whitti. As I kept my eye on this Cascade I sometimes thought the waters which composed it had a great friendship for each other, for on their arrival at the precipice, and as they were hurl'd down in contrary channels, all seemed eager for a speedy union when, on their arrival below, they could fondly condole on the dangers, separations and difficultys they had just escaped from, with the flattering prospects that their friendship would never again receive so bold and dangerous an assailance.

While witnessing this Scene it brought into my mind some reflections on Friendship. This is a subject concerning which I have

---

* Dionysius of Syracuse (d. 368 BC) constructed a rock-cave in which the acoustics enabled him to hear the softest whispers of prisoners plotting in adjoining confinement.

seen a great deal wrote, but every Author I have read has totally mistaken the business and dress'd it in some garb or other perfectly distant from its origin. His heart might probe and the Springs of Friendship be found out but his delicacy must have prevented him from committing his *real* Ideas on paper. It is an indisputable fact, firmly established in my mind, that no Friendship can exist but what it has *Love* for its basis. This perhaps is one of the boldest expressions that ever came from the mouth of Man as, on a superficial view, it seems to deny the existence of Friendship. But that by no means is my sentiments. My assertions are that *no* Friendship can exist where there is no reciprocal affection.

I have often been told by an acquaintance—"That I will serve you all that lies in my power." This is a strong and forcible manner of expressing our intention, and has led me more then once to ask of the Party an explanation. All I could draw from them was—"I tell you that I will serve you all that lies in my power, anything that is compatible for me to be, no more." Now the word power, as here made use of, clearly demonstrates that he tells you to call upon his property as a common stock of your own. Was I to reply —"I have a great liking to all the Cloathes you now have on your body, come strip yourself quite naked that I may array myself in your Garments"—the person must be staggered at the request; and when I saw him hesitate I should observe—"What, do you refuse to comply with your own proposals! Is this the manner you grant every favour in your *power*?"

"Oh, is it possible you could suppose me so foolish as to give you the Robes from off my back."

"Most certainly, for that is perfectly in your *power*."

He may talke of decency, propriety, consistency and suitability; but Sir, there are the cloathes on your back, and here is your expression—All in your power. Fullfill your word or you forfeit your consistency.

Friendship is a sentence concerning which almost every individual that has ever wrote a Letter has said something about. He who writes with the mind, and not from the heart, useth it the same as Weomen do Soap. The man who flatters jingles it in the Ear of his associates for the same purpose as the Country weoman strikes the door key on an old, broken Iron Vessel when a play of young Bees are taking an Aerial journey from their native Hive. The clink she riseth with her old Key is to entice, deceive, entrap and enslave. So everytime the flatterer writes the word Friendship may be considered as synonymous to the Knell of the old Weoman's Pan. Its sound is deception and every clang it sends forth is deceit, artifice, craft and treachery.

The trading friend is what may fairly be called the *valuable* Friend, and its degrees of *warmth* are measured by that popular standard Profitt and Gain. This is by far the most numerous Class in the Republic of Friends.

If I was in Trade and see a Housekeeper who I think can lay out Fifty pounds a year with me and I reckon on Ten pounds a year profitt I avail myself of every opportunity of complimenting him on the possession of qualifications he does not possess. He, being in Trade, makes the same average of profit on me and brandishes the Truncheon of flattery so bountifully that I am almost smother'd with abilitys that never belonged to me. We soon become *warm* friends, we drink our Nib of Burton togather in Gray's Inn Lane every Sunday evening, during which time a hidden contention exists of who shall outlye the other, or rip out most of his neighbour's teeth. Having brought more Trading Friends into our Society we deal, talke, drink and associate with each other untill some horrible *whirlwind* alights on our Shops, blows the money out of the Till, carrys the Goods out of the House, shoves the Books into the Street, our Furniture into the Auction Rooms, our Servants to find new Masters and our sweet, dear selves have an end put to our friendship. Our friendly intercourse is forever blasted, each being forced into a different quarter of the Globe.

When I stick myself behind my Counter and the Man of Independent Fortune appears before me and gives his orders, with ready money, I see in him a valuable Friend. According to the texture of his disposition and the pliability of his mind I should endeavour to slip a hook to a silky chain, softly to entangle my benefactor not to forget me, who was the humble object of his esteem and regard.

I am now arrived in the Thirty-First year of my age, and for the last Ten years of my life I have kept a list of my associates, commonly called Friends. This Catalogue is curious. The names amount to 108 who were all *close* and *firm* friends—acquaintainces I mean. I accustomed myself to sketch the little Biographical anecdotes of these people—you must pardon me for substituting the word people for that of Friends. I never hope to alter my opinion of you, so be not alarmed. On looking them over, at this period, I receive no small share of entertainment. These 108 people I have been forced to divide into divisions for minute examination. I find I have had, in Ten years, four Setts of friends. The first sett stuck by me four years. With them I was a fine fellow, and they, with me, were gay blades also. Some of them got marryed, three are laid in their Graves, the rest like a disbanded Regiment are dispersed. But every one on separation, ramed his friendship under the Cuff of his Coat, in order to be ready to shake it into the Fist of the first hand he should lay hold on whose finger was graced with a Diamond Ring.

This is a singular confession on my own part as it is a fair surmize that I was as great a changeling as the most inconstant amongst us. I shall admit that novelty was the ensign continually displaying itself before my Eyes. As I arrived at maturity my mind expanded, and not seeing any striking traits of foresight in the possession of my inmates we all parted by instinct; not on the same day, the same week, the same month or the same quarter, but fell off by degrees, like the leaves of the Holly. Different winds sent us in different directions. He that was drifted on the Ramparts of the City never put his head through the Port Hole to ask he who had taken up his abode in the midst of filth and mire in the Ditch if he would mend his Quarters. If I had told all my *Dear Friends* that I was going in full speed to the river Styx I have my doubts if any one would a pulled a single hair out of my Horse's tail in endeavouring to prevent so fatal a journey. This sympathy, or fellow feeling, was reciprocal to all. I cannot account for this behaviour of this society of *Loving* friends in any other possible method then by believing that we bore towards each other no *Love*, and consequently there did not exist any friendship between us.

It will smell very strong on the Extraordinary when I observe that I have often walked the Streets of London with an acquaintance; he has met his friend, and all the notice taken was a simple Nod of the head, and yet not a year had elapsed since it was understood that they were sworn friends. It may be said that had some fatal accident befell the one the other would have expressed grief by an external sadness of countenance, but all this semblance of vexation would be deceit, exhibited for the treacherous purpose of carrying on his fraud on divers persons. I have been in the Company with well informed men who aver that the kind of friendship last described abounds in the *polished* world upon an average of Fifteen

Thousand to the solitary number one. There is Fourteen Thousand, nine hundred and ninety eight rational creatures out of every Fifteen Thousand who never knew what Friendship is.

I will give you an account of the first *friend* I myself ever had and in what a praiseworthy manner we first became acquainted. We lived togather in the same Street, our circumstances and prospects in life bore an affinity, there was a parity of years between us. Although we had lived in the same Street for near two years, yet there was no connection. If we met we passed and took no notice of each other. But on a particular evening of the summer of 1778 Chance threw us togather, and I am not ashamed to confess that in the Society we were then in something occur'd which may, with propriety, be termed vice. This laid the foundation of our acquaintance, we were constant companions for upwards of Three years and in the Town of Ludlow, where we resided, it was remarked that there did not exist two such intimate souls as we were.

During this long period my friend, I believe, deposited every secret he had with me. I, in return, lodged all my private concerns with him. My confidence was never abused, but I discover'd symptoms of a disposition which were opposite to mine. I tryed to reclaim him, but in vain. As I saw, in every other particular, a good heart I could not persuade myself to withdraw from his society, and in time I found I had fell into the very errors which I had so loudly condemned in him. Being now alike in our principles our intimacy glided along smoothly. When I reflected, which seldom happened, I thought I possessed a friend which nothing but the Grave could disjoin. But this period tells me of the sophism of my Ideas. On ranging my recollection I find that our Friendship was of the Libertine kind in which each took a pleasure in relating his Amours. These were the secrets we had to keep, and what I then thought were the Traits of Friendship. We left the Country and came to London togather, but my friend not succeeding to his mind, returned again into the Country. Our residence togather being broke a correspondence continued for some years afterwards, but our Friendship, at this moment, I believe to be as cool as the Bed of the Bird called the Swallow, who in its torpid state during the Winter, lies congealed in a frozen mass of Ice and mudd. But in retrospect I must admit this connection, in some particulars, was sacred. In Justice to this Gentleman I cannot but observe but what he has treated me, when in the Country, with great respect and attention. As I always made his House my Home I have to ask his forgiveness for this narration. It will soon be obtained when it is known that I ask not for flattery, nor shall I bestow it on others.

There is a circumstance of Sisterly Love which befell a party who were within the circle of my acquaintance that places Affection between a Brother and a Sister in so strong and uncommon a light that I shall mention the affair. It was well known at the time, being published in most of the Provincial Newspapers.

Mr Turner, a very respectable Farmer of Menaughty, near Presteign in Radnorshire, amongst a numerous Offspring, had a daughter who was marryed to the Revd Mr Griffiths of Knighton, in that County. Mr Turner, at that time, had three Sons living at home. Two of them went out one day a Shooting. By accident the Gun went off and Killed one of them on the spot. Intelligence was sent to Knighton of the fatal catastrophe, to his Sister, Mrs Griffiths. She immediately set off for Menaughty. On her arrival there she went into the Chamber where her Mother, Mrs Turner, was seting. Says she, "Is it true that my Brother is *Killed*?" "Yes," reply'd the Mother, "Your poor Brother is *dead*." To which the sister answer'd—"Then I *cannot* live."—and instantaniously dropped down and died before her afflicted Mother. This is as forcible an example of affection as can be recorded. Old Mr Turner and his Wife I know well, having been often entertained at their hospitable House at Menaughty, and I think it is an honour to them to be the Parents of a Weoman who exhibited so noble an instance of affection for her Brother. I have frequently heard young Mr Edward and Mr Thomas Turner (who are Brothers to Mrs Griffiths that died) speak of this tragical scene in the mournfull language of sorrow and grief and I avail myself of this method of thanking those two Gentlemen and all that family for the civilitys which I received at Menaughty in the months of October and November in the year 1791.

[The tombstone to John Turner in Bledffa churchyard reads: "John, son of John and Mary Turner of Menaughty in this Parish, who was killed by his gun going off accidentally January 9th 1787 in his 27th year, also his sister Ann wife of George Griffiths of Knighton, who died of grief the same day, aged 34 years."]

As I mean not to lay aside my Pen from the subject of Friendship untill I have made an observation on a charge which I have heard brought in general terms, which complaineth of the few instances in which genuine friendship is to be found, I must admit myself as one of those in the list for finding fault on this head. It strikes me that more instances of Friendship would be met with, but are prevented from ever taking place, by the following reasons: A man may have a heart susceptible of pure Friendship, he may fall in with a person who meets his fancy and humours. On him he may bestow favours and marks of good meaning and kindness, and doth not discover, till it is too late, that he has been dealing with a Knave. He withdraws himself from this connection as soon as propriety will permit, but he is more circumspectfull in his next choice, but here his caution is upset and the same disappointments attends this as arose from his first companion. Completely foiled by these two instances he resolves to keep all Mankind at a distance and a revolution takes place in his temper, and even his face—the index of the mind—assumes a new appearance. You see an underlip jutting out beyond the upper one, which is a certain sign of a morose and acid disposition; and yet this disposition was not original, but became habitual from being duped, imposed on and disappointed by these in whom he had reposed his first confidence. I find myself prevented from further examination into the principles of Friendship. I shall quit it by asserting that no *friendship* can exist if there is no Love between the two partys.

I shall take my leave of my seat in the woods and proceed to Titti Whitti the singular situation of which I have before spoken of. The day being warm, on my arrival there my nose was refreshed with a fragrant smell, which is very common in this Country, and the best of the business was that I met with the flavour in its highest perfection. Most of the Fish Rooms in Newfoundland are built so that the cutting is over the water. The Fish, which are daily brought ashore, are operated upon in the Cutting Room, when their heads and filth are thrown into the Water. [*This offal*] the Tyde carrys away. At Titti Whitti these conveniences cannot be adapted, for the Fish Rooms, Flakes etc. are upon Broken Rocks and barren spots. The Codd's Heads and Offal are thrown on dry land, where they get putrid, breed Maggots and in this putridness send forth a most offensive smell which far exceeds the Effluvia arising from a collection of the Bones of Horses in the environs of an Ivory Black Manufactory.

I went into the House of a Fisherman who said he was so poor that he asked me for Charity. The cause of his distress, he said, arose from his being so unfortunate last winter as to have a Tilt he had in the Woods and a Bed burnt, add to which in the month of June last an Island of Ice had arrived in Titti Whitti Cove, without being sent for, and torn all to rags a large Salmon Nett he had placed there for the purpose of catching Salmon. Having seen the Island of Ice there myself I doubted not his story, but all I could do for him was to give him Six Shillings for a Gallon of Essence of Spruce, which he assur'd me he could sell for Ten, was he to carry it to St John's, which was not so much as two miles. At night I return'd on board the *Boston*. The next morning the poor Fisherman brought it on board but he could not quit the Ship untill he had solicited Charity from every Gentleman belonging to the *Boston*.

XII

Anecdotes and a Little History

At Sea, 9th September, 1794. Cape Spear distant 113 Leagues.

[*The log records "At noon Cape Spear distant SW 4 or 5 leagues".*]

We left the Harbour of St John's in company with the *Amphion* Frigate on Saturday the 30th August. We are to cruize about Longitude 42–8 examining such American Ships as we meet with. Yesterday we spoke the *Jay*, from New York to Cork,* and this morning we boarded a Ship from Baltimore to Rotterdam. From her we got some American Newspapers which are full of criticism on Lord Howe's Public Letter to the Admiralty on his Victory over the French Fleet. They are not a little impudent in their remarks, for they say that by His Lordship's Dispatches they must infer that his Admirals fought in the Tops, and conclude by saying that Lord Howe is better qualify'd for fighting then writing. But I am afraid they are not well pleased at His Lordship's success.

The Latitude we are now in is about the same we were cruizing in a month ago. From the circumstances of our falling in with a number of American Vessels and getting Newspapers from them we used, jocosely, to call these Latitudes our Coffee Room—here we come to read the News. Very few Vessels we boarded from Europe but what gave us Newspapers. As soon as a Sail was discover'd the cry on the Quarter Deck was "I see a Newsman Two Points to our Larboard Beam, I wonder if she is from Europe or America". After she had been boarded and the Officer return'd, the Buzz of "What News?" would be as violent on Deck for some minutes as the enquires "What Intelligence?" on the first appearance of a Gazette Extraordinary.

---

* According to *Lloyd's Register of Shipping* for 1793, the home port of the *Jay* was Boston. She was owned by nine Americans and a merchant of Canton, China, and managed by Stoker and Co., probably of Boston.

St John's Harbour, October 3rd.
We arrived in this harbour yesterday with our consort the *Amphion* Frigate. On Thursday the 25th September, on the Banks, we met a tremendous Gale of Wind which made us seek for shelter. We arrived off Aquafort Harbour the next day but the Wind being against us we could not get in, but we had better success at Capelin Bay, into which Harbour we got the same afternoon. The *Boston* had been at anchor in this Harbour once before this summer so that the environs of this place are well known to me. However on Saturday the 27th of September I had a cruize to myself around this Bay. In my perambulations I met with a few Mushrooms on the borders of a Bog, which was an article I had been told was never found in Newfoundland.

The only scene I met with worth mentioning occur'd at a House in the Woods, kept by an Irishman of the name of Poor, a man of about 40, who had marry'd a young wife, very fair and beautifull. They had four children, were tolerably well-to-do in the world and seemed a happy Couple. In this House I domesticated myself for some hours. The chiefe complaint of the Weoman was that her Fowls and Ducks laid their Eggs in the woods, then sat upon them, and before the Young Brood had sufficient strength to travel home after the old ones, they all died of fatigue in the march, or else the Wild Catts found their nest and destroy'd old and young togather. So heavy were her complaints on this head that she said her Geese, Cows, Horses, Ducks, Goats and Chickens would all get into the woods for a week and she would never be able to find one. She said that a few days ago she sent her eldest children after them and they got themselves lost and were a whole night in the Woods exposed to the Foggs. In the morning they were brought home in a Boat from Cape Broyle Harbour, to the head of which place they had straggled. It is a common thing at this season of the year for Horses, Cows etc. to stray into the Woods for they meet a continual feast of the most luxurious Berrys and will eat them eagerly and live entirely on them. Partridges and Deer or any Wild Bird or Animal that is taken at this season of the year are fat and plump by reason that they all live on Berrys.

During our stay at Capelin Bay I was at Ferryland. I viset'd my old acquaintances there but have nothing new to relate, only that I poked my Nose into a Hutt, a good Weoman of which told me that in her early days she had been much used to the Bon Ton, altho now the Wife of a Newfoundland Codd Hauler, having lived with a family of Rank in Hanover Square. Changing the East End of the Town for the West she there became acquainted with a Sailor, who she marry'd and came to this land of Frost and Fish, prefering the Society of the man she loved to the company of the Man of Fashion who would lead her to pertake of the pleasures of the Opera House and taste the fragrance of Kensington Gardens, amidst the Promenade there in Summer time. She told me that about a month ago she lost Four Sheep, which was all her stock, and she suppos'd at the time that they had stray'd into the Woods. A few days ago a person in Ferryland had opened a Potato Cellar, the door of which was only pushed to, and there found her four Sheep starved to death. This Cellar had for some time been empty and the door was left to play with the Wind. When it was open the Sheep went in, accident shut the door and enclos'd them in the Tomb of death.

This circumstance puts me in mind of a transaction in some particular similar, which occur'd in England a few years ago, and is shortly this: In the Isle of Sheepy, in the County of Kent, is a small Island containing Four or Five Houses. It is called the Isle of Emley. It also has a Chapel, the Minister of which has Forty pounds a year. The frequency of the performance of Divine Worship may be guessed at when you are told that in the Chapel an Ox was not only found dead but was in a state of putrefaction. He got in and was enclosed under the same circumstances as the Sheep, but what was the more laughable part of the story was that the Clergyman (from Faversham), Clerk and Congregation all arriv'd at the Chapel togather, each ignorant of the despoiling carcase which lay within. When the door was thrown open and the corrupted mass was exhibited that, and the strong smell which must have escaped through the door place, must put the Parson and his Flock into a situation easier understood then described. It was a matter that made no little noise, at that time, in that part of Kent.

[log, 29–30 September: At anchor in Capilin Bay; 1 October, "Standing in for Bay of Bulls"; 3 October–2 November, "Moored in St John's Harbour".]

We left Capelin Bay in the morning of the first of October and anchor'd the same evening in the Bay of Bulls. That Bay we left the next morning, and the same afternoon arriv'd at our present moorings. We shall remain in this Harbour untill our return to Europe, during which time I shall give you detached scraps and little anecdotes, as they occur, without date or order.

I was walking amongst the Houses the other day when an alarm was given of Fire. I stopped at the House and the Fire issued above the Chimney. A Ladder was placed against the House and another so put as to accelerate a passage to the Chimney. A Flock of Geese was near the door, a man runs and lays hold of a Goose, another man ceazes a second Goose, with which they both run up to the Chimney and threw the Two live Geese down it, one after the other. This was, to me, a new and singular method of putting out a Fire in a Chimney; but by putting the Goose in with her Belly downwards she would keep a great fluttering with her wings and knock all the sut down before her. The Fire was put out by the Two Geese. The first that descended came down scortched and nearly Black, and was afterwards killed to ease her of her pain. The Second Goose that came down I believe will outlive this adventure as she was turned adrift again, but her old Mates did not congratulate her with their usual cheerings on her joining them, but hissed her as if she had been a stranger. Her colour was much alter'd and her smell, I presume was not very fragrant.

I sat in company the other evening with a poor but merry Fellow who told me that a Brother of his had been killed in the Woods last Winter, and as it tends to show the extreme severity of the Climate here I shall introduce the anecdote.

When the face of nature was cloathed with Snow in December last, two men of the names of Lacey and Connor went into the Woods to cut wood. It froze so strong that Icicles were form'd by the water that dropped from the Eyes and Nose. Lacey was bending his head down near to the Stick when Connor was cutting. Unhappyly the Ax missed the Stick, struck the frozen Snow, rebounded and fatally hit the neck of Lacey. This sever'd his head from his body. But Connor immediately laid hold of the decapitated head, placed it on the body again, which *froze* and united the body and head, and for the present saved Lacey's life. After this Lacey and Connor carry'd their load of Wood to St John's. Unfortunately Lacey went into a warm room where there was a good fire and, while he was relating the narrow escape he had had from death in the morning, he stooped over the fire to take some Fish out of a

Kettle which was boiling. In performing this office his head fell off (the warmth having thawed his neck), it fell into the Pott and his Trunk tumbled backward on the floor, and both perish'd at the same *moment*. . . . So much for Master Lacey!

In the same society, the same evening, a Taylor told me that in severe winterly weather he once heated his Iron Red Hott and, in carrying it across the Path to a Neighbour's House to press his Coat, one of his fingers got Frost burnt. *[The Water Street and Duckworth Street of today were then known as Lower and Upper Path.]*

Speaking of the method of putting out fires in Chimneys a few lines back, I forgot to tell you what kinds of beings they are here which perform the office of Chimney Sweep. You may laugh, but it is a Goose which acts the part of the Chimney Sweep here. The Goose is carry'd up and let down as often as necessity requires. By the flapping and fluttering of her wings, I am told, she doth it to perfection.

Doctors (Surgeons and Apothecarys) have a custom here which destroys that little dignity we sometimes find attached to the Sons of Galen. It is a rule with them for to give you Medicines for the Fishing or Summer Season. Ill or well the money must be paid at the Fall of the year. You enter your name on the Doctor's book on arrival and, if he doth not see you untill the close of the year, you pay all the same. If you propose to stop all the year round you must pay 10/– under the same regulation as the first. Having made these premizes, I have to mention that part of the business which reflects disgrace on these disciples of Warwick Lane. As soon as a Vessel appears in the offing the Doctors get into their Boats and scamper for the Vessel as fast as they can. He that gets first on board has the best chance to have most patients that is putting names in the Book. The bustle and chasing which these Blisterers and Purgers sometime get into exceeds the Tumult and Confusion occasion'd by an opposition of Pilot Boats when a Fleet of Ships appears off a Harbour they wish to enter, whose access is difficult. About three years ago their prices were 2/6d and 5/–, but now it is 5/– and 10/–.

In a former part of these Sheets I have told you that in the craggy and rugged precipices of these shores Eagles are to be found. A man in St John's has four of them, the produce of two nests which he took last Summer. He has brought them here for sale, from Fortune Bay. They are very large Birds, much bigger then those I have seen in the Tower of London. The fellow who has possession of them tells me a very comical story of an Eagle, many of which are often seen in the environs of the House. His Wife was frying Pancakes one day. She was a remarkable hand in turning them cleverly, so much so that she would toss a Pancake out of the Frying Pan, up the Chimney, and catch the same Pancake, fair and flat in the Pan, *outside* the House. Two men came in while she was at this business. They wagered with each other a trifling sum, concerning the possibility of this piece of dexterity in the Weoman, who promized on her part to exert her best abilitys. She Put the Batter in the Pan and fry'd it brown, she then gave it the *Grand Toss*—and fairly out of the Chimney it went. She ran on the *outside* of the House to catch the Pancake, but what was her surprize, for instead of finding the cake descending, it was ascending in the Claws of an Eagle! It seems strange, but it was told me as a fact. It may be believed when you are inform'd that the Chimneys in this Country are very wide, and also the Eagle, in his aerial flight over the focus of the Chimney, might be drawn down by the smell to the entrance of the Tube from whence the gratefull flavour issued.

I now come to a part of my promize, in the performance of which I am confident I shall not be satisfy'd with my own work; but as I never meant to give a complete History of Newfoundland, you must be content with what I have before given and take what follows as gleanings. I shall only attempt to give you the names of a few persons who have been Governors of this Island and relate the manner of its first Colonization and Discovery.

The Island of Newfoundland was discover'd by Cabot, a native of England, in the Reign of Henry the Seventh in 1498. Cabot is also called a Venetian, but this mistake ariseth from the circumstances of his being in the employ of that people, who at that time engross'd a very considerable share of the Merchandize of the East Indias.

The year 1500 is to be consider'd as the centre of Discoverys. This was soon after the finding out of the New World. There was not a Maritime Nation in Europe but what had Ships out, under hope of their revealing on their return Empires of Gold and Oceans of Pearls. Amongst these the Portuguese had an Adventurer out in the year 1500 who pretended to discover this Island. He landed in a Cove in Conception Bay. The Bay he named Conception, as Conception is the Mother of all things, and the Cove at which he landed he called Portugal Cove, in honour of his Country. From this person the Portuguese, or rather I may say the Spaniards, derive a claim to this Country; for at that time Portugal was subject to Spain, and was not acknowledged a free Nation untill the year 1668.

[In 1500 Emmanuel of Portugal commissioned Gasper de Cortereal to discover Baccalaos, which Cabot had previously coasted. He accordingly visited the island and gave Conception Bay the name it bears.]

The first Settlement that was made in this Island was at Placentia, by a Spaniard of the City of Tolosa, the Capital of the District of Guipuscoa, in the Province of Biscay, in Spain. He called it Placentia or Placencia, from the City of Placenzia, as in that City the Antients placed the Elysian Fields, its neighbourhood being full of odiferous flowers, Orange and Citron Groves, with every luxury that could please the Eye and satiate the heart. But the reason which gave birth to the name of Placentia in Newfoundland was of a nature far different to any of these qualifications. Its environs enjoy none of these recommendations, but its situation had merit, for on the arrival of the Spaniards they found the native Indians very troublesome; they made continual inroads upon them wherever they fixed their Residence. After they had ranged the Coast for some length they arrived at the spot now called Placentia. On surveying the place they found it to have a good Road and a perfect secure Harbour for Shipping, but what had more weight in rendering it to their notice was that it was surrounded by water, except where it was joined to the Mainland by a sandy beach, which was very narrow. This water, they conceiv'd, would serve as a Barricade against the Indians, and protect them from the sudden assaults of a Savage people. Therefore at this place they had a kind of Settlement which was only tenanted during the Summer, for at the Fall of the year they sailed back to their own Country.

The name Biscayne or Biscayneers and Guispusians are terms very common at the present period in Newfoundland. Their notoriety ariseth from the Tolosa Merchant who collected his followers from the Province of Biscay and the District of Guipuscoa. I have heard the word Biscayneer used by way of reproach. It means little less then a Pirate. For some years after Columbus discover'd this quarter of the Globe the Atlantic swarmed with Robbers and that people that were the most numerous had some ignominous name given them. But on the Piracys commit'd on these Shores I shall speak hereafter.

The Epoch I am now alluding to is about 1556, when there was so close a connection between Spain and England, by the marriage of our Queen Mary to Phillip the Second of Spain. This union of Crowned Heads, and the great partiality Mary had for Roman Catholicks induc'd her to show great favour to the subjects of Phillip, and this might not be a bad policy for at this time Spain was a most powerfull Crown, being in possession of the New World, the Netherlands and vast and valuable Countrys.

Altho England claimed Newfoundland by right of discovery yet from its Barren aspects and winterly Climate it was held of so little value that neare a hundred years elapsed before any serious thoughts of a British Settlement there were entertained. When it did take place it arose from the quarrel of Elizabeth of England and Phillip of Spain. In the Reign of Mary she permitted the Spaniards and the Hollanders (then subject to Spain) to catch and cure Fish in Newfoundland. The French also viset'd these Shores and it was common, at this period, for the English, French, Spaniards and Dutch to have their Vessels in the same Harbour and also to have their Fish Flakes mingled one with the other. But on the death of Mary a great change took place in Newfoundland, although trifling when compared to the effects it produced in Europe.

After Phillip had lost his wife he paid address to her Sister Elizabeth, but the Two Sovereigns were set by the Ears togather, and from it followed a War of Love. The consequences were extraordinary and the events well known. As to Newfoundland, in 1587 Her Majesty Queen Elizabeth granted a Charter of it to Sir Humphrey Gilbert, this being the first Chartered Grant of the Island. Sir Gilbert sent out some Adventurers, who return'd in the year 1581, but their report was not very flattering. However the rumours from other quarters being more promizing—particularly from the Straits and the Portuguese and Spanish Shores where the Fish were brought for Sale. These accounts stated that Fish were so plentifull on the Banks and Shores of Newfoundland that a Quintal *[100 pounds]* might be taken in Ten Minutes, with a Crooked piece of Wire.

In consequence of this information Sir Gilbert resolved to make a Voyage to Newfoundland himself and by his presence inform and gain that personal intelligence which is necessary to complete a perfect knowledge of the place as to its value and worth to the Parent State. Accordingly we find that he arriv'd in the Bay of St John's, now called St John's Harbor, in June 1583. He immediately published a Manifesto, in Her Majesty's Name, declaring the Gracious Goodness of the Queen in sending him out to so distant a place, solely for their future benefit. He enjoy'd all to be peaceable, and stated that all Foreigners would be individually protected.

He brought with him Her Majesty's Arms, curiously carved. These he set on a Pillar of Wood, which he erected at the landing Place in the Settlement of St John's. Before the Pillar he convened the Inhabitants and, after he had the persons assembl'd, they marched round the Wooden Column in solemn Procession, the Flag of England being display'd under the discharge of Guns. Sir Humphrey took possession of the Country in Her Majesty's name. He here deliver'd a Speech to the People, the same in purport as his Proclamation, and concluded his Oration by wishing that England might, to the end of Time, be as able to protect her Colonys as she was at that period, and that Britain would act the part of a Parent to Newfoundland. So, in return, he hoped that this infant Country would be an obedient and dutifull child.

In the year 1610 a Mr John Guy acted as a kind of Governor, he being Deputized by the Earl of Northampton and Sir Francis Bacon, who obtained the Second Charter of this Country. But these persons were soon out of conceit of their New Territory.

[John guy of Bristol was granted a charter to colonize Newfoundland on 27 April 1610, and with a considerable number of colonists settled on the north shore of Conception Bay. The settlement continued for four or five years in a fairly prosperous condition, after which Guy and some of the colonists returned to England. Those who remained moved to other localities. The failure was probably due to attacks from pirates.]

Soon afterwards Sir George Calvert was in possession of the Third Charter granting the Country to individuals. He was not long in discovering the fertile Country which now forms the Province of Maryland in America and the barren and forbidding face of things in Newfoundland. He carry'd all his attentions from this place to America, where he planted a Colony which flourished to such a degree that a County bears the name of Calvert, in the West Division of the Province of Maryland. Sir George Calvert was the original Grantee of that Province, on his death Lord Baltimore, as the heir to Sir George, became possess'd of all his inheritance in Newfoundland and America. But His Lordship's mind run all on America. In it he spent his time and embark'd all his Fortune. He extended, in a most extraordinary degree, the Settlements made by his Ancesters by bringing Roman Catholicks from Ireland and England so as to people a space of Country in Length 140 Miles and in Breadth 137 Miles. To it he gave the name of Maryland, in Honour of Mary, the Daughter of Henry the Fourth of France, who was King Charles's Wife. Lord Baltimore's vast success in America made him pay no kind of attention to his Lawfull Inheritance in Newfoundland. It was generally understood that he set no more value on it then he did on an Island of Ice.

It must be here noticed that *[the second]* Lord Baltimore was a strong favourite of Charles the First, and on the death of that King on the Scaffold, he lost *all* in America and Newfoundland; but at the Restoration he was reinstated in all his Possessions except only that he had but a part of Newfoundland Chartered to him, but this part containeth all the Best Bays and Harbours in the Island. This Land which was Granted him forms a Peninsulated space as Chappel Harbour, in Trinity Bay, on the Northern Shore and Come by Chance, in Placentia Bay nearly meet, and are separated from the Continental part of the Island by a neck of Land little more then Six miles across. *[The distance between the two bays is actually little more than a mile and a half.]*

The Chartered part of the Island he termed Avalon, from Joseph of Arithemea who was sent to establish the Gospel in England. He laid the foundation of the Christian faith at Avalon, afterwards written Inisartren, but now Glastonbury, in Somersetshire, where Joseph died and was bury'd. Inas, King of the West Saxons built the Great Abbey at Glastonbury, over the Tomb or Cell where the precious relicks of Joseph lay. When I was at Ferryland I questioned the Clergyman of that place (The Revd Mr Cole) as to the origin of the name of Avalon as apply'd to that part of Newfoundland. He told me that Lord Baltimore called it Avalon from an Estate he had in England which bore that appellation. But from the apparent embarrassment of the Rev'd Gentleman before he answer'd me I am confident he was not inform'd on the Subject, but wished to answer me some reason.

The Fourth Charter of Newfoundland was Granted, in 1620, to the Marquis of Hamilton, the Earl of Pembroke, Lord Holland and Sir David Kirke. *[Sir David Kirke went as Governor and lived at Ferryland in the house built by Lord Baltimore.*

Sir George Calvert, afterwards Lord Baltimore, chose Ferryland as the site of his colony and he built a fine mansion in which he resided. He took great care in selecting suitable colonists and he encouraged them to be industrious. He built fortifications for their protection and large storehouses and he expended a great deal of money on the settlement. It prospered for a time but the soil around Ferryland was not fertile, there were repeated raids from the French and he had no jurisdiction over visiting ship fishermen. He returned to England and got a grant of what is now Maryland in the United States. He died in 1632 but a new patent was issued to his son. Most of the colonists he brought to Newfoundland remained as residents.]

I shall now speak about the year 1650, which time Newfoundland was a continual scene of Rapine and Robberys. No Law was to be met with, and altho a Court was establish'd in St John's yet it was regarded no more then a Thiefe does a Pound for confining strayed Cattle. A few years afterwards, when the value of America became more known and the consequence of the New World expanded more largely, the discontented of all nations flocked to these parts before any regular system of Government could be adapted so as to inflict Punishment, in a speedy manner, on offenders. Piracys were as numerous as the hours of the day. The History of Newfoundland and America about this date is connected as far as it relates to the stealing and smuggling of men, and the Asylum each Country afforded to Pirates and Sea Robbers.

At this early time and infancy of the Newfoundland Fisherys it was customary for the Adventurers to arrive in the Spring and to return to England in the Fall of the year. The leading persons in the Trade brought from England Husbandmen, and any things that was healthy and strong. They paid them a stipulate price for the Fishing Season. Vessels from America were always in the Harbours of Newfoundland at the close of the Fishing Season. The Masters of these avail'd themselves of all opportunitys to ingratiate their persons with the Fishing people from Britain, and would prevail on numbers to go to America, under the Promize of Lands and very high Wages. Several of these people who went to America, instead of going back to Britain, had left a Wife and Children in England. These became chargeable to the Parish and these complaints accumulating every year induced the Parliament to pass an Act Inflicting a Penalty on the Master of every Vessel who was found carrying Men from Newfoundland to America.

We now draw to the year 1670, when we find that the Act passed by the British Legislature did not prevent the inveigling of men from this Country to New England or America. It was now common and notorious as ever. From Conception Bay a single Ship sailed with neare 200 men in her—but they were all *headed up,* and stowed away *in Casks.* Other Harbours and Bays were not behind in this clandestine intercourse. The reason given by the Americans for this conduct was that on the Shores Fish abound in great abundance, but men there paid more attention to Agriculture then Fishery so of course hands were not easily procur'd. Out of all these poor people that went to America, under these circumstances, it may be fairly infer'd that some were disappointed. It is a lamentable fact, but an undisputed one, that several of these Fellows were afterwards to be cruel and infamous Pirates.

1674 was a period which rung with complaints in this Island. The Planters, as they were called, grew jealous of the Fishermen and discord and contention was evident in every little Settlement. Very heavy murmurs and severe accusations were sent Home in a Petition, which prayed the King not to appoint a Governor. It stated that they were of little use, for on their arrival from Europe they stopped here only a few weeks and were ignorant of the Nature of the Fisherys and the business of the Country, that they resided intirely at St John's and sent inferior Officers to administer Justice at the Outharbours, that the persons so deputised were needy characters without property and very illiterate, that when Two opponents came before these men to seek recompense and Justice he who before had given the most Dollars or a Quintal of Fish, was sure to have satisfaction awarded him.

[*In reality the planters were suffering from the very repressive policy of the British Government who were influenced by the West of England Merchants and the shipowners engaged in the Newfoundland fishery. They were opposed to the appointment of any civil or permanent Magistrate or any Governor of the Island. The planters petitioned against the power of the Fishing Admirals.]*

In 1676 a Mr Dowling, a leading Merchant of St John's procured a Petition which had a number of signatures to it, to be sent home. This complained of the irregularitys commit'd in Summer time by the Adventurers and Fishermen in the Out-harbours, who robbed the Fish Rooms and had ruined many people, and that there was no Law to be got from the great distance of some of the Out-harbours from St John's. It was common for people to be plundered and put up with depredations rather then put themselves to the expense and loss of time in coming to complaine to the Chiefe Court of the Island, where redress was very doubtfull. It frequently happened that a man lost a part of his Salted Fish, and if by chance he learned where they were deposited, to go and ask the Robber who had stolen them to let him have some of the Fish again.

[John Downing, the son of a former governor, was elected by the inhabitants to defend their rights and so eloquent were his petitions that many of the West Country towns gave the settlers their support. The Lords of Trade sent out Sir John Berry, a naval officer, with orders to drive out all the fishermen and burn their dwellings. This was not strictly carried out as he and others came forward with arguments on behalf of the planters. In 1677 masters and seamen were ordered to cease violence against the settlers but further emigration to Newfoundland was forbidden.]

A year or Two before this I find that the Native Indians were very troublesome. They came in a body to Placentia and plunder'd the French, who at this time resided there. They also viset'd the English in Conception Bay and other places and much disturbed the Settlers. This, with the dissentions amongst the Fishermen, and other matters, was the cause of it being debated in the Council at Home of the propriety of totally abandoning the Island. It was observed that Sir John Berry was soon expected in England. The Council awaited for his arrival. On being examined he gave it as his opinion that the Settlement ought to be encouraged. From this time we find many Acts passed by the British Parliament for the better regulating of Newfoundland. One of these Acts is very ambiguous in one particular, and for my own part I do not understand its meaning. It says that no person shall inhabit within Six miles of the Shore. Now every person that has been to this Country knows that the Shores only are inhabited and that in few places, except St John's, is there a House to be met with half a mile from the Water's edge. *[This was one of the rules which were added to the old Western Charter when it was reaffirmed in 1675. The object was to discourage settlers.]*

I have already mentioned some of the circumstances with regard to fortifying some part of this Island. In addition to the works at St John's, in Queen Anne's Reign a Military Force was kept up here, and the following instance will show how abuses of every kind were practized in Newfoundland. About this period a Major Lloyd was Commandant of the Troops stationed here. This man used to let out his Soldiers to go afishing for others or for himself, when he allow'd them for their own Share One Eighth, taking all the rest for his own use. This person was try'd and was convict'd of this charge and most of his Officials were implicated in the Business.

[Major Lloyd was appointed Commander of the forces in Newfoundland in 1703, he had come to Newfoundland in 1700 as paymaster. Prowse described his character as typical of the military roué of that day—unprincipled, reckless yet as valiant a soldier as ever sought "the bubble reputation at the cannon's mouth". In 1705 complaints were brought against him to the Lords Commissioners for Trade and Plantations. These included the charges that he had devised base means to get money and that £660 of Queen's money to pay soldiers had been converted into trade. The charges were substantiated and he was suspended by petition of his own soldiers in 1704 but held a second term of office from 1705–08. On his return he told the planters that it had cost him a large sum of money to obtain reappointment and he meant to have it out of them. He was taken prisoner by the French when they took St John's in 1708, and was sent to France where he met a violent end.]

Amongst the regulations for the better administration of Justice in the Outharbours, and also for the encouragement of the Fishery, it was ordained that the Master of every Vessel from the British Dominions in Europe who should arrive first, after the 25th of March, in any Harbour, Bay, Creek or Cove in Newfoundland should, for that Season, be Admiral of the said Harbour, Bay, Creek or Cove. The Master of the Vessel which arrived second was the Vice Admiral, and the Master of the Third Vessel which arriv'd in the same Bay etc. was the Rear Admiral for the Season. This plan was adopt'd by the Government in consequence of the complaints of the want of Justice in the distant Settlements. To these Admirals they gave the power which had some semblance to the First State of Mankind. On the arrival of the Vessel in the Harbour, Bay etc. the Master was declar'd Admiral. He took possession of the best Fishing Room, which is annually assigned for the Admiral's use and has some little advantages of a pecunary nature. In his official capacity the original intent was that he should arbitrate between partys and settle petty differences. The use of the Fishing Room was esteem'd as sufficient Reward for his labour. These methods were much approved on at the time as it kept people from putting themselves to expense and loss of time in seeking redress at the distant Settlement of St John's. The Admiral, as I before stated, was a kind of Church Warden or Head Constable, and the Vice Admiral and Rear Admiral might be consider'd in the light of Constables. When this trio of Admirals were assembled, and the Complainants before them, the Judges and Plaintiff, Defendants and Evidence, being equal in Rank, a free communication was likely to take place between them. If *all* were disposed to an amicable adjustment their friendship and good neighbourhood was soon restored again.

The Rear Admiral has the Appellation of Lady. The functions of the Admiral is very great if he goes to Sea a Banking, he having Command of all the Vessels which are employ'd on the Grand Bank a Fishing. But this honor is perfectly nominal and the title Admiral is frequently derided and laughed at. This creation of Admirals was passed into Law in 1698 and the Preamble of the Act stateth—That the Fisherys of Newfoundland is valuable, for in return for the Fish we get Oil, Plate, Wine, Iron, Wool and other Commoditys, which are very useful to our Manufactory at Home.—The places from which these returns came was within and without the Straits and other Catholic Countrys, which parts, at this day, are the grand consumers of Newfoundland Fish.

[In 1698 the enactments of the Star Chamber were reaffirmed and extended in an Act which was passed by the British Parliament. The appointment of the Fishing Admirals, who were servants of the West Country merchants, obstructed all improvement in the country.]

By the Act of Parliament of which I am now speaking, the Admirals were required to keep a Journal, and in it to enter every Transaction that occur'd within his Harbour, as also the number of Vessels, Boats and Fishermen employ'd; but the Statute, in this particular, could never but partially be comply'd with for in the year 1728 out of all the Bays, Harbours, Creeks and Coves in Newfoundland only Four Admirals were to be found that could write. This seems extraordinary and I can but wonder how such illiterate men were trusted with the care of a Valuable Vessel to Navigate her across the Atlantic Ocean.

Her Majesty Queen Anne, in the Sixth Year of her Reign, passed an Act of high favor and indulgence to the New World, for it said that it should not be Lawfull for her Naval Officers to press the Seamen from Private Ships in America or Newfoundland, nor neither should they press persons who were on shores at these places. This Act was meant as a fostering Statute in assisting the Colonization of America. As, at the time, England was engaged in an extensive Continental War, and every man she left there promoted her contracting the Sinews of War in a double degree, as the event of their insurrection and their finally gaining their Independency in 1783 has fully shown, this Statute of Arms is now repealed.

In 1774 an Act was passed for the better encouragement of the Newfoundland Fishery. The Act declared that after the 1st of January, 1776, every Twenty-Five Vessels that should, at two trips to the Grand Banks, catch and bring to Newfoundland Twenty Thousand Fish, by tale or upwards, that each of these Vessels should receive from the Government the sum of Forty Pounds. That the succeeding one hundred Vessels which arriv'd afterwards at Newfoundland having catched at Two trips Twenty Thousand Fish, that each of these Vessels shall be entitled to the sum of Twenty pounds from the Government. That the following one hundred Vessels which should next arrive in succession, having catched Twenty Thousand Fish on the Grand Banks, at two trips, should be entitled to Ten pounds from the Government.

The same Act awarded Five Hundred pounds to the First Vessel that should sail from England and return with the produce of one Whale or Whales, killed on the Coast of the Island of Newfoundland or Labrador Shore, Four hundred pounds to the Second, Three hundred pounds to the Third, Two hundred pounds to the Fourth and one hundred pounds to the Fifth. But this Whale Fishery has not been very flattering to the projectors of the Bill, for altho the number of Whales are in the Seas, yet their quality is of so inferior a nature that few Masters of the Vessels chuse to go after them. During my stay in this Island I have not conversed with a single

Merchant whose knowledge leads him to say that there is a Vessel employ'd in this Whale Fishery this season.

[*English whalers, at this time, were frequently pursued by privateers and the French frigates kept a constant watch for them between Spitzbergen and Newfoundland.*]

There is an Act of Parliament in force which inflicts a Penalty of Two Hundred pounds on the Master of every Vessel who is found carrying Fishermen as passengers from Newfoundland to America. It is lawfull for the employer of every Fisherman to retain or keep back from the Wages of every Fisherman he employs the sum of Forty Shillings, which money is to secure the return of every Fisherman to England. Every Master who discharges a man, from caprice, or without just cause, is liable to forfeit Ten Pounds; and further if any Master becomes insolvent the Servants he has employ'd in the Fisherys have a prior claim to the Oil, Blubber and Fish to satisfy their Wages, before the demands of the other Claimant can be attended to.

Before the Law was administer'd so regular as it is at present in Newfoundland it was common for a Boat's Crew to be Fishing all Summer for a Master who supply'd them with a few necessarys, the men letting their Wages remain untill the Season was over. At this crisis the person who owed the Master a few Dollars would strip the Flakes of all the Fish, carry away the Oil and empty his Fishing Room of all its contents, leaving the Fishermen to bemoan their case, there being nothing left to pay them with, and every Fish which they themselves had taken stolen from under their Noses. Or perhaps a man would owe a few dollars to different people, these would carry away the Fish from off the Flakes, one after the other. Sometimes the Fisherman who catched the Fish would stop them, then a Riot would ensue and blood was often spilt; always a deal of Fish was lost and spoilt. Instances have occur'd where the contents of a Fish Flake have been thrown into the Sea in the Fray. When the Fish once got in the possession of the Creditor, even if he had Five times the value of his debt, nothing but downright force and violence could restore any part of it again.

I have before stated that every Master who brings a Servant or Fisherman from England has a right to retain Forty Shillings of his wages to enable him to return to England. This Law was made for the purpose of preventing emigration to America, to enforce the return of Fishermen to Europe to their Wives and Familys, and lastly, and particularly, to prevent Fishermen from wintering in Newfoundland. This, at first sight, appears singular, and its extraordinaryness ariseth from the supposition that the Residence of so usefull a people will hurt the public weal. I must say that in Newfoundland a Work House does not exist and Poor Rates are as great strangers as fertile fields and Cinnamon Groves. The Motto which is riveted on the minds of all Housekeepers here is that He who will not work shall not eat. This axiom is undoubtedly a good one and is more prevalent in America then in Europe. In Newfoundland a lazy idle man is consider'd by the Inhabitants in the same light as Bees do a Drone, where everyone assists in expelling him from the Hive. In this Land there is no Public Charity for the Sick and the Lame; even the Blind and Aged can have no assistance but what comes from the hands of Private Individuals. The Fisherman which Chance has left behind must be supported all Winter at the expense of the Master whom he serv'd during the Summer. It was his province to see that the Fisherman was sent Home at the close of the Fishing Season.

Numbers of Fishermen, at the Fall of the year (the 25th of October) on their term of serving being expired are paid the residue of their wages. With a little money in their pockets they precipitate themselves into every excess which Rum and Spiritous Liquors are capable of producing. A fortnight's debauchery and riotous and luxurious living reduceth them to their last pittance, so that in Fourteen or Twenty days they spend what they have been laboring hard amidst Foggs, Fish and Frost for Seven long months. When their money is all gone some of them will lett themselves out for the Winter as wooders, for their Victuals and Lodgings. To get a Berth of this kind is consider'd as lucky, for the Winters are long and severe. Provisions too bear a high price, no Fresh Meat can be bought for less then a Shilling a pound. In the Merchant's House it is consider'd as high living to have a joint of Fresh Meat on Sunday. Amongst the First Class of Inhabitants if they have a joint of Mutton, Beefe, Veal or Venison, they all dine off it togather and the next day another of the same party provides a joint and all go to eat off it. In the same manner the Dinner goes round till they have all had their turn. The living of the poor people is, of course, in the extreme, Salt Fish and Potatoes is the common Fare. Salt Pork and Salt Beefe comes within the denomination of good living.

I have wander'd from the distress'd Fisherman letting himself out for the Winter as a Wooder. Some of these poor Fellows are less fortunate. They are forc'd to become Dieters [*boarders*] with some Housekeeper, for which they promize to Fish for them the next season or pay them in cash at the next Fall. One season arrives after the other and the next Season follows that, but the Debt remains unpaid. All this time the Fisherman, like the Generalissmo of an Army, is firm at his post Codd Hauling and Fish catching as usual. I have enter'd under the Roofe of a poor Irish Family, more then once, when I have convers'd with a Fisherman who tells me that he has been in this kind of Thraldom for Five Seasons. He tells me that he expects this sort of bondage will fall on all his relations residing in Newfoundland, as they have all exhibited symptoms of a tendency strongly resembling his own. He has a Brother in Harbour Grace who is fetter'd with the same kind of links for the last two Seasons. When I hear tales of this kind, and from the mouth of the Hero of the action, I cannot but admire their Honesty in thus staying to work out their Debt, when opportunitys so often offer'd of leaving the Island. Situations of this sort are very common amongst the Irish. It is a National Justice to say that not a single complaint has reached my Ears where an Irishman has been backward in endeavouring all in his power to discharge those kind of obligations.

I find that in the year 1730 a Mr Larkins was sent out by Government to enquire into the abuses which then existed in this Country. On his return he reported that, in the year before his arrival, Captain Holdsworth of Dartmouth had brought out from England no less then Two Hundred and Thirty-Six Passengers. This Holdsworth was a man of affluence and carry'd high sway at St John's. The persons he brought out with him were mostly Bye Boat Keepers, which are people who possess a Boat and leave her all the year in Newfoundland. These persons he put into the best Fish Flakes and Rooms, and in more then one particular he acted contrary to the Law. In England Holdsworth people used to frequent the Fairs and Market Towns in Devonshire to pick up a supply of recruits for his Fishing Business in Newfoundland. These were easy to get, for he gave better terms then any other person, which he could afford to do, as for some Seasons he took all the Law and the principal part of the business of the Island into his own hands.

[Mr Larkins, a barrister, was sent to Newfoundland in 1701 by the British Government, to draw up a confidential report on English North American colonies.

Captain Holdsworth was the most celebrated of the fishing Admirals and Commander in Chief of the West Country Merchants in 1700 when he was also Admiral of the Harbour of St John's. He belonged to an old Dartmouth family, who were closely connected with the history of Newfoundland. A later descendant was Governor of Dartmouth Castle. He built a large stone house in Ferryland. The family owned much property in St John's and it is from them that Holdsworth Street takes its name.]

The Countys of Devonshire and Dorsetshire supply the greatest number of hands for the Newfoundland Fisherys yearly then all the rest put togather. Poole and Newton Bushell are the Emporiums for the Two Countys. Lads from the Plow, Men from the Threshing Floor and persons of all sizes, Trades and ages and from the Manufactorys flock annually, in the Spring, to Newfoundland. The desire of seeing a foreign Land and the hope of returning with Six or Ten Pounds in their pockets is the consideration which induceth many to leave their Native Country for a few months and viset this Land of Fish. The wages they get is as various as their qualifications. From Ten to Forty pounds is given, with a free Passage out, and some petty gratuitys are sometimes admit'd, such as a Cask of Codd Sounds, a Cask of Codd Oil, a few Quintals of Fish or some Blubber, to those who are alert in Baiting and active in taking Fish.

A Fisherman who works in a Banker on the Grand Bank has a most laborous life of it. I have raked my Brains for my memory to survey all the occupation London can produce, but I can find none bad enough for comparison. He is exposed to Wind and Rain, to Foggs and Frost, to live on Fish and to be always wett. But what is the finis or completion of the disagreeableness of the employ is the horrible Stink which ariseth from the Codds Heads and Offal which are retain'd for some time in the Ship, it being improper to throw them overboard as taken off, because if they were the Fish would eat them and thereby an injury would be done to the Fishing business. From the Heads, Offal and the accumulation of fishy, slimy matter a Stench or Smell is diffused over the Ship that would give a headache to the most Athletic Constitution.

There is a property in the Codd Fish not generally known, which is curious. A Codd has been haul'd in and when open'd a Stone has been found in him a pound in weight and sometimes more. They are frequently catched with Stones in them. Whenever this is the case it is a sure indication of an approaching storm, as the Fish swallow the Stone for Ballast to enable them the better to encounter the jaring elements.

A Banker is not a little proud of his Dog at Sea. This Creature exhibited his dexterity and usefullness to a surprizing degree. In addition to what I have stated before in the History of Newfoundland Dogs I shall mention the following trait as a good quality in their composition. The Fishermen, when they hooked a Fish, in drawing the line up *[find]* the Fish sometimes disentangled themselves. The Fish may sometimes float on the Water. The Dog, observing this, dasheth into the Sea and brings the Fish alongside. They then throw a Rope out and the Dog, with the Fish in his mouth, puts Head into the Noose of the Rope and Fish and Dog are hauled into the Vessel togather. At Sea those Dogs often pursue and kill Water Fowl. I have heard of a Dog who was absent from a Ship on the Grand Bank for Two days, on the Third he return'd with a Hegdown in his mouth. These Dogs have also been seen to dive after Porpoises but without success.

The following is the State of Population in Newfoundland, as taken in 1787:

Masters of Familys	2232
Men Servants	7718
Weomen Servants	1563
	877
Children	5338
Dieters *[boarders]*	1378
	19106

Summer Inhabitants who came from England and Ireland 28,018

Total 47,124

On the population of Newfoundland I have no further remark to make at present then to observe that it appears there is upwards of Nineteen Thousand Inhabitants who reside here all the year round and that they are settled in a Country and occupy a space of Earth containing near Thirty-Six Thousand Square Miles—and that this Nineteen Thousand Souls have amongst them Two Thousand Two Hundred and Thirty-Two heads of Familys, which so completely shows the sterile and unfruitfull nature of the Soil of this Country. *[The area of the island of Newfoundland is actually 42,000 square miles.]*

The very high price of Flesh and Fowl in Newfoundland is owing to neither Wheat or Barley growing here. I saw about Four acres of Oats in good condition, near Titti Whitti Lake, which I believe was raised in the District of St John's. An acre of such Meadow Land as environs the Castle of Kenilworth, in Warwickshire, would be a pretty little Estate for a man here. Very little Hay is grown here. I have paid Nine Pounds a Ton for Hay for some Stock we had on board the *Boston*. For the Summer months Cattle, Horses and Sheep fare well, but from the small quantity of Hay which can be housed little stock of Cattle etc. can be supported during the long Winters in this Island. From this circumstance ariseth the high price of Fresh Provisions. Live Stock are brought to this place from Nova Scotia and the States of America and sold at reasonable rates, but they fall into the hands of the Merchants and the Jobbers who retail them out at exorbitant prices to the Fishermen and inferior class of Inhabitants.

I now come to a Military transaction and the only one, I believe, wherein a Hostile Band from a civilized Nation has viset'd and succeeded in gaining possession of any Settlement in Newfoundland since England took this Island immediately under its protection. This was when War raged with France in 1762, when the French landed on the 27th of June and took possession of St John's, and it may be said of the whole Island, for the principal Inhabitants left all the Settlements and took their effects with them. The Fishery was abandoned, not as a matter of choice but as a matter of necessity. It was not untill this year that England discover'd the true value of Newfoundland, for this Season no Fish were caught by the English, nor carry'd to distant Catholic Countrys. England felt the loss of those returns which she gained by importing Newfoundland Fish into the Ports of Spain, Portugal and within the Straits.

[St John's was taken by the French in 1696, 1708 and 1762 and there were many other attempts.]

When the Intelligence of the Surrender of St John's arriv'd in America General Amherst collected One Thousand men, with which he sailed from Boston in the month of September to retake the place. On his arrival on the Coast he was joined off St Mary's by Captain Graves *[Governor of Newfoundland at that time]* in the *Antelope*. After this juncture our Naval Force consisted of *Gosport* of 40 Guns, Lord Colville, Commodore; *Antelope*, 50 Guns, Captain, now Admiral Graves; *King George*, of 22 Guns; *Syren*, Sloop of War.

With this Force the English appear'd off St John's Harbour. They afterwards sail'd to Torbay, a bad Harbour a few Leagues to the Northward. Here the Troop landed after receiving a few Shots from the French, who retir'd through an Indian Path to St John's. General Amherst arriv'd with the Troops under his Command the same night at an open space called the Grove, and encamped at some distance from the Garrison (now called the Old Garrison), having the Lake of Titti Whitti between him and the Enemy.

The French being in possession of Signal Hill it was thought prudent to Storm it in the night. The access was extremely difficult, Nature having fortify'd it in every part except one, where Spruce Trees and Brambles were interwoven amongst the Rocks and large Stones as to almost refuse all intercourse with the mainland. However it was attack'd by Assault and carry'd, but numbers were slain on both sides. Captain Mackinsee was killed by a piece of broken Rock falling on his head as he was climbing up the Rock. The French Garrison still held out, but some Works were thrown up over Maggoty Cove, which commanded the Garrison, and a few Bombs thrown from it. The French surrender'd at discretion.

[Captain Roderick McKenzie 77th Foot (Montgomery's Highlanders) was not killed but was badly wounded at the engagement of Quidi Vidi Pass, 13 September 1762, when the British drove the French from their forward lines on the southside of Quidi Vidi river and up Signal Hill.]

On the landing of the British Troops the Naval Force was to block up St John's Harbour, where the French had two Ships of the Line and Two Frigates, but Lord Colville and his Squadron were blown off the Coast in a Gale of Wind and in the interval the French Force came out of the Harbour and escaped. When the

French Flag was hauled down General Amherst had not an English Flag to hoist, so the Ensign Staff in the Garrison could not receive this ornament untill the return of the British Squadron, which was not before Two days had elapsed after the Capitulation of the French.

XIII

The Murder of Lieutenant Lawry

St John's, 31st October, 1794. I shall break into my narration to relate a very malancholy circumstance which has befell one of the Officers of the *Boston.* It was deemed necessary for the benefit of His Majesty's Service that a Boat should be manned from the *Boston* for the purpose of going ashore a Pressing. Lieutenant Lawry was sent with the Party. They return'd with some hands which they had pressed. The next day, Saturday the 25th of October, Mr Lawry was sent ashore with two of these men in order to get their Cloaths and the Wages from the persons whom they had served as Fishermen during the Season. They landed at the upper end of the Harbor, on which Mr Lawry took Four of the Boat's Crew with him, as the men had a few yards to walke. They passed under some Fish Flakes, When suddenly a number of Irishman, armed with Wattles [*sticks*] surrounded Mr Lawry and Three of the Boat's Crew. They rescued the Impressed Men, and then beat Mr Lawry in so unmercifull a manner that he *died* the next morning of the wounds he had received in this fray. Two of the Boat's Crew were beat in a terrible manner, and their lives for some time dispaired of. One other got off with a few strokes, and his Messmate got off, perhaps with his life, by running for, and gaining the Boat.

By the death of Mr Lawry the persons who composed the party in this rescue and killing the Lieutenant were, in the Eye of the Law, Guilty of *Murder*. For Altho the Men were Impressed yet they had said they would enter, and Mr Lawry was on shore with them in a *Civil*, as well as a Military, capacity.

This Murder made a great noise and Partys of Marines from all Men of War then lying in the Harbor went on Shore on the following Sunday, when near one Hundred Fishermen and Shore-men were brought on board the Ships and detained, others were sent to Gaol. No information was gained so as to find out the persons who gave the deadly blows but an Irishman who was the principal, when he found his own Neck was in danger, turn'd King's Evidence. He swore positively to Three Men who struck the Deceased. Two of them were taken, Try'd on Wednesday, Condemned on Thursday, and Suffer'd death on Friday 31st of October, on the Barrens, near the New Garrison.

Had this transaction happened in England a great scope offer'd itself for the pleading of Counsel. They would a spoke on the *right* and *necessity* of Pressing, on Volunteers and Impressed Men, on the Verdict given by the Jury, which was Guilty of Striking, on the circumstances of the Governor, Admiral Sir James Wallace, taking people on board his Ship and telling them he would hang them instantly at the Yard Arm if they did not disclose and inform who the Murderers were, with some other circumstances which, in the hands of an ingenious Counsel might a been played upon. The Two Men that were hanged were Natives of Ireland and most deservedly met their deserts.

Mr Lawry was Bury'd in St John's Churchyard on the Monday after he was Murder'd. His body was removed from the *Boston* to the Shore in the same Boat in which he went to lose his life. His Corpse was attended on the Water by a Boat from the *Monarch*, one from the *Amphion*, one from *Pluto*, one from *Bonette*, one from *Lutine* and Two of our own Boats. They contained every Officer of the Squadron. The Boats took a circuitous route in the Harbor and moved in a slow and solemn manner. On his Coffin was placed his Uniform Hatt, his Sword and Dirk. On landing at the King's Warfe all the Marines of the different Ships, who had been previously landed, *[and]* the Three Companys of St John's Volunteers Received his Body, which was carry'd to the place of enterment in a great funeral parade, attended by all the Captains of the Squadron and the Principal Officers, several Gentlemen of the Town, all the Volunteers, and all the Officers and Troops stationed here.

There is a circumstance or two attending the execution of the Two Men I wish to mention, and that is relative to the dress of the Hangman and the dress of the Malefactors. An Executioner is so detested in this Country that were he known he would entail disgrace on his posterity. The person who filled this office to the Murderers of Mr Lawry did his business in disguise. He wore a Wigg made of Black Sheep's Wool which cover'd his head and shoulders, he had a Mask on, and was cover'd with a large long Cloake. The Two Culprits walked from the Gaol to the fatal spot. Each wore on his head a kind of Bonnet or Turban made of fine Linnen, which contained Three or Four yards at least. The Hangman, Malefactors and Priest (for they were Roman Catholic) walked in a Group and were surrounded by the Military, who formed a very strong guard.

[The log of the ship records the events as follows:

"Sunday, October 26th, 1794 . . . At half past one Lieut Lawry died of his wounds received from the mob. Carpenters employed making a coffin for him. Sent a party of Marines on shore in search of Murderers.

Tuesday, October 28th—Lieutenant Lawry interred with military honours.

Saturday, November 1st—Sent a party of Marines on shore to attend the execution of Richard [Power] and Garrett Farrell, two of the men that murdered Lieut Lawry."

The name of the first man executed was indecipherable in the log but is given as Richard Power in the Colonial Secretary's correspondenee where there is also reference to a reward being offered of £50 for the apprehension of Wm Burrows. According to "Pedley's History of Newfoundland" the Boston *was short of fourteen men.]*

On the *27th of October* we had a very heavy fall of Snow here. The face of the Country exhibited the extreme of Winter and its effects were keene and acute. What I felt and saw of it induceth me to believe some of the many storys, which often before I considered improbable. I am told that persons are often Frost bitten in the face and they themselves do not know it untill they are told by another person.

It is an extraordinary circumstance to see an Island of Ice on fire. It is a fact that two Ice Islands have produc'd so strange a phenomena. After a great fall of Rain Trees, Bows and Sticks are forced down the Rivers, these empty their Waters into the Bays and Harbours. In some of these are floating Islands of Ice. Some of these pieces of Wood are jammed in between Two Ice Islands. The motion of the waves, and the ponderous weight of the Ice cause a most violent friction and from this rubbing and friction heat is produc'd, which catcheth fire and riseth into Flame.

When you get Two Leagues at Sea the Settlement of St John's has a very pretty effect. The White Fort on the left, Signal Hill on the right, the high Cliffs on each side which forms the Narrows and the distant Hills produce a pleasing Landscape. The Harbour's mouth, called the Narrows, is defended by Fort Amherst and Two other Batterys. The Guns of the Old and New Garrisons will also defend the entrance. On the whole, St John's is very well fortify'd. The new Garrison is also called Fort Townsend. It has been built since the French viseted the Island.

The air of Newfoundland is considered as salubrious, it agreeing with most constitutions. Here the Merchant makes his Fortune before the Physician, whereas in the West Indias the Physician gains a Fortune before the Merchant.

The Newfoundland Banks are the most celibrated in the World for Fish. They cover a space of more then Fifty Thousand Square miles. The shape is not unlike a Trout with his mouth open and its back and Belly Fin extended, only its Tail part ends like an Eel. This description applys to the Grand Banks. In all there are Nine Banks. No dangers exist amongst them but in one place on the Grand Bank where there is a Rock called the Virgin Rock which is sometimes seen above water.

The assemblage of Fish of various kinds which inhabits these Banks surpasseth the belief of numbers of people; Codd Fish are the Sovereign specie and are so numerous as to be jigged. This is letting a Line down with Hooks on it, and then pulling it up quickly and on each Hook will be catched a Codd. The Vessels which are most abounding in the Codd Fishery are small Shallops, with four or Five hands in them, who go out every morning and return at night with their Fish which they always catch on the Banks which run off the Shore. Briggs and Sloops and other large Vessels proceed to the Grand Banks to Fish and are then termed Bankers.

The process of Curing Fish is curious. The names of Header, Cutt Throat, Carver, Splitter and Salter are the appellations given to the Fishermen who perform the various offices in the stages or in the Rooms. After the Fish have lain a certain time in Salt they are put on a Fish Flake, which is a broad, flat stage raised with Wattles or Sticks. On this stage they lay the fish to dry with the skin uppermost. When the Fish becomes more dry they are placed in heaps like the Roofe of a House and they are then called Faggots. Afterwards they are raised into heaps which are called piles. Here they lie for some days, when they are once more spread on the Flakes and Housed for exportation with the *Spirit* of the *Sun* in them, that is they are taken off the Flakes before the Sun is set.

The Newfoundland Fisherys employ a great number of Vessels and is a good nursery for Seamen of the British Navy. In one of our Cruizes we met a Brigg coming from the Grand Banks who had been afishing for Twenty-Two days, in which time she had caught Twenty one Thousand Codd Fish. We also passed a Shallop, with five men in her, who had been out Sixteen days and had catched Nine Thousand Fish each weighing from Seven to Thirty pounds. The Liver of the Codd Fish is valuable, from it is produced the Oil called Codd Oil. The Livers is thrown into large Casks with Spruce Branches placed about the Bung Hole, the head of the Cask being out. They are exposed to the Sun to rott. After lying in this situation for some time the Casks are headed up and the Bung Holes placed downwards. When the Oil drains off the Spruce branches serve the purpose of a seive and prevents the Liver from egressing. When the oil is all drained from the Liver the remains fall under the denomination of Blubber. This name the dealers in Satire often Christian the Aldermen and Citizens of London with, probably from their immersing themselves in fat Dishes, rich Soups and Savoury Sauces in Guildhall, which is considered the Baptismal Font for a corpulent man. If he Dines off a poloo or a Saddle of Mutton it is a chance if he is not called Citizen Poloo or Alderman Mutton.

There is a Fish found on the Banks and on the Shores of Newfoundland after the Capelin time is over which is the most curious I ever saw from its shape and colour and propertys. Its weight and length is about equal to a small Herring, its composition is a transparent jelly with a small substance in the middle. It is called a Squid. Its formation is very singular. Its Tail is like the Fluke of an anchor; from the head part extends Six fibrous and gluninous tubes ending in a point, the inner part looking like a saw has the property of adhering to any pungent substance it toucheth. Within its mouth is a Beak alike and as hard as the Beak of a Parrot. Right down the centre of his gummy body is a tube, a part of which is filled with a Liquid, as Black as Ink. This engine, so charged, he can command as freely as an Elephant can his Trunk, and whenever a Squid is hauled out of the Sea he is sure to discharge this Liquid at you, he generally aims at your face. The colour of the Squids is very beautifull. No Confectioner, when assisted by painted glass windows and a full Sun, can give his jellys half the variegated hues which are exhibited by the Squid when dying, and yet a Whale is Bait for them. The Squids go in large shoals and with their suckers will fix on a Whale and gnaw and torment him with their Beaks in such a manner as to worry him to death. When these teasing Creatures are ferreting a Whale he is followed by an immense train of Squids. If any danger suddenly shows itself they discharge their Black Fluid, by which the Ocean is so discoloured that they escape from the enemy. A Squid can move backwards and sideways. He is also said to be the largest Fish in the Sea, but this is fabulous. I never met a person who ever saw one that weighed more then Four Pounds, but I have heard storys at St John's of one being caught on the Grand Banks which Eight men could not haul into the Boat, and also of the horn of one being found cast ashore in Freshwater Bay which Two men with difficulty could carry. Whenever Squids are found is also found a Fish called Jumpers, or Squid Hounds, from the avidity with which they pursue and eat Squids.

[*The squid* (*Illex illicebrosus*) *follows after the caplin and is used as bait for cod. The description is apt. It has ten arms and not six. As anyone who has been on the squid jigging grounds knows, the jet of ink that is released when the squid is pulled from the water will hit the face of the inexperienced but a dexterous fisherman learns to point the squid away from him. The colour changes which ripple over a squid occur as the many chromatophores spread throughout the skin expand and contract and they are a beautiful sight. It is actually the whales which prey on the squids. Currently in Newfoundland the names "jumper" and "squid hound" are used rather loosely by fishermen for two common species of dolphin. These are often found feeding on squid in close association with pothead whales* (*Globicephala melaena*) *and it is conceivable that it is to this species which feeds almost exclusively on squid while in the Newfoundland area that the author is referring.*

The reference to the large squid is no doubt an allusion to the species of giant squid which has been found more commonly off Newfoundland than anywhere else and is now the subject of considerable research.]

Signal Hill is a place which I have mentioned before. On this Hill are Three Ensign Staffs on which are display'd annexed Flags. They denote the approach of Ships and Convoys. The utility of these Signals are very great, for as soon as a Signal is hoisted the Inhabitants looks at them from his door, then refers to a copy, which most Housekeepers provides themselves with, and he knows what is coming in from the Northward or Southward, without asking any questions.

[The page opposite to this is blank and no flags are annexed. Until 1948 this custom was carried on. The mercantile firms had distinctive house flags and on the approach of a ship the appropriate flag was hoisted for all St John's to see.]

XIV

The Return Journey

8th November, 1794. Latitude 47—N Corvo One of the Azores Islands Distant 249 Leagues.

We left the Harbour of St John's on Sunday, the 2nd of this month and are bound with a Convoy for Spain and Portugal. The Admiral, in the *Monarch*, is at present in Company, he being bound for England. We expect to separate from him every hour. By Signal by the *Monarch* I have sent a few Letters to my acquaintance in England, which I hope will reach their consignment safe.

We have already had some blowing weather and while I am seting below in my Cabin, with the Purser's dull Rush Light before me its horrible glance gives so deadly a hue to all around that I sometimes fancy myself in the Regions below, amongst my ancestors in our Family Vault. So dismal is the Light of my Candle, and so Black is the Table on which I write, that the other day I thought I was using my Pen on the Lid of my Great Grandfather's Coffin. I was awoke from this soon by our Boatswain's Trumpet, whose noise is as shrill, and whose voice is as sonorous as any Naval Man's in the world, when I found that I was alive and that the Boatswain was Piping all hands to Quarters. When I am possess'd with these malancholy Ideas I often contrast my present situation with that which I was in the year 1780, when going to Sea was never an Iota of my thoughts. I then resided in England, at a Town called Ludlow in Shropshire, a place which is ornamented with an antient Castle, beautifull walkes, a fine River of Water, a cheap Market, hospitable Inhabitants, a healthy air, Valuable Coal Mines, Gentlemen's Parks, plenty of Corn, Orchards of Apples, good Society and everywhere surrounded by the most luxuriant fields and fruitfull soil. But amongst these blessings I remember that I was not a whit happyer then I am at this moment, cooped up in so narrow a compass with near 300 of His Majesty's *best* Subjects, as I am at present. At that time I rose early, walked in the fields over a Hill called Whitcliff, where I often sat down and read. That time I never thought but what *[it]* was a sorry period, because my relations would not permit me to follow the bent of my inclinations. I wanted then to see the world and every day I hoped such a wish nearer the accomplishment. It is the misfortune of all *living souls* never to be satisfy'd with what they possess. Something is ever wanting. The man with an affluent Fortune is as uneasy in his mind, and the desire of possessing his Neighbour's Field makes his situation as dissatisfactory as the Sailor who labours in the cause of his Country for Seventeen Shillings and Sixpence a Month.

Great Britain is a Country famous for Charitable Foundations and Public Contributions but there is one method of asking relief and another method of giving it which has often struck me as not a little singular. I have seen in the Newspapers an Individual solicit Charity from the humane, and the Advertizement generally concludes with saying that donations will be thankfully receiv'd and *Publicly Acknowledged.* This expression *Publicly Acknowledged* is what I lay my stress upon, for I am fully aware that the Advertizement's Ideas are the same as my own, viz. That numbers of people subscribe a Guinea for the purpose of having their name in Public Prints, thereby endeavouring to tell the World that they are the most *humane*, tender hearted and Charitablest Souls in His Majesty's Kingdom. *Real Charity* consists in doing good to others in so private a way as only the Donor and the Donee are privy to the transaction. If I give a man a Shilling, and want afterwards to tell of it, it is exposing the wants of the poor man, and the *Charitable* intent is done away. In a list of Subscribers to a Charitable use where I see Initials only opposite a sum I consider that as coming from the hand of *real humanity*, but you will generally see in the List the residence of the Subscriber so minutely described that one would suppose the Donation had been sent from the East Indias, and had travelled through Persia, over the Black Sea, into Turkey and found its way into London by way of Italy and France. How can it be reconciled to *Necessity* if I am disposed to give a Guinea to a Charitable use to give so long a direction as to say Mr Aaron Thomas, 8 Orlton Lane, Boston Street, Cavendish Square, London?

Confinement is the Parent of Meditation. I have seen many good things come from within Prison walls and I have heard some bright Ideas, with pleasing imaginations, started within the sides of a Ship. This is a White Apology for a Black Subject.

I Dined one day at a Table in St John's. Amongst the things serv'd up was a Dish of Stewed Eggs, with a remarkable large one in the middle, as big as the Body of a Goose. It was cut in Halves so that the White and the Yolk showed distinctly and there was no deception. I thought an Egg of so large dimensions not a little extraordinary and was curious enough to enquire the name of the Bird who generated the Egg. I was told by the Master of the House that it was produc'd by his Cook, who was an Irishman, who could make an Egg of any size, from a Tennis Ball to that of Blanchard's Balloon. I afterwards learn'd the process of Egg Making, which is simply thus:—Separate the White and the Yolks of Eggs boil the Yolks, have a Machine or Cloathe, then pour the White of the Eggs round the Yolks, tye the Cloathe in the same shape of an Egg, boil it, and when cold it will turn out a perfect Egg.

In Newfoundland they have a strange method of milking Cows and Goats. The Girls in Cheshire will never believe me I am sure. You have heard of Guy, Earl of Warwick's Red Cow and the Sieve. Do you know that in this Country, in the Winter time, a girl can Milke a Cow into her *Apron* and carry the Milke home in it? If she Milkes the Cow in the open air the intensity of the weather will freeze the Milke as it falls from the Cow into the Apron and *[it will]* remain there, a hard, conglutinated, frozen mass, untill melted by heat.

Grog Shops are very numerous in St John's. Rum here is very cheap, it being brought from the West Indias and only pays 1/– a Gallon Duty. Three Shillings and Sixpence is the common price to the consumer. A person who is fond of Malt Liquors will find them very dear. One Shilling a Bottle of London Porter is the regular price.

I am told that the Wolves of Newfoundland eat one another. A Hunter, whom I have often convers'd with, says that last Winter he was pursued by a Flock of Wolves and in imminent danger of his life. They were within Gunshot of him and no hope left of escaping, except that of firing amongst them and killing some of them so the rest would stop to devour the Carcases of those Slain. He try'd the experiment and killed one. They stopped, but again followed him. He fired and Killed a Second, a Third and a Fourth under the same circumstances, but they followed him to his Tilt, where some people were, on seeing of which they retreated. Cattle turned on the Barrens often get into the Woods and the Owners never find them again. Brine, a well known Butcher in St John's, had some Cattle strayed into the Woods last Summer. Some people went after them and shot two of them. As they were carrying the Flesh home they heard the cry of Wolves, they were on the scent of the blood of the Cattle, but luckily they made for the spot where the Cattle were shot and left the men to pursue their journey Home in peace.

November 18th, Boston at Sea, Cape Finisterre Distant 256 Leagues.

[The log gives Cape Finisterre S 79 E 96 Leagues.]

We parted with the *Monarch*, Admiral Wallace, the 13th Inst, he going for England and us continuing our Course for Spain. On the afternoon of this day we had a hard Gale of Wind, some desperate Seas struck the *Boston*, one of which threw such a Deluge of Water over the Weather Gangway that to those who were under the Half Deck it appear'd like an immense Cascade. At the moment it happen'd I was in the Galley, and I hope my credit will not be *disputed* if I hazard an assertion by saying that one *Pint of Water more* would a made the quantity *equal* to that which glides down the Fall of the celebrated Cataract of Niagara.

We have had a heavy Sea and blowing weather for some days. The accidents are many, but serious ones befell the Platters and Earthen Ware. If we do not get to England soon the Supernumeries—Wooden Bowls and Spoons—must come in general use. As to my own part I am very unfortunate in all my undertakings. During my Emigration in Newfoundland I collected a small assortment of Birds of the Country. These I got stuffed and had them hung in my Berth. They consisted of Lews, Wild Ducks, Sea Parrots etc . . . From the excessive rolling of the Ship her seams are a little opened so that the Leaks between Decks are very considerable. The Water, at times, poured down the Ship's sides in my Cabin so plentifully as to represent a spring of some magnitude. A few mornings ago I went to turn out of my Cott and found my Berth ankle deep in Water; travelling a few inches further I put my foot against one of my stuffed Hegdowns. Putting my hand down to satisfy my mind I got hold by the Neck of a Lew which was riding Buoyant on the Water. I had so much Water Fowl about me I began to have my doubts wither I was not in a Trance and wadling in a Fish Pond in Kensington Gardens. Groping on in the dark I put my hand on some White Moss of a curious kind, which I meant to take to Europe. This assur'd me of a certainty that I was in a Pond and that the Moss was the coating of the Dam Head. I was afraid to advance Fore or Aft lest I should plunge o'er Head and Ears and be drown'd. At this moment the Ship gave a roll, I was thrown down on my side and half immers'd in Water, but grabing something on the Ship's side, which I took to be the Stump of an old Tree, I held on to it, attempting to raise myself. In the effort it gave way with a crackling noise like the parting of an Island of Ice. On this the Lights came in, when they found me nearly up to my knees in Water, and the suppos'd Tree Stump was the neck of a Wine Decanter which I had hauled down with a Frame and a long train of Goblets, Decanters, Glasses and Tumblers—and all broke to Atoms.

On Board Ship there is generally a Goat. The Sagacity of these Animals is well known. In the blowing weather, when the Decks were wett, a Goat we had, for the sake of warmth got into the Oven. When she got in the Door, fatally for her, was shut. Next morning the Fire was lighted as usual in the Ship's Coppers and Grate. About Eight O'Clk the Oven Door was open'd, when the Goat was found baked to death.

I have often wondered that Artists do not exercise their talents in picturing a Captain's Cabin after a Gale of Wind. I can only account for it by supposing that few men of abilitys make long Voyages at Sea. Quadrants, Chairs, Compasses, Tables, Quoins, Guns, Tackle, Ports, Maps, Pistols, Tomyhawks, Lanthorns, Windows and Quarter Gallerys—Split, Cract, Stoved, Rended, Dash'd and broke all to pieces, would form a good subject for a humourous Limner. Possibly such a Picture may be in existence but it has never fell my way.

When the Wind was violent, the atmosphere cloudy and the Sea furiously raging I sent a Boy that belongs to my Berth one day on Deck, to see at what distance a particular Ship of our

Convoy was. He return'd and gave me the following ludicrous answer—That he could not get a view of her altho he could see *beyond sight*.

We have (had, I mean, for he is now run away) a Man on Board who has fought for many European Nations. He has fought under the Banners of France, Holland, England, Turkey and Spain. He was in a Dutch 64 in the engagement off Dogger Bank, where he receiv'd a British Bullet which went in at one corner of the mouth and out at the other, so that he had Three Holes on his mouth and could smoak Three Pipes at one time. When he was on board our Ship he acted as Boatswain's Mate and could blow the Call through his mouth and his Two side holes. He got Three smart Tickets for accidents he met with in the British Services, all of which were in different names. He is not more then Thirty and when the *Boston* was in England last Winter he deserted from her. Probably at this time he is fighting under the Colours of the French Republic.

Captains of 74 and larger Ships of the Line generally have a Cow on board at Sea, which they take for the sake of her Milke. This is a practize which I mean to find fault with. Although the expense comes from the Captain's private Purse, yet the Public may be said to have a property in one of her caretakers, he being paid by them. This being the case, when a Sailor, in the morning, is seting on a Gun eating Dry Biscuit or Oatmeal and Water, and sees a Bowl of new Milke carrying to the Captain's Table I wonder what he thinks of it—particularly if he is on a long Voyage and that morning had carry'd his Flour and Plumbs on the Quarter Deck, and there mixed his Puding before the Officer of the Watch, in order to prevent him embezzling of Water. A Cow will drink Seven Gallons of Water a day if given to her and I need not comment by asking how usefull this Seven Gallons would be to Seven Messes, when under the vertical Sun. Cheesecakes, Custards, Cream etc. which are produc'd by the new Milke are desirable delicacys, but the Sailor and the Admiral are born with the same appetites. It must be admit'd that it is a little irksome to the Seaman to see a Train of Seventeen or Twenty Dishes borne in State to the Great Cabin—full of Savoury Meats and Vegitables, with Jellys and Blomonges, when they themselves have din'd off a Gob of Fatt Pork or Pease and Water.

It was my good Fortune to serve, in a Ship of the Line, a Great

Officer who had the following singularitys, pecularitys, odditys or Whims. I shall relate them in a Hodge Podge way, without order, just as my recollection falls on them.

He had Three Servants in his Suit, all of which were discharged within a month. The first he Discharged for cutting the Soft Bread for Dinner *two minutes* before the Company sat down to Table, by which he was depriv'd of the refreshing smell of a New Cut Loaf. The next he turn'd away for cuting up the Salad in the Bowl before he was told, from which he lost the fragrance produc'd by the first mixture of Vegitable and Vinegar. The Third Commit'd a Grand Fault for cutting some Slices of Corn'd Beefe for Breakfast behind his Master's back, when he ought to have done it under his Nose that he might a receiv'd the Flavour arising from the concoction of Beefe, Salt and Parsley, with which it was stuffed. But the circumstance of giving a Dried Neat's Tongue to the Cook to boil before he showed it to his Master was fatal to the Servant's remaining in that situation, as the Officer said that a Smoked Tongue was his Thermometer to know the weather by.

He once had a Rascal for his Valet, who stole all his Body Linen. He prosecuted at the Old Bailey and laid the Indictment for privately Stealing, in a Dwelling House. This is Capital, if found Guilty. The Jury gave a Verdict of Guilty of Stealing to the Value of Four Shillings and Ten Pence, which takes the Capital part away and saves the man's life. However somebody was at the Public Office the next morning enquiring about a Hatt which was lost the day before at the Session House, insinuating that a Jury Man who presided at a Tryal the day before was seen to look very hard at it.

He was very much troubled with Corns. For the sake of ease he never changes his Shoes. He calls them his Starboard and his Larboard Shoe. He always orders them to be laid by his Bedside Fore and Aft, the Starboard Shoe on the Starboard side and the Larboard on the Larboard side so that in case he should be called up in the night he might not put the Left Foot in the Right Shoe. Rising one morning and finding his Shoes placed wrong he rung the bell in a passion, and order'd his Servant to be turned before the Mast for putting his *Starboard Shoe* on the *Larboard* side, as such Villany deserved the most *exemplary* punishment.

At a particular period, being without a Body Servant, his Cook officiated in that employ. The Cook was one night putting his Master to Bed. He asked for a Nightcap, but the Cook by mistake gave him a Puding Bag in which he had that day boiled a Plumb Puding. The Gentleman put it on and did not find out the exchange untill the next morning, when half a Dozen Plumbs tumbled out of the corners. He apply'd some harsh words to the Cook, but the Cook had the boldness to affirm that all His Honor's Nightcaps were Puding Bags.

During the late Peace he made what is called the Grand Tour. When he was in Turin he wore a Coat the body of which was made of Red Velvet, the Arms of Green and the Collar Yellow, the Cuffs White and lined with Silk, in the manner of Harlequin's Diamonds. He wore on his finger a Ring as big as a Pigeon's Egg, which was raised in the shape of the Globe. He had been in most of the Habitable World and the Ring put him in mind of the dangers he had undergone. By some accident he got a Bruize on the finger, which became a wound. He had, soon after, a Quarrel with a young Savoyan who, pointing to his finger, said that a Ring on a Scabby finger did not much symbolise a Gentleman. He retired to Constantinople in disgust. When walking on a Parade on a sunshiny day he held up his finger which had the Globe on it; the Company were immediately enveloped in so dark a Shaddow that everybody believed that there was an Eclipse. He was a very conspicuous Character there for months, generally appearing in Public with a *Compass* painted on his Hatt, which made the English residing there call him the E. O. Table. [*This probably refers to a table at that time used in the Navy showing the deviation of the ship's course from the true bearing.*]

When he was a young man he made a Gentleman a present of Two Chinese Geese. Under their Wings he put a Letter which was designed for the Gentleman's Daughter; but they miscarry'd. From this circumstance he was known for many years by the name of the Navy Gull.

Since he has turned Fifty he has a Strong Partiallity for Spectacles, almost constantly wearing them. For the convenience of *Backsight* he has a pair of plated Glass ones, made so curious as not to be discover'd. When he has a new Servant he makes use of them, and also sometimes at Breakfast. The Scenes that he gains a view of by these Backsighters, he says, is Food for a King.

He once commanded a Vessel in the Merchant Service and

being bound, with another Vessel, in the Slave Trade to the Coast of Guinea, he wished the Captain of it to Dine with him; for this purpose he order'd his Mungo to hang a Table Cloath through the Stern Cabin Windows as a Signal to Come to Dinner. When Mungo went to take in the Table Cloath a Large Shark, from the greasy texture *[of the cloth]* had swallowed a part of it. He thought himself a fit companion for the Captain's Society and permit'd his slippery Carcase to be hoisted in before he had receiv'd the regular summons from the Captain's mouth. Mungo, being a youth of humour, placed the Dinner on the Table and went on Deck and informed his Master that his *Visetor* was in the Cabin and Dinner was on the Table. On his entering the Appartment the Shark coiled his Body and distorted his Mouth into a ghastly shape at the Captain, strongly indicating his hunger, but making a movement which portended to *embrace* his Legs. The Captain declined the close connection by running out of the Cabin, swearing that his visetor wanted to *eat him.* This strange Visetor, introduced in so singular a manner, is not a bad subject for comment. Many a man has a Shark at his Table, by his side, in his House, within his confidence. For my part I can say that I have entertained a Lamb at my Table and in my House, but the Lamb in the end became a Shark.

He once belonged to a King's Ship lying at Spithead. He then had to serve his person, a Raw and newly imported Slave from the Coast. Wanting to go on board after night when there was a Fogg he desired Mungo to put a Compass in the Boat. Mungo, who was but a splatterer at English, mistook the word *Compass* for *Comfort* and positively put a Bottle of Brandy in the Tiller Box, instead of the Compass. They rowed along shore to Fort Monkton, but being by then some distance from the Ship and enveloped in a thick Fogg, the Compass became a necessary instrument to steer by.

"Give me the Compass," says the Commander.

"Here it is, Sir," replys Scripie, at the same time putting the Bottle of Brandy into his Master's hand. He was immediately convulsed with anger, but had enough strength left to poise the Bottle and aim a backhand stroke at Mungo's head. Luckily it hit the fleshy part of the Coxwain's Arm, who catched the Bottle free from flaw. The Commander never spoke a word in the Boat after untill he got into his Cabin, when such a *Storm* arose that the Boatswain came Aft to know if he should Pipe all hands to assist in securing the peace of the Ship.

I had it on good authority that on this occasion his anger rose to such a height as to create such a degree of heat as to *fire off* a Gun which was in the Cabin. The breath from his Nostrils produced a Vapour as great as the Foggs on the Banks of Newfoundland. The end of this man I know not, but I am told that he died suddenly, in a great passion. A relation of his once told me that his anger would arrive one day and accumulate to such a degree that he would *burst*!

It was his custom when reading to fill the Margin of the Book of every Author he laid hands on with his own comments and explanatory notes. He subscribed to a Public Library, the Keeper of which brought an action against him for defacing a Volume of Bruce's Travels. It seems that our Commentator had alter'd the Source of the Nile, as laid down by that Pedestrian, chang'd the Boundarys of Cairo and deny'd the fact of his eating Raw Beefe. He was in possession of a Scot's Family Bible, where the Reverend Gentleman has been elaborate in expounding the Sacred Text. Every hair's breadth of vacant paper is filled with his remarks in denying the hypothesis of the learned Doctor.

I once heard him assert that the people of England were men of Landed Property and Manufactorys and that those employ'd in Agriculture formed *no part* of the People of Great Britain. They, he said, might hang their Bags across their shoulders and march off to any Country. Were these people to hop off, as here desir'd, I should be glad to know what would become of the Lead, Tin and Coal Mines. Our Manufacturing Towns, when all the Artificers are gone, must flourish when the men of Landed Property are left behind! Every Man that drinks a Pint of Porter assisteth the Revenue. We Naval Men are paid, consequently we compose a part of the people of England.

I have had occasion to find fault with the Texture of the paper on which I write, but it matters little in regard to its quality. An Order on a Banker written on coarse paper is as valuable as if written on the finest that is manufactured, but a Manuscript is more desirable when written on clear, good paper. I am led to this observation from a circumstance that fell under my notice, where an Individual had received a Letter from a *Friend*, written on Paper little better than Whitty Brown. He was complaining of the disrespectfulness of his acquaintance in this little Transaction but I told him that being once in Wales a person in Montgomeryshire had occasion to write to me; having no Wax or Wafers to hand he sealed the Letter with *Pitch,* which happened then to be melting on the fire for the purpose to mark the Sheep with. With this *cement* it came safe to hand to me, who was then at Presteign, in Radnorshire. I told him that this letter was valuable to me, not withstanding its smeary and pitchey external, because it came from a person whom I *respected.*

This brings me to say what a pleasing sensation may be given to the Lover on *coarse* paper. The gilded edge, the fine Fabric of the paper, the colour'd Wafer, the Vermillion Wax, the elegant folds of the Epistle are no recommendations. The *words* that are written *from* the *heart* on coarse paper find their way *to the heart,* and when once lodged in so sacred a depot every vein is instantly filled with the most enlivened extacys of pleasures and joys.

I know a young Lady who had receiv'd a Letter from a Gentleman, the contents of which were so pleasing that she could not resist from uttering a Soliloquy. She received the Charming Lines in the night and fell into a violent rhapsody by saying "What a devine fellow. O! how warm are his expressions. I am almost in a Flame while I am contemplating his fond words." What passed further I was not able to learn, but I am told that she put the Letter to her bosom and pressed it there, when it suddenly took fire and burned untill it was consumed to ashes.

No person who has not been in a Ship can credit the various reports which are flying about every day, or rather every hour. These are termed Galley Packets. A stranger to a Ship wonders what subjects can arise for conversation, but persons who are acquainted with the Royal Exchange or Coffee Houses of capital resort well know the familiarity and method of starting a topick for the Company to join in discanting on. Thus, in a Ship, some transaction is every half hour arising for comment. The Foremast man ingratiates himself with the Wardroom Boys; every word he hears the Officer speak is brought out and immediately told at the Breechen of every Gun in the Waiste, to this is always added a thousand falsitys. Everyone who relates the story adds something. If a Servant says the Chaplain and the Purser broke a Wine Glass today at Hob Nob the story goes the Purser cut the Slit in his Tongue with a piece of Flint Glass which the Chaplain put in his Rice Pudding. The most trifling disaster which occurs in the Captain's Cabin is magnify'd to the Galley as a most momentious Calamity for the sake of laughing at the misfortunes which attend their Superiors.

I myself have put some drollery in motion to create a little mirth amongst the men and enliven their spirits. I always found it lost nothing in the travelling. Like a Comet it whirled its tail all round, keeping its head to the centre of the Sun. So these kind of Tales *[are]* told in the Galley (which is like a Barber's Shop or Pott House in London). Here the heat is sometimes as great as wood and coals can produce, the men around like so many Satellites, move off with what fresh News they can catch, and disperse it over the Ship with as much expedition as the Secretary of State transmits good News to the Gazette Office.

It is the misfortune of us all not to be over tender for our Neighbours, and we frequently give ourselves some trouble in probing concerns that neither relate to us, the Public, Religion or our Country. In Ships this banefull desire is almost universal. It is surprizing to see how quickly Scandal is circulated on board. Sailors indulge themselves much in this practize, and yet the instant they are discharged on Shore the Seaman whom he abused he will put the utmost confidence in. I do not know how to account for this, unless it arises from thoughtlessness and saying what they doth not mean, which is much attributed to Seafaring men.

XV

Cadiz, Lisbon and Spithead

16th December, 1794, Cadiz Bay. We arriv'd in this place on Thursday the 4th December having had a long passage from Newfoundland. We made Cape Finisterre the 24th of last month and were Nine days beating the Coast of Portugal and Spain before we made this place. The Shores of Portugal appear in general high land, Rocky and but indifferently interspersed with cultivated spots. Yet there are some fine openings where Rivers empty themselves into the Sea, by which you obtain a View up the Country when rich landscapes are exhibited to the Eye. The Ports of Viano [*do Castelo*] and Figeuro [*da Foz*] are objects of this kind and afford a pleasing prospect as you pass them Two or Three Leagues at Sea. This Coast is free from danger. The principal obstruction which is hazardous to Navigation is the Barlinques, or the Berlings, a sett of Rocks about Two or Three Leagues from Cape Fiscron. Some of them are very large. One of them, when viewed from a certain situation, represents the Hull of a Vessel turned upside down.

The City of Cadiz, viewed from the Sea, forms a magnificent spectacle. The immense Ramparts which encloseth it, the height of the Houses, their being White, the curious architecture which adorns them, the Turret which ariseth out of every House (there being no chimneys to be seen), the Domes which rear their heads from the Religious Houses and the Public Buildings all concur in giving Cadiz an air of Splendour which no City in England can display. This City contains more then 70,000 Inhabitants, and is full of Commerce and Oppulence.

This City was founded by Herculus, who in his travels came into the Isle of Leon (in which Cadiz stands). It is joined to the Continent by a Bridge. When he arriv'd at the head of the neck of land on which the City now stands he conceiv'd that there was no land further. In consideration of this he built a Tower which is now called Herculus's Pillar. He also built a Fort and some Houses and threw up an Embankment. The Phoenicians added greatly to the place and so rich was the Kingdom of Spain when the Carthagenians came here that their domestic Vessels, and even Ploughshares, were made of Silver.

I cannot attempt to give a History of Cadiz. That would be a Herculean work indeed. I propose to give you anecdotes and sketches only—and that in a detached manner.

In the War between Queen Elizabeth and Phillip Cadiz was a grand sufferer, for the Earl of Essex and Lord Howard came here with a Fleet and Army, took and plunder'd the place and carry'd off immense Riches. The memory of Essex is, at this day, much detested at Cadiz, for he sent away all the Ornaments, Pictures, Jewells, Gold and Silver and everything he could find within the Churches. The few Pictures he left behind he order'd his Soldiers to destroy, which they accomplish'd by running their Swords and Bayonets thro the Canvas in all directions. Some of these mangl'd Pictures are now in Cadiz, and for several years after Essex was beheaded the day on which he suffer'd death the Monks used to employ in returning thanks to the Almighty for executing Justice (as they say) on so great a Sinner. Numbers of the most valuable pictures, which were shipped to England, were sold, and purchased by Roman Catholics, who shipped them for Spain after the War, when they were replaced in the Religious Temple at Cadiz again.

In Queen Anne's War this City was in the hands of the English under the Duke of Ormond *[in 1702]*. He was also at Port St Mary's, on the other side of the Bay, where great numbers of his men died owing to their eating the New Fruits and Drinking Wine. Cadiz is situated in the Province of Andalusia, 300 miles South West of Madrid and only 56 miles from Gibraltar. It is the See of a Bishop who has 12,000 Ducats per year. Here is a new Cathedral, a Prodigeous Pile. It has already been upwards of Sixty years in hand and the Roofe is only just completed. All the inside is entirely the most highly polish'd Marble. The Pillars and Columns are all of Marble and of the richest workmanship. About Two years ago the King of Spain inform'd the Architect that if it was not finish'd in Ten years he should put him in the Inquisition.

Cadiz has within its Walls one Church, one Cathedral, Thirteen Convents and some other Religious Foundations. They are all wonderfull Rich and Splendid. A person who has never been in a Catholic Country can have but a sorry Idea convey'd to his mind by paper of the astonishing Grandeur, Magnificence, Pomp and Splendour which the inside of a Roman Catholic Church exhibits. In Cadiz there are some which vie with any in Spain. The College of the Jesuits is so richly embellish'd with Gold and Silver Ornaments that the Walls are most profusely cover'd with such costly decorations. The Convent on the Mall is also superbly and grandly ornamented with Statues as large as life, enclosed with Glass and Gold Frames, standing in Niches, arrayed in Velvet or Silk Robes, Gold and Silver Lace and every other habiliment corresponding with this extravagant description. All the Altars and the walls of the Building are loaded with most sumptious Roman Relicks and adorned with beautifull embroidery. To enter a Religious House so richly bedecked must create *Awe* in the human mind. This description is not overpainted and will serve for most of the Churches in Spain. These are the admiration of all Travellers.

The Convent which I have last spoken of has a very rich appearance from Cadiz Bay, its external being highly decorated with Gothic Architecture. The North West Front is nearly cover'd with a grand Marble Monument at the Summit of which is a Statue of the Virgin Mary with the Infant Jesus in her Arms. In the front of this Convent runs the Mall, which answers to our Mall in St James Park. It is the Promenade for the Inhabitants of Cadiz, who come here for the cooling Sea Breezes. It is situated on the City Ramparts, commands a fine view of the Ocean, is planted with Trees which are but yet in an infant state, and has Marble Seats for the accommodation of the company. At one end of it is a Fountain and a Statue of Herculus.

Cadiz labours under one considerable difficulty, which is the want of fresh water. None of this usefull article is to be met with in all the Isle of Leon, except what is caught on the tops of Houses. Cadiz is supply'd with this usefull Beverage from Port St Mary's, a Town on the other side of the Bay. It is sold in the City at the rate of Two Pence for Five Gallons. It appears strange to an Englishman, in going thro the Streets, to behold the number of *Water Shops* which, every moment, falls in his way. They are as numerous as the Oyster Stalls in London and at them is sold only water. Great numbers of Men get their living by selling Water about the Streets. They carry a Jar upon the Shoulder, a Glass to drink out of, some drops of the nature of Carraway Comfits to add to the flavour of the Water, a Glass swab to clean the Glass with. With these Vessels they travell about the Streets, or rest, as necessity of occasion requires.

Other Inhabitants catch great quantitys of Rain Water for their domestic use from what falls on top of their Houses, they being built with Flatt Roofs and bricked with Channels which convey the water into a Cistern at the bottom of the House. The Rain, in some parts of Spain, being periodically very heavy what they catch supplys their wants.

Cadiz is strongly fortify'd. I walked round the Ramparts one day and counted 407 Pieces of Ordnance, most of which were of Brass—from Six to Twenty Four Pounders. The Bay has some natural Bulwarks such as the Diamond and Porpoises Rocks which display to the Mariner a hideous Picture of Horror when there is a strong Sea. The Inner Bay and the Road of Cadiz is defended by the City Ramparts—Forts Sebastian, Rota, Lauret, Matagorde, St Catherine, Cuelo, Cindat, Fortens, Douane, Fort Real and Craugue so that it would be a difficult business to obtain possession of the Shores which surround this grand rendezvouz of the Spanish Fleets and Galleons.

The Late General O'Reiley (whose history is well known in Europe) was Governor of Cadiz at the time of his death. He was a Great Benefactor to this place. He built a magnificent Range of Buildings fronting the Landport, the Square where Bull Fights are exhibited, that immense Pile of Buildings which are the Barracks on the City Wall. He caused a sewer to be made which runs through the centre of every Street in Cadiz in order to carry off the filth. He built a Church near Puntala and converted the sandy tract of land near it into beautifull Gardens, erected machines by which water was carry'd into every direction amongst them and vegitation produced where nothing but Sand was before to be found. [*Count Alexander O'Reilly, General in the Spanish army, was born in Ireland 1722. While on the Havana station he conducted a successful operation against rebels in New Orleans (lately ceded to Spain by France). Subsequently he was entrusted with the reform of the Spanish army, but fell from favour after an unsuccessful action against the Moors in Algiers in 1775. Appointed as Governor of Cadiz, he held the post until the death of Charles III in 1788 when he went into enforced retirement. He died shortly before taking up a last official appointment to command in the East Pyrenees in 1794.]*

Cadiz is supply'd with every description of Vegitable and Fruit is abundant and cheap. The Fresh Meat Market contains a particular which no place of the kind in England can produce. The price of Meat here is regulated and in a conspicuous place in the Market is a Board on which is painted the representation of a Cow, a Hogg, a Sheep and a Calve. Opposite to each Animal is marked its particular price, for less then which no Meat can be purchased. This price is stated every morning. Every House in Cadiz has a Turret for the benefit of the family taking the air and cooling breezes in it. These Turrets rising from every House add greatly to the appearance of the City. I was upon the Roofe of the House of Mr Duff, the British Consul, and from it I had a fine view of the surrounding Country.

The Rota and St Mary's, Fort Real, Medina Sedoni, all the Country richly scatter'd with Houses, Orange and Olive Groves, with a multiplicity of Spanish Ships of War and the Lofty Sierra Morena or Snowy Mountain form a scene of vast Oppulence, as well as exhibiting a grand natural landscape.

I have heard much of the filthyness and lazyness and cruelty of the Spaniards. Of the first and second I have to observe that I believe it is quite as fashionable in England; as to the last—they are charged with Cruelty viz.—in Drawing and Stabbing for the most trifling assaults. On this remark I have nothing to say but that I have walked in Spain in all hours of the night but never met with the smallest incivility.

The Horses in Spain are very beautifull Creatures. They are decorated in a curious manner by their Jockeys. Their Hair is cut so as to represent Diamonds, Stars and a variety of zig-zag work. I could not refrain from lamenting the fate of some fine Horses which I saw carrying Paniers and loaded with some burdensome weights. Had they been in England the Stud at Tattersalls would a been graced with their presence.

The method by which a House to be Lett is advertized in Spain is not a little singular from its simplicity. When a House wants a Tennant the person to whom it belongs sticks a bit of *Blank* white paper on the Door or Window. This is sufficient signification to denote its being in want of a Tennant.

The Shop Keepers in Cadiz are not a little particular in regard to their being disturbed at their Dinner Time. They generally allow themselves Two Hours every day for that purpose, during which space most of their Shops are shut up and they will not serve any of their Customers.

While our Ship lay in Cadiz Bay I viset'd Port St Mary's, a large Town on the opposite side of the Bay. I went into the Country to Xeres De La Frontera, a considerable Inland Town on the River Gaudaleta. The Road on each side is planted with Orange Groves and Fig and Palm Trees. The Orange Trees were loaded with Fruit, even at this Season of the year. Some of the Groves had not the smallest fence from the highroad and yet the Oranges were lying under the Trees very plentifully. About half way to Xeres, on a Hill, is a pretty little House surrounded by Olive Trees, where are sold Viands, etc. People halt here with their Mules and Horses. There are seats cut out of the Rock for the Passengers to set on. What render'd the House remarkable to me was its Front being stuck with *Horns* which were put on the Wall when the House was built. The use they were apply'd to was to hang the Horse's Bridles on while their Rider was refreshing himself within doors.

A circumstance struck me in a House which I thought would not be misapply'd if adapted to our little Shop Keepers in England, amongst whom petty Robberys are very common. I observed that within the Drawer or Till, where the Master of the House kept his money, was fixed a little Bell. Every time the Till was touched the Bell would jingle, the sound of which would convey to the Ear of the Owner that something was going on in his Shop.

The Neighbourhood of Xeres De La Frontera produceth the Wine so well known in England by the name of Sherry Wine. At Xeres liveth a Mr Gordon, a British Merchant, who yearly sends great quantitys of that Wine to England.

Great numbers of Boats ply between Port St Mary's and Cadiz. Passengers are very numerous. It is carry'd on in the same manner as the Boats which ply between London and Gravesend with this difference—that all hands in the Spanish Boats have a general set to at Prayers before any person in the Boat goes on Shore.

4th January, 1795, River Tagus.

We left the Bay of Cadiz on Saturday the 27th of December in company of His Majesty's Sloop of War the *Bonetta* and a Fleet of Merchantmen bound to this place and afterwards England. I find myself much cramped for time therefore no leisure to relate particulars, only that we anchor'd opposite the City of Lisbon, in this River, on Thursday the 1st January, having had a fine Wind from Cadiz. Cape St Vincents, so well known to Navigators, is the only Land I sketched. The Cape is very remarkable, having a Monastery on the Edge of the Rock. The reason of its being built in this situation is not a little singular, therefore I shall relate the cause.

St Vincent is a Saint held in high Esteem in Portugal. He had wander'd to the Seashore and arriv'd at the Cape which now bears his name. He was there murder'd and his Body thrown into the Ocean. A short time afterwards his Body was washed ashore on the Sands when it was surrounded by a Flock of *Ravens* and, contrary to their general custom, they had not touched the Body but had watched and protected it from being mangled and mutilated by any Beast or Bird of Prey. When met with it was known to be the remains of St Vincent. His Body was brought to Lisbon and deposit'd in the Great Church and an Altar was erect'd. To this day Two Ravens are kept alive in the Church as a Monument of their Piety in protecting the Body of so great a Saint. There is a Box attach'd to one of the Pillars in the Church for receiving the Contributions of Charitable persons for the support of these Two Holy Ravens.

The City of Lisbon, view'd from the Tagus, has a splendid appearance. The Houses are all White. The Streets are crowded with people and the Exchange and the Custom House and Quays exhibite scenes of Business and Traffick which show that the Portuguese are a Trading people. The new Streets that are built where the Earthquake was felt the most severest can vie with any in the world.

[*On 1 November 1755 when the churches were crowded for All Saints' Day masses, a dreadful earthquake occurred. In less than fifteen minutes two-thirds of the city was in ruins, it was followed by a tidal wave which inundated low lying areas. Thousands of people were killed.*]

The Statue of the late King Joseph on Horseback in the Great

Square is a massy and noble work. The fountains and Statues in Lisbon are numerous. Their Churches are rich and the Magazines where the Jewellry, Gold and Silver articles are exposed for sale produce solid marks of Oppulence and Wealth.

The Aquaducts in and near Lisbon, by which the City is supply'd with Water are very curious. That at Alcante is a wonderfull performance. It crosseth a Valley and is so high that a First Rate Man of War may, with ease, pass under its Arches. There are Operas and Plays every night and the rich people display much Grandeur when they go out. Begging is common here and *Stars and Garters* also. I was addressed by a poor Knight who wore a *Star* pendant to a Blue Ribbon for *Charity*. Religion is rigidly observed in Portugal. I had a part of a Boat's Crew follow me one day through the Rue Agusta at the time that the Holy Sacrament was passing. One of the Sailors did not pull off his Hatt as early as he ought so a Portuguese immediately walked up and took it off.

I have a variety of subjects to comment on which apply to Lisbon but I must pass them all over, not having time, as we sail in a few days for England. I shall leave this place with regret. Altho it is now the middle of January yet the Fields are full of Vegitation and the weather as warm as it is with us in the middle of May. I assure you that I feel a strong attachment to the Portuguese and whenever opportunity offers I shall speak of their generosity and Civility.

4th February, 1795, Spithead.

We left Lisbon the 12th January and anchor'd in this place the 31st having had a bad Passage and much blowing weather. There left the Tagus with us Twenty Three Sail of Merchantmen and the *Bonetta* Sloop of War, all of which parted company with us. We had a perfect Hurricane in the night of the 23rd. The morning display'd to our view the *Myrtle* of Poole with all her Masts gone. Fortunately the weather moderated; when our people got the people out she was scuttled.

The first English Land we made was the Lizard. Off the Bill of Portland we met our Fleet going out. We learned the French Fleet was at Sea but we saw nothing of them. On our arrival at this place I was concerned to find such deplorable Pictures of our Armys on the Continent, and the total discomfiture of the

Allies, with the aggravating circumstances of the French being in possession of Holland and the whole of its Navy.

I now draw towards the Conclusion of these Sheets, but in looking them over I find that I have promized more then I am able to perform. I have met with some disappointments which prevents me from completing my remarks on Dryed Fish Imported from Newfoundland into Portugal and Spain and within the Straits.

There is other subjects which I meant to have been somewhat more elaborate upon, and other details which I have intirely omited. My time between Lisbon and England was occupyed in a manner different to what it was at any other period of our Voyage. I therefore shall soon lay aside my Pen. My Notes, which remain undigested may be ramed into some unfathomable hole, where, like the memory of their original owner, they may become a wreck, and rot in everlasting oblivion.

I make no doubt but before you get half through these pages you will exclaim—"From such another voluminous Letter as this, Good Lord deliver me."—It is the Rules in the King of England's Navy to permit every Sailor to have a Weoman on board, if they chuse. And generally most of them have a poor unfortunate creature to pertake of the comforts of their Hammock. These virtuous Ladys are obliged to attend Devine Service, when performed by the Chaplain on Board. At the time the Clergyman recites—"From fornication and all other Deadly *Sins*" etc.—At this Crisis, I should like to know what are the sensations of the Congregation. A Painter who could manage his pencil in a masterly style would have some capital originals to produce a plate of Phizs from—And yet in perusing these Sheets, where I talke of my morality, I am afraid you will reckon me one of this sinfull Congregation. In another part of our Service the Clergyman says—"From Battle and Murder etc., etc." To which the people reply—"Good Lord deliver *us*." These words, when spoken on board a Ship of War, whose very *business* it is to *fight*, and inflict *sudden* death appears not a little singular and in my opinion ought not to be repeated at Sea, in time of War.

But to apply this observation to myself—in looking over these lines I am sure you will say "From such stuff as this good Lord deliver me." But let me hope that such an expression was uttered as a matter of course, as unmeaning as the Sailors who is seeking the French, and yet in the Chase says "From Battle and Murder, good Lord deliver us."

I now conclude. Had I wrote with a Bar of Gold my performance would a been capital. Had I used a Silver Marlinspike it might a been passable. Had I used a Crow of Iron there would a been *heavy* arguements. Had I wrote with a *red hot* Skewer there would a been furious reasoning.—But alas!—I wrote with the quill of a Goose. A simple Animal. Therefore all my subjects are flat, mucid, rough, heavy and creative of lethargy, into which state permit to be consigned your humble Servant

AARON THOMAS.

Bibliography

ANSPACH, LEWIS. *A History of the Island of Newfoundland.* Sherwood, Gilbert and Piper, 1827.

BONNYCASTLE, SIR RICHARD H. *Newfoundland in 1842.* London, Colburn, 1842.

CARTWRIGHT, GEORGE. *A Journal of Transactions and Events During a Residence of Nearly Sixty Years on the Coast of Labrador.* Newark, printed and sold by Allin and Ridge, 1792. 3 vols.

CHAPPELL, LIEUT. EDWARD, R.N. *Voyage of His Majesty's Ship Rosamund to Newfoundland.* J. Mawman, 1818.

CLOWNES, W. LAIRD. *The Royal Navy. 1899.*

DEVINE, P. K. and O'MARA. *Notable Events in the History of Newfoundland.* St John's Trade Review Office, 1900.

FAY, C. R. *Life and Labour in Newfoundland.* University of Toronto Press, 1965.

HARVEY, MOSES. *Textbook of Newfoundland History.* London, Collins, 1890.

HOWLEY, JAMES P. *The Beothucks or Red Indians.* Cambridge University Press, 1915.

HOWLEY, REV. M. *Ecclesiastical History of Newfoundland.* Boston, Doyle and Whittle, 1888.

INNES, HAROLD A. *The Cod Fisheries.* Yale University Press, 1940.

JAMES, WILLIAM. *The Naval History of Great Britain.* London, Bentley, 1886. 6 vols.

MURRAY, JAMES. *The Centenary Magazines,* June 1896 and February 1898. St John's.

The National Dictionary of Biography. 1897.

OLDMIXON, JOHN. *The British Empire in America,* London, J. Nicholson, 1708. 2 vols.

PEDLEY, REV. CHARLES. *The History of Newfoundland.* London, Longmans, 1863.
PERLIN, A. B. *The Story of Newfoundland.* St John's, 1959.
PETERS, HAROLD S. and BURLEIGH, THOMAS D. *Birds of Newfoundland.* Dept of Natural Resources, Newfoundland, 1951.
POYNTER, F. N. L. *The Journal of James Yonge.* London, Longmans, 1963.
PROWSE, D. W. *A History of Newfoundland.* London, Macmillan, 1895.
REEVES, JOHN. *A History of the Government of the Island of Newfoundland.* London, J. Sewell, 1793.
SMALLWOOD, JOSEPH R. *The Book of Newfoundland.* 2 vols.
TEMPLEMAN, WILFRED. *The Life History of the Caplin in Newfoundland Waters.* 1948.
TOQUE, REV. PHILIP. *Newfoundland As It Was and As It Is in 1877.* Toronto, John P. Magurn, 1878.
Wandering Thoughts. London, Richardson, 1846.

Other Sources

Reports of the S.P.G. 1792–1796.
Independent Chronicle, May and June 1794. Boston Atheneum, Boston, Mass.
Letter Books of Colonial Secretary's Office. Vol. SI.12. Nfld Archives.
Parish Records of Wigmore Church, Herefordshire
Admiralty Papers in Public Record Office, London:
ADM. 36/13726 Muster Book of H.M.S. *Suffolk*
ADM. 51/874 Log Book of H.M.S. *Suffolk.*
ADM. 51/1146 Log Book of H.M.S. *Boston.*
ADM. 36/11913
13728

Index